MISBEHAVIOR IN CYBER PLACES

*The Regulation of Online Conduct
in Virtual Communities on the Internet*

Janet Sternberg

University Press of America,® Inc.
Lanham · Boulder · New York · Toronto · Plymouth, UK

**Copyright © 2012 by
University Press of America,® Inc.**
4501 Forbes Boulevard
Suite 200
Lanham, Maryland 20706
UPA Acquisitions Department (301) 459-3366

10 Thornbury Road
Plymouth PL6 7PP
United Kingdom

Library of Congress Control Number: 2012948299
ISBN: 978-0-7618-6011-2 (paperback : alk. paper)
eISBN: 978-0-7618-6012-9

Dedicated to

my mother, Eileen Sternberg
my father, Norman Sternberg
and
my great-aunt, Marietta Sternberg

Contents

Preface:
The Internet at the Turn of the Century

When the opportunity arose to publish as a book this research about misbehavior in virtual communities, I considered how to update the work, originally reported in my 2001 doctoral dissertation in the Media Ecology Program at New York University. To publish one's dissertation is not unusual. What is unusual is to publish the research a decade later, particularly with time-sensitive topics like digital media and the Internet.

Yet I decided not to undertake a major update of the original work, and to limit the scope of the revisions, maintaining the same overall structure, perspective, and tone, especially vis-à-vis the related literature, for several reasons. First, the research reported in this book has historical relevance, documenting the initial phase of Internet activity, up to the end of the twentieth century. Second, this book has theoretical relevance, discussing the earliest stages of Internet research, and also laying out fundamental ideas about the media ecology intellectual tradition, while presenting a picture of both realms of study at a specific point in time, the turn of the century. And third, this book has ongoing social relevance, as people continue to misbehave, and interest is growing in distinguishing misbehavior and rule-breaking from crime and law-breaking, in all kinds of environments, offline as well as online.

Research about the Internet at the turn of the century has historical relevance because digital technologies and online environments have changed dramatically since the dawn of the new millennium. This book provides a historical snapshot of the first period of the Internet, up to the year 2000, a valuable record of an online era before social media, a time that youth today barely remember. For instance, the infamous text-only "rape in cyberspace" originally recounted by Dibbell in 1993 seems ancient, quaint, and tame to today's hyper-connected multimedia digital natives, so familiar with cyberbullying. The research reported in this book portrays the early Internet, a universe of cyber places where amateurs prevailed rather than professionals, where digital immigrants explored online frontiers and founded virtual communities, just as e-commerce was starting to emerge. This book offers details about the first wave of Internet activity, before the Web and omnipresent commercialism began to dominate the second wave of activity on the Internet in the new millennium.

The early period of virtual community participation during the first wave of Internet activity set the stage for social media, with Internet activity migrating from desktop computers to laptops to notebooks to cell phones to multi-function handheld devices. In many respects, social media grew out of virtual communities, so studying virtual communities helps us better understand present online environments. Furthermore, many virtual community genres described in this book still survive, like mailing lists, discussion forums, and Internet Relay Chat. These old-time virtual communities coexist with their descendants, newer varieties of digital gathering places such as the massively multi-player online role-playing games called MMORPGs, virtual worlds like Second Life, and social networks such as Facebook and Twitter, among others.

This book also has theoretical relevance in showcasing and providing context and references for early Internet scholarship, some of which is discussed and cited even now (e.g., Rheingold, 1993). And virtual misbehavior keeps on attracting academic scrutiny (see, e.g., Bruckman et al., 2006; Foo, 2006, 2008; Selwyn, 2008; Williams, 2006). Moreover, to date, this book constitutes the only systematic investigation of virtual misbehavior in general across a wide range of online environments.

There is theoretical relevance as well in the media ecology scholarship analyzed in this book, particularly discussions of space and place and of mediated interpersonal communication, topics which continue to provoke intriguing questions in our current media environments. A young field of study, media ecology is evolving and advancing, and in the past decade, important works on media ecology theory in general have appeared (see, e.g., Albrecht, 2001; Lum, 2006a; Moran, 2010; Strate, 2006, 2011). Since the turn of the century, more media ecologists have written about computer-mediated communication and about social media (see, e.g., Barnes, 2001, 2003; Levinson, 2003, 2004, 2009; Maushart, 2010; Rushkoff, 2010). Yet little has changed in the intervening years regarding media ecology approaches to space and place, and even to mediated interpersonal communication. Therefore, this book calls attention to pioneering media ecology research still pertinent for the study of mediated interpersonal communication (e.g., Gumpert, 1987; Gumpert & Cathcart 1979, 1982, 1986a; Meyrowitz, 1985), refreshing our appreciation of their insights and introducing their research to additional generations of media scholars. Similarly, this book cites rare, hard-to-find seminal texts of limited distribution, notably, Nystrom's writings on media ecology. Thus, this book contributes to the theoretical framework of media ecology, and helps clarify the media ecology perspective.

So much has changed in so many online environments since the 1990s, when most of this investigation was conducted, that whole new sets of research conditions and questions have arisen. Entirely new projects would be required to study misbehavior in the social media that have replaced virtual communities as venues of choice for today's Internauts. Due to advanced digital technologies and transmission capabilities, online environments have gone beyond simple text-based functions to complex multimedia combinations. Taken for granted nowadays, high-speed bandwidth and wireless connectivity so abundant in modern urban environments make digital misbehavior easier than ever. Ubiquitous mobile handheld hybrid devices like smartphones and tablets are becoming as common as desktop and laptop computers, thereby changing our media practices and social habits.

But despite technological changes, this book about misbehavior in virtual communities continues to have social relevance because human nature has not changed—we are not so different now than we were at the turn of the century or than we will be decades in the future. The basic findings of this report about the Internet at the turn of the century furnish general background for ongoing current discussions of digital media in the new millennium. Social media may have replaced virtual communities, but in many respects, social media offer cyber places that resemble those described in this book. These new cyber places likewise provide venues where people interact in private, public, and semi-public conditions, and the potential for misbehavior online has only increased with the development of sophisticated always-on mobile multimedia technologies.

With more people and devices connected to the Internet in more ways, there are simply more opportunities to misbehave. Smartphones and social media introduce new digital ways to create trouble and to inflict pain, as we carry with us wherever we go the possibility of becoming victims or perpetrators of mediated misbehavior. The old-fashioned flame wars of Usenet newsgroup days are reflected in the present epidemic of incivility in online venues such as comments sections of news sites and shouting-heads clips in public video collections. Cybercrime has become more prevalent and more threatening around the globe. Virus protection and firewall use are commonplace routines in daily living, but instead of fewer attacks, we have more genres of malware appearing on a growing array of devices. Hackers now target not only computers and printers connected to the Internet, but also smartphones, game consoles, and other digital hybrids which are succumbing to viruses as well.

We still face similar problems today managing conduct with social media as we did with virtual communities, even in commercial for-profit online environments. The past decade of Internet activity has brought a proliferation of user-generated content; but this same user-generated content, in turn, multiplies exponentially the potential for virtual misbehavior. Contemporary commercial online systems, such as Facebook, Google, LinkedIn, MSN, Twitter, Yahoo, and YouTube, among others, must pay a price to monitor and moderate such user-generated content in order to minimize involvement with virtual misbehavior and cybercrime. In short, virtual misbehavior has increased, and people remain concerned with the regulation of conduct in all sorts of online environments.

This book about the regulation of conduct in virtual communities is also relevant with respect to growing interest in distinguishing misbehavior and rule-breaking from crime and law-breaking, both online and offline. In the twenty-first century, the social and physical environments we inhabit are in constant flux. Online and offline activities increasingly blend and overlap, creating new sorts of challenges for controlling conduct. As questions arise about appropriate behavior in a wide range of social and physical environments, perhaps local self-regulation based on informal rules of the type often found in virtual communities will prove more flexible and suitable than centralized institutional regulation based on more rigid formal legal systems.

Finally, this book offers the double perspective of a participant as well as a scholar. I bring to this research the personal viewpoint of someone who spent years actually dealing with virtual misbehavior as an enforcer on Internet Relay Chat, with exposure to international online contexts, not just those related to the USA, giving me broader experience. I myself did not engage in ethnographic field work for this research, but the fact that I actively participated in regulating online conduct in virtual communities on the Internet, in addition to studying them as a scholar, adds extra value to this book. At the turn of the century, as people gathered for social interaction in cyber places on the Internet, I was there.

Janet Sternberg
Bronx, New York
October, 2011

Acknowledgments

I welcome this opportunity to express my gratitude and appreciation to those who helped and supported me in this enterprise over the years.

In the academic realm, I thank my professors, advisors, and doctoral committee in the now defunct Media Ecology Program at New York University: Joy Gould Boyum, Terence Moran, Christine Nystrom, Henry Perkinson, Neil Postman, and Lance Strate. I also thank Amy Bruckman, Frank Dance, Nicholas Frota, Bruce Gronbeck, Joshua Meyrowitz, Camille Paglia, Shelley Postman, and Douglas Rushkoff, as well as colleagues from the Media Ecology Association, for encouraging me along the way.

In the online realm, I thank various groups and participants on Internet Relay Chat, especially those of the #brasil and #jazz channels on the EFnet and DALnet IRC networks. In particular, I thank Márcio Guidorizzi de Siqueira for first calling my attention to the significance of misbehavior in virtual communities; Flávia Rodrigues Alves Camargo Mariano for her friendship both online and offline; and Amit Peleg of InterJazz and the Blue Note jazz club, Orlando Sodré of Sodre.net, and the IRCops and KLine teams of DALnet for allowing me to help administer their cyber places.

In the offline realm, I thank my mother, Eileen Sternberg, and my father, Norman Sternberg, for everything they have always done on my behalf, as well as my great-aunt, Marietta Sternberg, for inspiring me to continue my studies. I also thank Patricia Keeler, dear friend and president of my fan club, for listening patiently, commenting thoughtfully, and offering wise advice at key times. And last, but certainly not least, I thank the series of fabulous felines who have provided the most constant companionship over two decades, my cats past, Lola (1991–1999) and Moe (1991–2006), and present, Isabella Pearl and Theodore.

Introduction:
Athenians and Visigoths in Cyberspace

If you build it, they will log on.
> Neil Randall, *The Soul of the Internet* (1997, p. 19)

If you build it, some will abuse it.
> John Suler, "The Bad Boys of Cyberspace" (1997b)

I want to tell you about two groups of people who lived many years ago but whose influence is still with us. They were very different from each other, representing opposite values and traditions. . . . The first group lived about 2,500 years ago in the place which we now call Greece, in a city they called Athens. . . . The second group of people lived in the place we now call Germany, and flourished about 1,700 years ago. We call them the Visigoths. . . .

The Athenians and the Visigoths still survive, and they do so through us and the ways in which we conduct our lives. All around us—in this hall, in this community, in our city—there are people whose way of looking at the world reflects the way of the Athenians, and there are people whose way is the way of the Visigoths. . . .

To be an Athenian is to understand that the thread which holds civilized society together is thin and vulnerable; therefore, Athenians place great value on tradition, social restraint, and continuity. To an Athenian, bad manners are acts of violence against the social order. The modern Visigoth cares very little about any of this. The Visigoths think of themselves as the center of the universe. Tradition exists for their own convenience, good manners are an affectation and a burden, and history is merely what is in yesterday's newspaper.

To be an Athenian is to take an interest in public affairs and the improvement of public behavior. . . . A modern Visigoth is interested only in his own affairs and has no sense of the meaning of community. . . .

Eventually, like the rest of us, you must be on one side or the other. You must be an Athenian or a Visigoth.
> Neil Postman, *Conscientious Objections* (1988, pp. 186–189)

Wherever people gather in cyberspace to interact with one another, Athenians and Visigoths can be found: Athenians who follow the rules of civilized online behavior, and Visigoths who break those rules and misbehave. Nowadays, Visigoths misbehave so often in so many gathering places on the Internet that dealing with online misbehavior has become a prominent concern for civilized Athenians around the globe. As group interaction online has evolved, generating a growth of interest in social aspects of cyberspace, issues related to virtual misbehavior have begun to preoccupy laypersons and scholars alike.

First as a layperson and then as a scholar, I became fascinated with the activities of Athenians and Visigoths as they confront each other in virtual communities on the Internet. I decided to investigate the types of misbehavior in which people engage and the ways people deal with such misbehavior in a variety of online environments. To introduce the study reported in the pages that follow, here is a brief account of the path that led me to this research.

The seeds of my interest in virtual misbehavior and the regulation of online conduct were sown during my own experiences on a system for live, typed conversation among individuals and groups known as Internet Relay Chat ("IRC"). On IRC, people gather in cyber places called "channels" to "chat" by typing to each other in real time. In December 1994, I stumbled onto IRC for the first time, and there I immediately began to notice things that drew my attention to online misbehavior. I returned to IRC many times, and gradually came to suspect that dealing with misbehavior is a central part of life in this set of virtual communities.

Initially, I noticed that the IRC software itself includes features that anticipate a need to regulate conduct, as if predicting that participants will misbehave. Created in 1988 at the University of Oulu in Finland by a computer programmer named Jarkko Oikarinen (Oikarinen & Reed, 1993; see also Cheung, 1995; Reid, 1991; Rintel, 1995; Rintel & Pittam, 1997a, 1997b; Surratt, 1996), the original IRC program contained two features that remain key elements of the many versions of IRC released since then and still in use today. First, every participant has access to an "ignore" command, which blocks incoming messages from selected other participants. Second, each IRC channel is controlled by certain participants called "operators." Channel operators have access to special commands (unavailable to ordinary users) to "kick" participants out of a channel or even "ban" them from entering a channel at all. Thus, participants can ignore others whose comments they deem undesirable, and operators can kick and ban troublemakers so as to maintain order in their channels. These features of IRC (and there are others) provide built-in tools for dealing with misbehavior and regulating online conduct.

The next hint I received that misbehavior figures prominently on IRC came from observing that IRC participants misbehave as often as they discuss rules of online conduct, which is to say, all the time. Misbehavior is a daily occurrence on IRC, something encountered routinely, dealt with constantly, and argued about incessantly. For years now, IRC users around the globe have been debating issues related to virtual misbehavior, on hundreds of channels on dozens of

IRC networks, as well as on IRC-related electronic mailing lists, message boards, and sites on the World Wide Web. In venues like these, IRC users manifest their preoccupation with misbehavior by discussing various aspects of the regulation of online conduct.

I ultimately became convinced that misbehavior is a focal point of attention on IRC when I accepted the status of operator on several channels I had been frequenting for a while. Channel operators use their special powers to enforce the rules and discipline those who misbehave. The commands to kick or ban are simple, but figuring out when to use these commands can be complicated. As operator and rule-enforcer, I had to recognize when someone was breaking the rules and misbehaving, and decide what to do. My fellow operators taught me how to enforce various rules that people might break. Some rules applied to IRC in general, some to specific channels only. Some rules related to common-sense and politeness, and others to technical aspects of IRC. There were even rules for enforcing the rules! As I developed and exercised my abilities as operator, I learned firsthand that IRC participants do indeed devote a lot of time and energy to issues revolving around misbehavior and the regulation of online conduct.

Once I realized the extent to which IRC participants concern themselves with misbehavior, I began to wonder whether this might be the case elsewhere online. After all, IRC is just one kind of environment where virtual communities develop—there are many others. How prevalent was misbehavior in other places where people gather online? How prominent were issues related to the regulation of conduct in online environments besides IRC? I set out to explore these questions in the two main types of text-based environments in which people gather to interact on the Internet: chat systems and post systems (see, e.g., Cutler, 1996, pp. 321–322; Herz, 1995; Rheingold, 1993, pp. 110–196; Strate, 1996b, p. 369; Strate et al., 1996b, pp. 8–9; Surratt, 1996, pp. 28–34).

Chat systems such as IRC employ synchronous communication: participants hold live conversations by typing to each other almost simultaneously, which requires them to be present online at the same time, much like chatting on the telephone. Besides IRC, at the turn of the century, people gather for real-time typed conversation on the Internet in the "chat rooms" of America Online and the "CB channels" of CompuServe, and they also chat on Web sites. Some synchronous systems, known as Multi-User Dungeons or Domains ("MUDs") and MUDs-Object-Oriented ("MOOs"), allow users to combine chat with role-playing and text-based props and scenery. And synchronous chat systems such as the Palace incorporate graphics in addition to text: users appear on screen as images called "avatars" and interact with graphical props and scenery, as well as typing to each other.

Post systems, on the other hand, involve asynchronous communication: participants conduct non-simultaneous, delayed typed conversations, reading and replying to each other's posts at different times as suits their individual convenience, similar to snail-mail paper correspondence or to notices on traditional bulletin boards offline. At the turn of the century, countless asynchronous post systems exist on the Internet. Electronic mailing lists called "listservs" circulate posts among subscribers, and the international system of public message boards referred to as Usenet newsgroups, as well as a growing multitude of private and commercial posting sites on the Web, are frequented by hordes of participants. People also post in asynchronous discussion conferences on independent bulletin board systems ("BBSs") such as Echo, FidoNet, and the WELL, and in asynchronous message boards and forums of mainstream networks such as America Online and CompuServe.

Visiting and reading about chat and post systems like these, I satisfied my curiosity regarding the prevalence of misbehavior in a range of virtual gathering places and the importance that participants attribute to the regulation of online conduct. For both chat and post systems, as for IRC, my preliminary investigations uncovered ample evidence to suggest that people are definitely concerned with regulating conduct in their online environments.

First, I discovered that almost every chat and post system has built-in features for dealing with online misbehavior. Most systems offer ordinary participants an equivalent of the IRC ignore command to block messages from users whose comments they prefer not to receive. In addition, systems usually have some sort of rule-enforcer or "superuser" analogous to the channel operators on IRC, although their presence is not necessarily apparent to average users. Depending on the particular system, enforcers go by titles as diverse as "sysop" (BBSs and CompuServe), "wizard" and "god" (MUDs, MOOs, and the Palace), "moderator" (listservs and Usenet newsgroups), and "community leader," "ranger" and "guide" (America Online). IRC itself has higher-level enforcers than channel operators: the IRC server operators called "IRCops," who may use extended privileges to remove troublemakers not only from channels but from entire IRC networks as well. The precise responsibilities of rule-enforcers such as these vary as much as the technical features of their respective systems and the rules they enforce. But most enforcers have special powers, analogous to the kick and ban commands used by IRC channel operators, for disciplining those who break the rules.

Next in my quest for information about misbehavior in online environments, I found that in most chat and post systems, people do in fact misbehave quite a bit, and others spend a good deal of time and energy discussing how to handle troublemakers. In practically every virtual gathering place I looked at, participants engage in the same sorts of ongoing debates as IRC users about misbehavior and the regulation of online conduct. In chat systems and post systems alike all over the Internet, participants are preoccupied with misbehavior in their virtual communities.

Then I came across a wealth of online documentation produced by and for users themselves, pertaining to rules of conduct. Such documents typically set forth rules of conduct applicable in different online environments, stipulating policies for enforcing rules as well as sanctions for breaking them. Some documents are informal primers on proper network etiquette, often referred to as "netiquette." Some are compilations called Frequently Asked Questions or "FAQs," and others are more formal agreements known as Acceptable Use

Policies or Terms of Service. In addition, guidelines for conduct often appear in the help features and manuals of software used to participate in online environments. The existence of such an abundance of documentation provides further evidence that the regulation of online conduct figures prominently in a wide range of virtual gathering places.

Finally, convinced by these preliminary explorations that misbehavior on the Internet is widespread, and that the regulation of online conduct is critically important to those who participate in virtual communities, my curiosity as a scholar was aroused. I began to wonder what others, besides virtual community participants, had to say about misbehavior and the regulation of online conduct. I felt sure there must be research about online misbehavior, and began to look for literature on the subject. Indeed, I discovered quite a bit of material related to troublesome behavior in cyberspace, in academic publications as well as the popular press, both in print and online. But the more I read, the more it seemed that although many had commented on the topic, nobody had yet undertaken a systematic investigation of virtual misbehavior in general across a wide range of online environments.

Meanwhile, as I conducted these informal investigations of virtual misbehavior, I was also pursuing a doctoral program in media ecology. During my studies, I learned to approach communication contexts as environments; to be aware of conditions of attendance in communication environments, conditions such as such as co-presence in time and space (or the lack thereof); and to examine various aspects of the relationship between media and culture. Among the key principles I absorbed from the media ecology perspective is that the introduction of new media technologies alters the balance of a culture's communication environments, provoking changes in ways of thinking and behaving, including changes in conceptions of time, space, place, and community. Because of this media ecology training, throughout my experiences online, I was highly conscious of cyberspace as environment, especially the differences among conditions of attendance in face-to-face versus computer-mediated communication environments, as well as the different sorts of co-presence involved in synchronous versus asynchronous online environments.

As I became familiar with literature in the media ecology canon, two books in particular resonated with what I was discovering about cyberspace and struck me as especially pertinent to the study of virtual misbehavior. The first book, a classic in sociology, was Erving Goffman's *Behavior in Public Places* (1963), in which he discusses the social organization of face-to-face gatherings, emphasizing the significance and function of rules and rule-breaking in social situations. On the very first page of this text, Goffman mentions situational "improprieties" and highlights the importance of studying public behavior that is "inappropriate in the situation. . . . misconduct" (1963, p. 3). The second book that haunted my thoughts as I traveled online was Joshua Meyrowitz's *No Sense of Place* (1985), concerning the impact of electronic media, primarily television, on social behavior. A seminal work in media ecology, Meyrowitz's book is arguably the most significant extension of Goffman's ideas about face-to-face encounters to the realm of mediated interpersonal communication. Although barely touching on computers (understandable given the date the book was published), Meyrowitz proposes that physical place and media are both information systems, and therefore, functional equivalents (1985, pp. 35–40), which accounts for the ability of electronic media to complement and even substitute for, if not altogether replace, physical place (1985, pp. 1–9), especially with respect to social experience.

Throughout my explorations in cyberspace, these two books kept coming to mind because I did have strong perceptions of the online environments I visited as *places*. But these online places were of a vastly different nature than traditional places offline: these were *cyber places*, digital rather than physical locations, symbolic as opposed to tangible, constructed of information and communication, built with clicks instead of bricks.

Eventually, because misbehavior in cyber places proved so compelling a subject, and because the subject presented such a promising opportunity to apply the ideas of Goffman and Meyrowitz in a new context, I decided to focus my doctoral research in this area. I owe a special intellectual debt to both these scholars, for Goffman's *Behavior in Public Places* gave me inspiration for the title as well as the topic of this report on misbehavior in cyber places, and Meyrowitz's *No Sense of Place* helped me to understand that online environments offer us the prospect of developing a new sense of place.

And now, to wind up the tale of how I came to study misbehavior in virtual communities on the Internet, a few words about storytelling. Having begun this introduction with Postman's comparison of Athenians and Visigoths and the respective traditions and values of these two ancient cultures, it seems fitting to end by citing his views on the purposes of social science in modern culture. Postman describes social research, including media ecology, as "weaving narratives about human behavior. . . . a form of storytelling" (1988, pp. 12–13; see also Gencarelli, 2000, pp. 101–102; Nystrom, 1989). As Postman explains:

> The purpose of social research is to rediscover the truths of social life, to comment on and criticize the moral behavior of people; and finally, to put forward metaphors, images, and ideas that can help people live with some measure of understanding and dignity. Specifically, the purpose of media ecology is to tell stories about the consequences of technology; to tell how media environments create contexts that may change the way we think or organize our social life, or make us better or worse, or smarter or dumber, or freer or more enslaved. (1988, p. 19)

In the pages ahead, I discuss in detail the scholarly rationale and academic goals of this research project. But in addition to these formal purposes, as the work of Postman and Nystrom has led me to understand, this report is also my chance to tell stories about what happens when Athenians and Visigoths confront each other over misbehavior in cyber places.

Chapter One
The Research Objective

This study of misbehavior and the regulation of online conduct in virtual communities on the Internet is based on two premises. The first premise is that the field of media ecology lacks applications of existing theory to the analysis of interpersonal communication in mediated environments, especially those which involve online computer-mediated communication ("CMC"). The second premise is that significant research and data exist, related to online CMC in general and to virtual communities in particular, which suggest the need for a more thorough and comprehensive investigation of misbehavior in online environments than has been undertaken so far. Support for these two premises is presented below and examined further in Chapter Two, which provides a more substantive discussion of the theoretical context of this study.

For scholars in the field of media ecology, broadly defined as "the study of complex communication systems as environments" (Nystrom, 1973, p. 3), there is little doubt that electronic media have had tremendous impact on human affairs (e.g., Carpenter & McLuhan, 1960b; Frommer, 1987; Gozzi, 1999; Gumpert, 1987; McLuhan, 1964; Noone, 1986; Ong, 1982; Perkinson, 1991; Postman, 1982, 1985; Quarles, 1986; Strate, 1991). Although most media ecologists would agree that human communication and interaction have been dramatically affected by computers, at the turn of the century, limited research has been carried out in this area from a media ecology perspective. For the most part, studies in the media ecology tradition have focused on the computer itself as a medium, approaching the subject from cultural, economic, educational, historical, philosophical, political, psychological, and technical points of view (e.g., Barnes, 1995, 2000; Barnes & Strate, 1996; Beniger, 1986; Bolter, 1984, 1991; Levinson, 1997, 1999; Papert, 1980; Perkinson, 1996; Postman, 1992;

Roszak, 1986; Turkle, 1984; Wachtel, in press; Weizenbaum, 1976; Wiener, 1950/1954).

Recent decades have brought the rise of online CMC, which has changed forever the landscape of electronic media and human interaction. Nevertheless, at the turn of the century, research on the interpersonal aspects and social consequences of online CMC from a media ecology perspective has only started to emerge (e.g., articles in the anthology on communication and cyberspace edited by Strate et al., 1996a; Barnes, 1996b; Conforti, 2001; Mineo, 1998; Strate, 1996a, 1999). That there are relatively few media ecology studies of online CMC can perhaps be attributed to a larger imbalance in the field: an overall lack of applications of media ecology theory to contexts involving mediated interpersonal communication.

Informed by the work of foundational scholars such as Carpenter (1960), Eisenstein (1983), Ellul (1954/1964), Havelock (1982), Innis (1951), Langer (1942/1979), McLuhan (1964), Mumford (1934), and Ong (1982), among others, media ecologists have concentrated on media in relation to mass communication and *intra*personal communication, as opposed to studying the role of media in *inter*personal communication, especially with respect to electronic media. As a result, mediated interpersonal communication has been comparatively neglected in the field of media ecology. At the turn of the century, exceptions to this pattern include articles in the series of anthologies on mediated interpersonal communication edited by Gumpert and Cathcart (1979, 1982, 1986a), Meyrowitz's landmark study of the impact of electronic media on social affairs (1985), and anthologies edited by Gumpert and Fish (1990b) and Drucker and Gumpert (1997).

Media ecology research on interpersonal communication draws heavily on the ideas of sociologists such as Mead (1934) and Goffman (1959, 1963), who represent what is often referred to as the symbolic interactionist approach to social affairs. Symbolic interactionists view social relations as transactional phenomena involving active meaning-making by participants. Goffman's work in particular has been identified as furnishing one of the fundamental paradigms for media ecology research (Nystrom, 1973). This sociological approach is described by Meyrowitz as "situationism" (1985, pp. 23–33), as opposed to what he calls "medium theory" (pp. 16–23). Whereas medium theory concentrates on media technologies as cultural and psychological environments, emphasizing mass and intrapersonal modes of communication, situationism can be construed as focusing on environments as media (i.e., how people make meaning from various aspects of social situations), emphasizing interpersonal modes of communication.

These two perspectives, media as environments and environments as media, are combined in exemplary fashion by Meyrowitz, who explores the social impact of electronic media by applying Goffman's ideas about face-to-face encounters to the realm of mediated interpersonal communication (1985). As Meyrowitz argues (pp. 33–34) and demonstrates throughout his work, a combination of medium theory and situationism offers a rich theoretical framework for studying interpersonal communication in mediated environments. As explained in Chapter Two of this study, areas of concern in such a framework include the relationships among media and environments, on the one hand, and on the other, conceptions of space and place, as well as the significance of situations, rules, and rule-breaking in social affairs.

Writing some 25 years ago, in the dawn of the computer era, Meyrowitz charted new waters in applying a combined media ecology approach to the analysis of how electronic media, primarily television, affect social interaction. Today, this type of media ecology framework, grounded in sociological as well as communication and media theory, cries out for further application, especially to the mediated situations involved in online CMC, which, at the turn of the century, have only begun to be explored by media ecologists, as noted above and discussed in Chapter Two. The investigation of misbehavior in online environments provides an excellent opportunity to apply such a media ecology approach in the domain of computer-mediated interpersonal communication.

Although at the turn of the century, media ecologists have not yet produced a great deal of research on interaction in computer-mediated environments, scholars in related disciplines have been investigating various social aspects of online CMC for quite a while. As described in Chapter Two, several groups of research themes have emerged as focal points of attention in studies of online CMC. Among such online CMC research themes, those which address what have come to be known as "virtual communities" stand out as the most relevant for investigating misbehavior in online environments.

The idea of virtual communities began to appear in both scholarly and popular accounts of computer use several decades ago (e.g., Hiltz & Turoff, 1978/1993; Rheingold, 1993; M. A. Smith, 1992; Stone, 1991). Since then, substantial research on virtual communities has accumulated. Reviewed in Chapter Two, such research includes theoretical debates about conceptions of community, as well as surveys of virtual communities in general and case studies of particular virtual communities.

Among the topics which have captured the attention of virtual community researchers is misbehavior in online environments. However, research directly addressing this subject is still relatively scarce. As discussed in Chapter Five, at the turn of the century, such research consists mostly of limited studies, focusing on issues related to behavior management and social control, which examine either specific aspects of online misbehavior, or misbehavior in specific virtual communities. To date, no overview, general survey, or book-length treatment appears to have been published about misbehavior in online environments.

Nevertheless, in the research related to online CMC and virtual communities, there are three bodies of literature which offer ideas and information relevant to the study of misbehavior in online environments. Each of theses areas is examined more closely in a separate chapter of this report: Chapter Three reviews literature related to trouble brewing in cyberspace; Chapter Four reviews literature concerning cybercrime and law-breaking on the Internet; and

Chapter Five reviews literature which directly addresses misbehavior and rule-breaking in virtual communities.

Throughout these three bodies of literature, there is unanimous agreement that additional inquiry is needed into misbehavior in online environments (e.g., D. E. Denning & Lin, 1994; Dutton, 1996; Kollock & M. A. Smith, 1996; MacKinnon, 1997; Sproull & Faraj, 1995/1997). Moreover, as some researchers note, the need for research on the social organization of cyberspace is growing increasingly urgent (e.g., Kollock & M. A. Smith, 1996; MacKinnon, 1998). Thus, a comprehensive study of misbehavior and the regulation of online conduct in virtual communities on the Internet, grounded in a coherent media ecology theoretical framework, seems particularly promising as a way to shed light on social issues of importance in online environments that may well bear on social relations in the offline world.

As explained in the introduction, this study of online misbehavior grew out of my own experiences in virtual communities on the Internet. By participating in some virtual communities, and visiting and reading about others, I discovered that misbehavior is prevalent in a wide range of virtual communities, and that the regulation of conduct is a serious concern for participants in a variety of online environments. Intrigued by the types of misbehavior in which people engage online and the ways that people deal with such misbehavior in virtual communities, and convinced that a media ecology perspective could illuminate such matters, I decided to design a research project on this topic. But what sort of research into online misbehavior should I pursue?

In approaching online misbehavior as a research project, I originally expected to design an ethnographic case study of misbehavior in one type of virtual community—probably an Internet Relay Chat community, because of my experiences as both participant and rule-enforcer in this online environment. Reviewing the literature related to misbehavior and the regulation of online conduct, however, I gained a new sense of what sort of research was needed. As noted above and discussed in Chapter Five, empirical research such as I contemplated has already been carried out in various online environments, and at present, sufficient case studies exist to indicate beyond a shadow of a doubt that people misbehave in practically every gathering place on the Internet, and that the regulation of online conduct is a universal concern for participants in virtual communities. And in addition to scholarly research, accounts of online misbehavior surface frequently in the popular press as well.

Furthermore, as group interaction in online environments has evolved, participants themselves have developed a rich tradition of producing electronic documentation pertaining to appropriate online behavior, for the convenience and edification of their fellow users. Available on the Internet in diverse forms, varying in degree of formality and authority, such documents typically set forth rules of conduct applicable in different online environments, stipulating policies for enforcing rules as well as sanctions for breaking them. Some documents are informal primers on proper network etiquette, often referred to as "netiquette." Some are compilations called Frequently Asked Questions ("FAQs"). Others are more formal agreements known as Acceptable Use Policies ("AUPs") and Terms of Service ("TOSs"), as well as Network Working Group Requests for Comments ("RFCs"), a numbered series of Internet-wide proclamations. Additionally, guidelines for appropriate conduct often appear in the help features and manuals of software used to access online environments, as well as on electronic mailing lists, message boards, newsgroups, and Web sites related to particular virtual communities. Such an abundance of user-oriented documentation provides a great deal of basic information about the concerns of participants with respect to troublesome behavior in a wide range of online environments.

Yet despite this profusion of scholarly and popular material related to the regulation of misbehavior in online environments, there are no studies that survey the subject in general or consolidate what is known about the topic as a whole. At the turn of the century, existing studies of online misbehavior provide scattered glimpses of a larger picture which is still indistinct. Although they offer abundant data about particular virtual communities, about specific types of misbehavior, and about various means of regulating online conduct, existing studies require further interpretation and, especially, comparison with each other. The excellent arrays of ideas and questions that have been published so far deserve to be examined more closely and to be extended to a broader range of environments.

Many important questions remain unanswered, in particular, concerning patterns and differences in types of misbehavior and in the means used to regulate conduct across a range of virtual communities in a variety of online environments. For example: Do people engage in different types of misbehavior in different types of virtual communities or online environments—e.g., mailing lists, chat rooms, Web sites, etc.—and if so, what might account for the differences? Do some types of misbehavior seem more common than others, or more offensive? Are different means used to regulate misbehavior in different types of virtual communities or online environments, and if so, what might account for the differences? Do certain means seem more or less effective than others in regulating specific types of misbehavior?

To address questions like these, what is needed is research that sorts out and synthesizes, organizes and clarifies, and ultimately draws conclusions from what already is known about misbehavior and the regulation of online conduct, to provide a more coherent sense of the main issues and primary parameters in this area of inquiry. What is missing is the application of existing ideas from theoretical literature to existing information garnered from source literature so as to identify patterns and generalizations, and to uncover differences and similarities.

The gap which this study aspires to fill, then, is this distillation and combination of the results of scholarly and popular investigations through a careful consideration, informed by a media ecology perspective grounded in sociological as well as communication and media theory, of existing research on misbehavior and the regulation of conduct in virtual communities in diverse online environments. In this study, therefore, I examine and systematize the relevant scholarly and popular literature and derive answers to questions such as those above, by using a media ecology framework to analyze and assess how people deal with misbehavior in virtual communities in a variety of online environments.

In order to understand more precisely the nature of computer-mediated communication and human interaction online, it would be helpful to develop a clearer picture of troublesome behavior in cyberspace. By studying how people deal with misbehavior in online environments, we can enhance our understanding of the dynamics of both the symbolic and the physical environments we currently inhabit, our virtual communities online as well as our traditional communities offline. For instance, studies that elucidate misbehavior in virtual communities can contribute to clarifying the boundaries between law-breaking and rule-breaking, which are so problematic in offline environments as well as online. This could help assuage the general uneasiness caused by uncertainty about applying laws where rules might better serve, by the ambiguous delineation between criminal and prankster, and by overlapping circuits of internal and external jurisdiction. Moreover, this research is a step towards promoting vigorous discussion about internal attitudes and actions available to participants within their communities, whether online or off, that empower them to take command of their own circumstances and agendas, thereby freeing external authorities and resources such as law-enforcement agencies and judiciary institutions to attend to those cases and issues which cannot adequately be handled within community settings. For reasons such as these, the purpose of this study was to investigate how people regulate misbehavior in virtual communities on the Internet.

The results of this investigation are potentially significant in two domains. In the realm of media ecology theory, I hope to advance the study of interpersonal communication and social relations in computer-mediated environments by synthesizing knowledge about one area of computer-mediated social interaction, namely, misbehavior in virtual communities. I also hope this research will contribute towards balancing the field of media ecology itself, by extending the under-represented tradition of investigating interpersonal modes of mediated communication to the online gathering places of cyberspace.

In the sphere of everyday life, I hope to promote deeper understanding of several facets of the digital and physical environments we currently inhabit: to shed light on the dynamics of virtual gatherings, such an integral component of so many Internauts' online activities; to help clarify distinctions between misbehavior and cybercrime, and between rule-making and law-making, universal puzzles perplexing to scholars, professionals, and laypersons alike; to stimulate comparison between online misbehavior and troublesome offline behavior that burgeons around us in an infinite variety of contexts, contaminating all sorts of arenas and burdening all kinds of people in the offline world; and finally, to contribute to ongoing discussions of community and public space, prominent and vital social concerns nowadays that will surely continue to bid for attention in the future. One way to progress in planning and developing new communities and in managing behavior in new public spaces and social situations is to look at and learn from existing communities and gathering places, including those that flourish on the Internet at the turn of the century.

THE RESEARCH PROBLEM

The purpose of this study was to analyze and assess, on the basis of the literature, how people regulate misbehavior in virtual communities on the Internet.

Subordinate Problem 1: To construct, on the basis of the literature, a taxonomy of misbehavior in virtual communities in different online environments (i.e., post environments, chat environments, and meta-environments).

Subordinate Problem 2: To identify, on the basis of the literature, patterns and differences in types of misbehavior in virtual communities (according to online environments, virtual communities, and participants).

Subordinate Problem 3: To describe, on the basis of the literature, the means used to regulate misbehavior in virtual communities in different online environments (i.e., post environments, chat environments, and meta-environments).

Subordinate Problem 4: To identify, on the basis of the literature, patterns and differences in the means used to regulate misbehavior in virtual communities (according to online environments, virtual communities, and participants).

DEFINITIONS

Misbehavior. For purposes of this study, "misbehavior" refers to misconduct: behavior which does not conform to norms and which breaks rules. To misbehave is to conduct oneself in a manner perceived by others to be aberrant, anti-social, bad, delinquent, deviant, wrong or as sociologist Goffman puts it, "inappropriate in the situation. . . . felt to be improper" (1963, pp. 3–4). I favor the word "misbehavior" instead of synonymous phrases used by other researchers, such as "anti-social behavior" (e.g., MacKinnon, 1997; Reid, 1999; C B. Smith et al., 1998) or "deviant behavior" (e.g., Bruckman, 1994; Surratt, 1996), for several reasons. "Misbehavior" avoids certain connotations not applicable in all cases of rule-breaking: for example, "anti-" may imply purposeful intent and "deviant" may convey a sense of moral perversion; yet a great deal of misconduct is neither intentional nor perverted. The word "misbehavior" seems more general and neutral, in that it connotes conduct that does not follow norms, conduct that is awry, off, or somehow out-of-synch, anomalous or dysfunctional perhaps, but not necessarily intentional or perverted. In choosing "misbehavior" as the most adequate term, I also consider the recommendations of Becker, a sociologist specializing in deviance research, who suggests that "it might be worthwhile to refer to such behavior as rule-breaking behavior" and reserve the term "deviant" for other uses (1963/1973, p. 14). Deviance sociologists Pfuhl and Henry (1993) favor the phrase "rule-breaking" as well. Misbehavior, or *rule-breaking*, runs the gamut from playful and roguish pranks, tricks, teasing, and mischief that others find annoying, vexing, or irritating, to more serious and malicious offenses, violations, and transgressions that are judged nasty, evil, or injurious. In this study, a general distinction is made between misbehavior, which involves rule-breaking situations and internal rule-making and rule-enforcement; and *crime*, which involves law-breaking situations and external law-making and law-enforcement.

Behavior. For purposes of this study, "behavior" and "conduct" are used synonymously to mean observable human activity; an aggregate of responses to internal and external stimuli; a person's demeanor, deportment, and manner of acting. This definition follows Meyrowitz's use of the term "in its broadest sense to include all that people do in conscious and unconscious expression and communication" (1985, p. 335).

Regulation of misbehavior. For purposes of this study, "regulation of misbehavior" refers to how people address misbehavior; what people do when confronted with misbehavior; the technical and social means people use to deal with misbehavior. Regulation of misbehavior includes, on the one hand, *rule-making* (activities revolving around establishing, revising, and disseminating rules of conduct); and on the other hand, *rule-enforcement* (administration and application of rules of conduct through activities related to detecting and tracking misbehavior, as well as implementing sanctions to punish those who misbehave).

Rule. A regulation, principle, guideline, or custom governing behavior; what a person must or must not do in relation to various elements of a situation. As Goffman describes them, rules are "social norms regulating behavior of persons," "the regulations of conduct characteristic in . . . gatherings" (1963, pp. 17, 20). Rules evolve from behavioral *norms*, which are the standards, models, and patterns of conduct generally considered to be typical of particular social groups. For purposes of this study, rules refer to internal regulations, expressed in varying degrees of formality, developed and enforced within communities by community members themselves. Rules are distinguished from *laws*, which refer to external, highly formalized legislation, developed and enforced by authorities and institutions outside particular communities.

Internet. This study considers the Internet at the turn of the century, before the advent of numerous other online activities developed since the year 2000. Thus, this report does not cover subsequent waves of online activities sometimes referred to as social media, participatory media, Web 2.0, or what Levinson prefers to call "new new media" (2009, pp. 4–5), characterized by collaborative sharing of user-generated content and by user-centered design, as well as by multimedia systems which typically incorporate smartphones and similar hybrid devices with high-speed mobile computing. Although this study is limited in time up to roughly the year 2000, "Internet" is meant here in a wide sense to cover a variety of online environments, including post, chat, and meta-environments as explained below. There is ample precedent for this usage in other scholarly definitions. For example, Chen and Gaines define the Internet as "a network of networks based on the TCP/IP protocols; a community of people who use and develop those networks; [and] a collection of resources that can be reached from those networks" (1998, p. 222; see also Gumpert & Drucker, 1996, p. 28; S. G. Jones, 1998b, pp. xiii–xv; Rheingold, 1993, p. 83; Schnurr, 2000, p. 22; Strate, 1996a, 1999; Surratt, 1996, pp. 24–27). Strate et al. view the Internet or "Net" as "the sum total of this network of networks" (1996b, p. 8). Danet et al. broadly define the Net as "the worldwide system of commercial and noncommercial computer networks and gateways that includes the Internet, BITNET, USENET, FidoNet, Freenet, CompuServe, GEnie, America Online, Delphi, BIX and The WELL" (1998, p. 42). Similarly, Sproull and Faraj define the Net as "all interconnected, interoperating computer networks including commercial services such as Prodigy or CompuServe, and dial-up bulletin board services" (1995/1997, p. 35).

Virtual community. For purposes of this study, "virtual community" refers to a variety of places on the Internet where people gather for online group interaction. In characterizing virtual communities as online gathering places, I follow S. Johnson (1997), who uses the phrase "digital gathering place," as well as Sproull and Faraj (1995/1997), who describe virtual communities as "electronic gatherings." Gatherings have been defined by Goffman to include "all occasions when two or more persons are present to one another," with emphasis on participants' immediate co-presence in shared physical space (1963, p. 9), but his notion of gathering to can be extended to cyberspace, where different sorts of co-presence reign. Precedent for applying Goffman's ideas about face-to-face encounters to online environments can be found in the related literature (e.g., Aycock & Buchignani, 1995; Barnes, 1996b; Cheung, 1995; Cutler, 1996; Donath, 1999; Gotved, 2000; Hiltz & Turoff, 1978/1993; Lee, 1996; H. Miller, 1995; Rheingold, 1993; Rintel & Pittam, 1997a, 1997b; Rutter & G. Smith, 1999a, 1999b; Samarajiva & Shields, 1997; Surratt, 1996; Tapscott, 1998). In this study, virtual communities are distinguished from *offline communities*, where participants engage primarily in face-to-face communication, requiring each other's immediate physical and temporal co-presence. Such offline communities of co-presence are those of the traditional sort: not virtual, not in cyberspace, not online. The extension of conceptions of community from traditional offline contexts to online environments reflects a "loose consensus around community as referring to a multi-dimensional, cohesive social grouping that includes, in varying degrees: shared spatial relations, social conventions, a sense of membership and boundaries, and an ongoing rhythm of social interaction" (Mynatt et al., 1997). Virtual communities develop and exist in different sorts of online environments which, for purposes of this study, are organized into three categories, explained below: post environments, chat environments, and meta-environments.

Online environment. For purposes of this study, "online environment" refers to a variety of contexts in cyberspace where people gather to interact by means of networked computers, contexts which provide the locations, settings, sites, or venues where virtual communities develop and exist. Online environments vary according to prevailing technical and social conditions and influences. In this study, for convenience of organization and exposition, online environments are grouped into three categories: first, environments dedicated to posting; second, environments dedicated to chatting; and third, meta-environments which allow both posting and chatting.

1. *Post environments* involve asynchronous communication, that is, interaction without temporal co-presence. In post environments, participants conduct non-simultaneous, delayed conversations by posting messages at different times, reading and replying to each other's posts as suits their individual convenience, similar to correspondence or to notices on traditional bulletin boards offline (see, e.g., Igbaria et al., 1998, pp. 237–238; Strate, 1996b, p. 369; Strate et al., 1996b, p. 8). For purposes of this study, post environments on the Internet include: electronic mailing lists called "listservs," which circulate posts among subscribing members; and the international system of public message boards known as "Usenet newsgroups."

2. *Chat environments* employ synchronous communication, that is, interaction requiring temporal co-presence. In chat environments, participants hold live conversations by typing to each other almost simultaneously, for which they must be present online at the same time, much like chatting on the telephone (see, e.g., Igbaria et al., 1998, pp. 237–238; Strate et al., 1996b, p. 8). For purposes of this study, chat environments on the Internet include: Internet Relay Chat ("IRC"), where people gather for real-time typed conversation in "channels"; Multi-User Dungeons or Domains ("MUDs") and MUDs-Object-Oriented ("MOOs"), which permit users to combine chat with role-playing and text-based props and scenery; and "Palace" sites, which incorporate graphics in addition to text, participants appearing on screen as images called "avatars" and interacting with graphical props and scenery, as well as typing to each other.

3. *Meta-environments* include both asynchronous post environments and synchronous chat environments. For purposes of this study, three types of meta-environments are distinguished, as follows. First, independent bulletin board systems ("BBSs"), such as Echo, FidoNet, and the WELL, which provide both post and chat features. Second, mainstream networks such as America Online ("AOL") and CompuServe, as well as other Internet Service Providers ("ISPs"), which furnish both post and chat facilities. For example, AOL includes asynchronous message boards as well as synchronous "chat rooms"; CompuServe has special interest forums for posting, and also "CB channels" for chatting. And third, the World Wide Web (the "Web"), which houses an ever-increasing multitude of private and commercial sites for posting as well as chatting.

DELIMITATIONS

Misbehavior Versus Crime in Cyberspace. People engage in a broad spectrum of troublesome behavior in cyberspace, ranging from playful and mischievous pranks to serious and malicious transgressions. As mentioned in the preceding definitions and discussed in the chapters which follow, although this study focuses on the lower end of the spectrum of troublesome online conduct (i.e., misbehavior in virtual communities), some aspects of the higher end of the spectrum (i.e., cybercrime on the Internet), will be taken into account. Nevertheless, it must be stressed that the primary scope of this study is misbehavior in virtual communities, and not cybercrime on the Internet.

Types of Online Environments. Although this investigation was designed to cover a wide range of virtual communities in a variety of online environments on the Internet at the turn of the century (as explained further ahead in the section on methods), the following types of online environments were excluded from the study.

1. Online environments which primarily emphasize individual rather than group communication were not included: for example, personal email (versus group mailing lists), one-on-one instant message programs like Unix "talk," AIM (http://aim.com), and ICQ (http://icq.com) (versus group chat systems like IRC). Although AIM and ICQ provide some group activity, these environments are mostly oriented towards one-on-one dialogue rather than group conversation; furthermore, AIM and ICQ were introduced more recently, and limited research about these systems exists to date.

2. Online environments depending heavily on multimedia properties like sound and graphics were not included: for example, conference software incorporating audio and video such as NetMeeting (http://microsoft.com/netmeeting) and Cu-SeeMe (http://cuseeme.com). Not only are such environments relatively immature in terms of community development and research, but also, the reliance on sound and graphics in addition to text overly complicates such environments for purposes of this study. Text is still the most common mode of communication throughout the Internet, and sufficient text-based environments were available for this investigation. However, findings from this report about misbehavior in text-based environments may be applicable to future investigations of complex multimedia environments.

3. Online environments revolving around virtual games were not included, such as Ultima Online (http://uo.com; for descriptions of this gaming environment, see, e.g., Bruckman, 1999; Kim, 1998). Not only do such gaming environments employ multimedia capabilities, but also, thematic violence is typically an intrinsic part of the game (e.g., "outlaw" character roles, built-in "player-killing" routines). In addition, multi-player online games have internal game rules, and would therefore require sorting out the game structure type of rule-breaking from the misbehavior type of rule-breaking. From the point of view taken in this study, online gaming environments like Ultima Online bear greater resemblance to multi-user computer games played offline than to text-based virtual communities, the focus of this investigation.

4. Online environments developed since the turn of the century, from the year 2000 onward, were not included. This study does not consider numerous other online activities developed since roughly 2000. Sometimes referred to as social media, participatory media, Web 2.0, or what Levinson prefers to call "new new media" (2009, pp. 4–5), such activities are characterized by collaborative sharing of user-generated content and by user-centered design, as well as

by multimedia systems which typically incorporate smartphones and similar hybrid devices with high-speed mobile computing. Examples of more recent online environments not considered in this study are, among others: Blogger (1999), EverQuest (1999), Facebook (2004), Flickr (2004), Friendster (2002), LinkedIn (2003), LiveJournal (1999), Myspace (2003), Second Life (2003), Twitter (2006), Wikipedia (2001), World of Warcraft (2004), and YouTube (2005). However, findings from this report about misbehavior in turn-of-the-century online environments may be applicable to future investigations of newer online environments.

METHOD

The research method used for this study was philosophical inquiry. The corpus of data examined consisted of three bodies of existing literature (reviewed in Chapters Three, Four, and Five) related to the regulation of misbehavior in virtual communities on the Internet in a variety of online environments. For reasons discussed above in the rationale for the study, examining existing literature afforded a better point of departure for research into online misbehavior than conducting new ethnographic case studies. The accumulation of published accounts and analyses of such environments and associated issues, from both scholarly and popular literature, as well as the abundance of documentation produced by and for users of online environments, contained a wealth of information and ideas. From this existing literature, useful insights were extracted, and then explored, expanded, and integrated into a systematic analysis and assessment of how people regulate misbehavior in virtual communities (presented in Chapters Six and Seven).

Thus, the data for this study were obtained by examining what others have written, rather than through direct observation. In accordance with Emmet's (1968) description of philosophical inquiry, the research method consisted of "going and seeing" what has been said in the relevant literature, "sitting and thinking" about the findings, and ultimately, drawing conclusions. Nevertheless, this study transcends a simple review of the literature in that the literature served merely as a point of departure, providing data for the research. By analyzing and synthesizing the observations of others and drawing my own conclusions, this study presents an original contribution to communication and media theory in the form of an assessment of misbehavior and the regulation of conduct in virtual communities.

Two types of sources, principal and supplementary, were used to provide documentary evidence for analysis. The principal sources included published analyses and accounts of misbehavior and the regulation of conduct in online environments, from both scholarly and popular literature, available in print as well as electronically. The supplementary sources involved literature pertaining to regulation of misbehavior produced by and for users of online environments, including: prescriptive documentation available online such as Acceptable Use

Policies ("AUPs"), Frequently Answered Questions ("FAQs"), Network Working Group Requests for Comments ("RFCs"), and Terms of Service agreements ("TOSs"); guides, manuals, and primers; material from electronic mailing lists, message boards, newsgroups, and Web sites; and finally, help files incorporated into software programs used to access online environments.

With respect to subject matter, the principal sources included three bodies of related literature: first, accounts of the emergence of troublesome behavior in online environments and the evolution of a frontier mentality in cyberspace (reviewed in Chapter Three); second, material concerning cybercrime on the Internet from computer science and jurisprudence perspectives (reviewed in Chapter Four); and third, studies of misbehavior in virtual communities from communication and media theory perspectives, in particular, those focusing on behavior management and social control (reviewed in Chapter Five). These sources were chosen because they appeared to contain the most fertile and provocative ideas and information about misbehavior and the regulation of conduct in virtual communities on the Internet in a variety of online environments.

In order to facilitate the research process, source literature for data about online environments considered in this study was organized into four categories as follows: first, sources of data on the general cyberspace environment (the Internet overall, including material on cybercrime as well as surveys of multiple environments); second, sources of data on post environments (asynchronous); third, sources of data on chat environments (synchronous); and fourth, sources of data on meta-environments (both asynchronous and synchronous). Listed below are the four categories and nine groups of online environments which were considered in this study:

General Cyberspace Environment
    1.   The Internet overall
Post Environments (asynchronous)
    2.   Electronic mailing lists ("listservs")
    3.   Usenet newsgroups
Chat Environments (synchronous)
    4.   Internet Relay Chat ("IRC")
    5.   Multi-User Dungeons or Domains ("MUDs") and MUDs-Object-Oriented ("MOOs")
    6.   The Palace
Meta-Environments (asynchronous and synchronous)
    7.   Independent bulletin board systems ("BBSs") such as Echo, FidoNet, and the WELL
    8.   Mainstream networks such as America Online ("AOL") and CompuServe
    9.   The World Wide Web

Besides considering the general cyberspace environment in order to distinguish cybercrime and law-breaking from misbehavior and rule-breaking, the post, chat, and meta-environments selected for this investigation were restricted to those which met certain criteria at the time the study was designed, as noted above under delimitations. First, they had to be environments in which group interaction predominates, as opposed to one-on-one interaction. Second, they had to be environments that rely primarily on text-based communication, although environments which incorporate comparatively simple graphics (i.e., the Palace) were included as well. Third, they had to be mature environments with an ample supply of related documentation and literature, as opposed to more recent environments still in their infancy, for which there has not yet been enough time for data and research to accumulate or become available. And fourth, they had to be environments developed before the turn of the century.

This study was guided by questions based on ideas developed while reviewing related literature, as well as on Lasswell's classic summary question for communication inquiry: "Who, says what, in which channel, to whom, with what effect?" (as cited in Agee, 1985, pp. 22, 30). Modified to apply to misbehavior in virtual communities, Lasswell's question becomes: "Who, does what, in which online environment under what circumstances, to whom, with what effect?"

Subordinate Problem 1: To construct, on the basis of the literature, a taxonomy of misbehavior in virtual communities in different online environments (i.e., post environments, chat environments, and meta-environments). The purpose of this problem was to construct a taxonomy of misbehavior in virtual communities in different online environments. The data needed were information and ideas from the source literature about misbehavior in different online environments. The data were organized and analyzed according to type of misbehavior, type of online environment, and type of virtual community. From the results of this analysis, a taxonomy of misbehavior in virtual communities in different online environments was constructed. This taxonomy is presented in Chapter Six.

Subordinate Problem 2: To identify, on the basis of the literature, patterns and differences in types of misbehavior in virtual communities (according to online environments, virtual communities, and participants). The purpose of this problem was to identify patterns and differences in types of misbehavior in virtual communities. The data needed were the results of Subordinate Problem 1 as well as information and ideas from the source literature about patterns and differences in types of misbehavior in virtual communities. The data were organized and analyzed according to type of misbehavior, type of online environment, type of virtual community, and type of participant. From the results of this analysis, patterns and differences in types of misbehavior in virtual communities were identified. These findings are also presented in Chapter Six.

Subordinate Problem 3: To describe, on the basis of the literature, the means used to regulate misbehavior in virtual communities in different online environments (i.e., post environments, chat environments, and meta-environments). The purpose of this problem was to describe the means used to regulate misbehavior in virtual communities in different online environments. The data needed were information and ideas from the source literature about the means used to regulate misbehavior in virtual communities in different online environments. The data were organized and analyzed according to type of means used to regulate misbehavior, type of misbehavior, type of online environment, and type of virtual community. From the results of this analysis, descriptions of the means used to regulate misbehavior in virtual communities in different online environments were derived. These findings are presented in Chapter Six as well.

Subordinate Problem 4: To identify, on the basis of the literature, patterns and differences in the means used to regulate misbehavior in virtual communities (according to online environments, virtual communities, and participants). The purpose of this problem was to identify patterns and differences in the means used to regulate misbehavior in virtual communities. The data needed were the results of Subordinate Problem 3 as well as information and ideas from the source literature about patterns and differences in the means used to regulate misbehavior in virtual communities. The data were organized and analyzed according to type of means used to regulate misbehavior, type of misbehavior, type of online environment, type of virtual community, and type of participant. From the results of this analysis, patterns and differences in the means used to regulate misbehavior in virtual communities were identified. These findings are also presented in Chapter Six.

CHAPTER SUMMARY

This report is organized into seven chapters. Chapters One and Two present the study and its theoretical context; Chapters Three, Four, and Five review the source literature used in the study; Chapter Six presents the findings of the study; and Chapter Seven evaluates the results of the study. The content of each chapter is summarized below.

Chapter One describes the general purpose and structure of the investigation, explaining the rationale and need for the study, stating the research problem and its component sub-problems, defining key terms, and reviewing the method used in the investigation.

Chapter Two sets out the context of the study, reviewing two bodies of theoretical literature relevant for the investigation: first, literature related to media ecology approaches to communication; and second, literature related to CMC in online environments and to virtual communities.

Chapter Three reviews source literature related to the emergence of troublesome online behavior, an ensuing frontier mentality in cyberspace, and the evolution of two types of approaches for dealing with troublesome online behavior.

Chapter Four reviews source literature related to cybercrime on the Internet, primarily from computer science and jurisprudence perspectives, representing approaches which focus on technological and legal dimensions of troublesome online behavior.

Chapter Five reviews source literature related to misbehavior and rule-breaking in virtual communities, primarily from communication and media theory perspectives, representing approaches which focus on sociological and psychological dimensions of troublesome online behavior.

Chapter Six presents the findings of the study, describing three sets of issues: first, how rules are broken online, including the types of misbehavior in which people engage, as well as the types of people who break online rules; second, how rules are made online, including the types of rules applicable in online environments, the processes of rule-making and rule-dissemination, and the types of people who make online rules; and third, how rules are enforced online, including strategies and techniques of rule-enforcement, types of sanctions and penalties for rule-breaking, and the types of people who enforce online rules.

Chapter Seven evaluates the findings of the study, assessing the results and implications of the investigation, drawing overall conclusions, and offering suggestions for further research.

Chapter Two
The Context of the Study

MEDIA ECOLOGY:
THE STUDY OF MEDIA ENVIRONMENTS

Media ecology is a branch of communication and media studies that is still unfamiliar to many, having developed only over the past several decades. A succinct definition of media ecology as "the study of complex communication systems as environments" comes from Nystrom's unpublished doctoral dissertation, *Toward a Science of Media Ecology* (1973, p. 3). In this work, identified by Strate and Lum as "the first major treatise on media ecology as an emerging discipline" (2000, p. 56), Nystrom also quotes a more elaborate working definition of media ecology presented some years earlier by two pioneers in the field, her dissertation advisor, Postman, and his colleague, Weingartner:

> Media ecology is the study of transactions among people, their messages, and their message systems. More particularly, media ecology studies how media of communication affect human perception, feeling, understanding and value; and how our interaction with media facilitates or impedes our chances for survival. The word *ecology* implies the study of environments—their structure, content, and impact on people. An environment is, after all, a complex message system which regulates ways of feeling and behaving. It structures what we can see and say and, therefore, do. Sometimes, as in the case of a courtroom, or classroom, or business office, the specifications of the environment are explicit and formal. In the case of media environments (e.g., books, radio, film, television, etc.), the specifications are more often implicit and informal, half-concealed by our assumption that we are dealing with machines and nothing more. Media ecology tries to make those specifications explicit. It tries to find out what roles media force us to play, how media structure what we are seeing, why media make us feel and act as we do. Media ecology is the study of communications technology as environments. (Postman & Weingartner, 1971, p. 139, as cited in Nystrom, 1973, pp. 22–23, 120)

More recently, Nystrom describes media ecology as "a branch of environmental studies especially concerned with the human species and how we use information to adjust to our physical and social environments—and ourselves to them—in order to survive," and she suggests that the primary concerns of media ecologists are "ecologies of information and their consequences for human affairs" (1989, p. 2). Another recent definition comes from Lum, writing as guest editor of a special issue of the *New Jersey Journal of Communication* devoted to the intellectual roots of media ecology:

> Media ecology is the study of the interaction among various forms of media in the struggle for their own niche and survival in a complex ecology of social forces. Such is a good initial conception of what media ecology is because it points to one of media ecology's major concerns, that is, the complex symbiotic relationship among the media and, on another level, between media and the various forces in society. (2000, p. 1)

Yet another current definition of media ecology is provided by the Media Ecology Association ("MEA"), a professional organization founded in the late 1990s by researchers in the field. As recorded in the minutes of a business meeting held at the MEA's inaugural convention in 2000, after considerable debate, members voted to incorporate the following statement into the MEA's constitution: "media ecology is defined as the study of the complex set of relationships or interrelationships among symbols, media, and culture" (reported in Sternberg, 2000b, p. 15).

That even today media ecologists are still preoccupied with defining the field reflects the fact that media ecology is a relatively young discipline. According to Nystrom's early assessment, "media ecology has begun to take shape in recent years. As a systematic field of inquiry, it is still in its infancy and not as yet very well defined" (1973, p. 111). And in an essay published just a few decades ago, entitled "Social Science as Moral Theology," Postman emphasizes that the field continues to develop:

> The subject known variously as "Communication," or "Media Studies," or . . . "Media Ecology" . . . takes as its domain the study of the cultural consequences of media change. . . . As a young subject, media ecology must address such fundamental questions as how to define "media," where to look for cultural change, and how to link changes in our media environment with changes in our ways of behaving and feeling. (1988, p. 5)

Reviewing the rise of media ecology "as both an intellectual tradition and a theoretical perspective," Lum cites Postman's evaluation to underscore its ongoing validity, even today:

> Media ecology should be viewed as a field of study that is ever evolving. . . . media ecology is still a relatively new, if not strange, subject to many scholars

and students in culture and communication. In short, the intellectual terrain of media ecology has yet to be fully explored, mapped, and defined. (2000, p. 4)

As for the goals of media ecology, Nystrom provides perhaps the most straightforward summary statement:

Media ecology takes as its primary goal . . . to increase awareness and understanding of the processes of communication and of the effects of complex communication environments—including media, techniques, and technology—on human perception, feeling, value, and behavior. (1973, pp. 120–121)

And Postman offers a similar explanation:

The purpose of media ecology is to tell stories about the consequences of technology; to tell how media environments create contexts that may change the way we think or organize our social life, or make us better or worse, or smarter or dumber, or freer or more enslaved. (1988, p. 19)

The phrase "media ecology" is generally acknowledged to have come from McLuhan by way of Postman. Nystrom claims that "the term 'media ecology' itself was first employed in November of 1968 . . . Neil Postman used the term in a major address. . . . The first formal program in media ecology was established in the School of Education at New York University in 1971" (1973, pp. 111–112). Lum's account of the origins of the phrase and the discipline differs slightly from Nystrom's, but concurs in spirit:

While it has been suggested that McLuhan (1964) might have been the first person to use the term media ecology in the 1960s, it was Neil Postman who first gave media ecology a formal institutional base and a supportive intellectual forum where it began to take shape as a new field of media and communication studies. Postman founded the graduate Media Ecology Program at New York University in 1972. . . . Postman took McLuhan's ideas and his method of inquiry seriously not only because of McLuhan's intellectual brilliance but also because of Postman's own profound interest in understanding media as environments and environments as media. (2000, pp. 2–3; see also Gencarelli, 2000, pp. 91–92; Strate & Lum, 2000, p. 56)

Key to understanding the scope and goals of media ecology is the concept of information environments, analogous to physical environments, but composed of symbolic as opposed to physical matter. In *Teaching as a Conserving Activity*, a book about education which also serves as a primer on principles of media ecology, Postman offers the following explanation of information environments and their significance in human affairs:

Every society is held together by certain modes and patterns of communication which control the kind of society it is. One may call them information systems, codes, message networks, or media of communication. Taken together they set and maintain the parameters of thought and learning within a culture. Just as the physical environment determines what the source of food and exertions of labor shall be, the information environment gives specific direction to the kinds of ideas, social attitudes, definitions of knowledge, and intellectual capabilities that will emerge. . . . The means by which people communicate comprise an environment just as real and influential as the terrain on which they live. . . . When there occurs a radical shift in the structure of that environment this must be followed by changes in social organizations, intellectual predispositions, and a sense of what is real and valuable. (1979, pp. 33–35)

A concept similar to information environments is proposed by Meyrowitz, who studied with both Postman and Nystrom at New York University. Building on his 1979 doctoral dissertation in media ecology about the social impact of electronic media, in *No Sense of Place* Meyrowitz refers to "information-systems," which he defines as "set patterns of access to information about others" (1985, p. 333). According to Meyrowitz,

Media tend to create different types of social information-systems because they generally differ in terms of complexity of "access codes," physical characteristics, extent of "association" with content, "conditions of attendance," the degree to which an individual's access to information through the medium is public and explicit, the extent to which the form of information fosters personal or impersonal messages and responses, and the degree to which the medium strengthens or weakens the relationship between physical location and social experience. (1985, pp. 334–335)

What Postman's concept of information environments and Meyrowitz's concept of information-systems have in common is that both direct attention to the form and structure of communication rather than its content. In this sense, Postman and Meyrowitz continue a line of thought expressed in McLuhan's famous aphorism, "the medium is the message" (1964, p. 23).

To summarize, media environments, sometimes called information environments, communication environments, symbolic environments, or semantic environments, are the contexts, situations, settings, conditions, and circumstances in which we communicate. Media ecologists think of media environments as complex, dynamic, and interrelated systems that include communicators and their messages as well as the technologies and techniques used to communicate. Media ecology deals with discovering and exploring how media environments affect what we see and hear, how we feel and think, and what we do and say, in all areas of life. Media ecologists investigate how different media environments encourage and discourage, facilitate and impede, allow and deny, foster and prevent certain ways of perceiving, feeling, thinking, behaving, and evaluating ourselves and the world around us.

Despite the fact that media ecology is still an evolving discipline, two basic intellectual traditions informing the field can be distinguished. On the one hand, there is a tradition in media ecology of studying media as environments, focusing on mass communication and on *intra*personal communication. On the other hand, there is also a second tradition of studying environments as media, emphasizing *inter*personal communication.

The distinction between these two intellectual traditions, the study of media as environments as opposed to the study of environments as media, has been suggested by others in the field (e.g., Lum, 2000b, p. 3; Lum, 2006a, pp. 28–31). A clear articulation of the differences between these two intellectual traditions comes from Meyrowitz, who compares the two approaches underlying these traditions, which he prefers to call "medium theory" and "situationism":

> (1) "medium theory"—the historical and cross-cultural study of the different cultural environments created by different media of communication, and (2) "situationism"—the exploration of the ways in which social behavior is shaped by and in "social situations." These two fields have developed independently of each other and the main questions explored in them have traditionally been far removed from the main concerns of most mass communication researchers. Yet each of these areas of inquiry offers partial clues to a detailed theory of the effects of electronic media on social behavior. (1985, pp. 15–16)

Meyrowitz describes medium theorists as concentrating on characteristics of individual media as information-systems (pp. 16–23), noting that "the best known and most controversial of these scholars are Harold Adam Innis and Herbert Marshall McLuhan" (p. 16). Situationists, however, concentrate on characteristics of social situations as information-systems (pp. 22–23), according to Meyrowitz, and "the situationist whose approach may indirectly provide the most clues to the impact of new media on social roles is Erving Goffman" (p. 28).

The approach Meyrowitz calls "medium theory," construed here as the intellectual tradition of studying media as environments, focuses on media technologies as cultural and psychological environments, drawing on disciplines such as history, philosophy, psychology, literary studies, economics, and political science, and emphasizing investigations of mass and *intra*personal modes of communication. In contrast, the approach Meyrowitz calls "situationism," construed here as the intellectual tradition of studying environments as media, focuses on the ways people make meaning from various aspects of social situations, drawing on disciplines such as sociology and anthropology, and emphasizing investigations of *inter*personal modes of communication.

Unfortunately, scholars rarely combine these two intellectual traditions. As Meyrowitz observes, researchers taking the medium theory approach tend to concentrate on mediated environments, with scant consideration of social interaction in face-to-face communication environments; whereas those who follow the situationist approach tend to concentrate on face-to-face environments, with little attention paid to social interaction in mediated communication environments. Meyrowitz elaborates on these deficiencies and points to the resulting lack of integration between the two approaches:

> The medium theorists describe how media reshape large cultural environments and institutional structures; but they do not tell us much about the ways in which media reshape specific social situations or everyday social behaviors. . . . the situationists focus almost exclusively on face-to-face interaction and ignore interactions that take place through media. Yet beneath the surface, both perspectives . . . focus on the overall effects of the larger structure of the environment. . . . The largest problem in integrating these two perspectives is the theoretical gap in our understanding of the relationship between media and situations. The medium theorists discuss media as if they have little to do with the dynamics of face-to-face interaction, and the situationists barely seem to notice that media exist. (1985, p. 33)

Studies that link media and behavior in social situations, Meyrowitz argues, can help bridge this theoretical gap (pp. 13–34), and he demonstrates the power of combining medium theory and situationist approaches in his own work on the social impact of electronic media. Nevertheless, as discussed further ahead, Meyrowitz remains one of the few researchers to apply such a combined media ecology perspective in the realm of mediated interpersonal communication. But before addressing in more detail the relative scarcity of media ecology research that applies both these intellectual traditions to the study of mediated interpersonal communication, each of these traditions bears closer scrutiny. Therefore, the first tradition of studying media as environments is reviewed next, followed by a review of the second tradition of studying environments as media, with particular attention to key concerns of this latter line of inquiry, including conceptions of space and place, as well as the significance of situations, rules, and rule-breaking in social affairs.

MEDIA AS ENVIRONMENTS

The intellectual tradition in media ecology which studies media as environments, referred to as "medium theory" by Meyrowitz (1985, pp. 16–23), emphasizes technological aspects of particular media, especially their cultural and psychological impact. In this sense, media ecology involves "the study of media and technology *as* human environments" (Strate, 1996a). Scholars following this approach concentrate on investigations of mass communication and intrapersonal communication, drawing on disciplines such as history, philosophy, psychology, literary studies, economics, and political science.

This tradition of approaching media as environments is sometimes characterized as representative of the Toronto and New York schools of media ecology (e.g., Lum, 2000a, pp. 1–4; Strate, 1996a; Strate & Lum, 2000, pp. 56–57). According to Strate (1996a), the Toronto school includes scholars such as Carpenter (1960), Havelock (1982; see also Gronbeck, 2000), Innis (1951), McLuhan (1964), and Ong (1982). Strate includes in the New York school, among others, Gumpert (1987), Meyrowitz (1985), Mumford (1934; see also Strate & Lum, 2000), Perkinson (1991, 1996), and Postman (1979, 1982, 1985,

1988; see also Gencarelli, 2000). In addition to scholars like these identified with Toronto and New York, inquiries into media as environments have also been pursued by other major figures in media ecology, such as Eisenstein (1983), Ellul (1954/1964; see also Gozzi, 2000), and Langer (1942/1979; see also Nystrom, 2000).

Scholars following the intellectual tradition in media ecology of studying media as environments have generated an abundance of research on the impact of electronic media on human affairs. Concentrating on investigations of mass communication and intrapersonal communication, various media ecologists focus on electronic media as information environments from cultural, economic, educational, historical, philosophical, political, psychological, and technical points of view. Perhaps more than any other single work in the media ecology canon, McLuhan's groundbreaking speculations about a wide range of communication technologies in *Understanding Media* (1964) laid the foundations and set the agenda for research into media in general and electronic media in particular. This watershed publication was preceded by another milestone in media ecology, McLuhan's prior collaboration with Carpenter as editors of *Explorations in Communication* (Carpenter & McLuhan, 1960b), a collection of essays by various authors that includes discussions of electronic media.

McLuhan, Carpenter, and others mentioned above paved the way for subsequent work by scholars who have developed and extended the intellectual tradition of studying electronic media as environments. For example, Ong discusses electronic media in relation to what he calls "secondary orality" in *Orality and Literacy* (1982). Postman considers the cultural impact of television in *The Disappearance of Childhood* (1982), as well as the consequences of television for public discourse in *Amusing Ourselves to Death* (1985). The relationship between electronic communication technologies and the contemporary church is examined by Noone in *The New Reformation and the Electronic Media* (1986); while the role of television in promoting moral progress is evaluated by Perkinson in *Getting Better* (1991). In *Videotex and Conceptions of Knowledge* (1986), Quarles undertakes a historical analysis of the epistemological consequences of this electronic technology; and Frommer compares the expectations of Samuel Finley Breese Morse, Thomas Alva Edison, and Alexander Graham Bell about, respectively, the telegraph, phonograph, and telephone, with the consequences that actually ensued from these older electronic media in *How Well Do Inventors Understand the Cultural Consequences of Their Inventions?* (1987). Gumpert devotes several essays in his collection entitled *Talking Tombstones* (1987) to the effects of electronic media related to telephone and audio-video recording technologies; Strate explores the relationship between conceptions of the hero/celebrity and electronic media environments in *Heroes and Humans* (1991); and Gozzi addresses *The Power of Metaphor in the Age of Electronic Media* (1999).

The tradition of studying electronic media as environments includes numerous studies of the computer as medium, focusing on issues related to mass communication and intrapersonal communication. Researchers following such

lines of inquiry concentrate on computers as technologies for processing information, rather than as technologies used for social interaction. (Echoes of this
view of computers as information-processing devices can be found in present-
day visions of the Internet primarily as a source of information and data rather
than as a constellation of environments where people gather for social
interaction.)

Various scholars in the field of media ecology have studied computers as
media of mass communication and intrapersonal communication, approaching
the subject from cultural, economic, educational, historical, philosophical,
political, psychological, and technical points of view. For example, in *The
Human Use of Human Beings* (1950/1954), Wiener provides a seminal
discussion of cybernetics. Another early work in this area is Weizenbaum's
Computer Power and Human Reason (1976), which explores the differences
between human judgment and computer calculation. In *Mindstorms* (1980),
Papert examines how children learn by programming computers; while in *The
Second Self* (1984), Turkle considers the influence of computers on conceptions
of identity and self. The technological and economic origins of the information
society are analyzed by Beniger in *The Control Revolution* (1986); and the relationship between computer data processing and human thought is examined by
Roszak in *The Cult of Information* (1986). Bolter provides a historical perspective on the evolution and influence of computers in Western culture in *Turing's
Man* (1984); and in *Writing Space* (1991), Bolter examines computers and
hypertext in connection with the history of writing. In *Technopoly* (1992),
Postman considers the relationship between computer technologies and culture;
while in *No Safety in Numbers* (1996), Perkinson claims that computers have
caused people to quantify everything and become risk-averse. Barnes documents the development of graphical user interfaces in the evolution of computers in her doctoral dissertation (1995), following up this topic in a journal
article (2000). Barnes also collaborates with Strate in an article about educational implications of computer technology (Barnes & Strate, 1996). Levinson
applies a historical perspective to analyzing the present and future of the information revolution in *The Soft Edge* (1997), as well as in *Digital McLuhan*
(1999). And Wachtel addresses the interplay of art, technology, and perception
in *From Cave Walls to Computer Screens* (in press).

Studies such as these of computer technologies as media environments have
contributed enormously to our understanding of the cultural and psychological
impact of computers on mass and intrapersonal modes of communication. Yet
one area of inquiry remains largely unexplored by media ecologists: interpersonal communication in computer-mediated environments. As discussed in more
detail further ahead, over the last several decades, the rise of computer-mediated
communication ("CMC") in online environments has changed forever the landscape of electronic media and human interaction. Nevertheless, research on the
interpersonal aspects and social consequences of online CMC from a media
ecology perspective has begun to emerge only recently, perhaps because the
study of media as environments has attracted more attention in the field than has

the study of environments as media. This second intellectual tradition in media ecology is reviewed next.

ENVIRONMENTS AS MEDIA

If the first intellectual tradition in media ecology of studying media as environments is more prominent, in the foreground of the discipline, as it were, then lurking in the background is the second intellectual tradition in the field: the study of environments as media. Less familiar to many media ecologists, especially those primarily oriented by what Meyrowitz refers to as "medium theory" (1985, pp. 16–23), this second intellectual tradition of studying environments as media is informed by what Meyrowitz calls "situationism" (pp. 23–33; see also Cutler, 1996, p. 318). In contrast to the study of media as environments discussed above, the intellectual tradition of studying environments as media focuses on characteristics of social situations as information environments and the ways people make meaning from various aspects of social situations. Scholars following this second intellectual tradition in media ecology concentrate on investigations of interpersonal communication in contexts of group behavior and social interaction, drawing on disciplines such as sociology and anthropology.

This second intellectual tradition in media ecology of studying environments as media is effectively explained and demonstrated in Nystrom's little-known manuscript entitled *Media Ecology: Inquiries into the Structure of Communication Environments* (1979). In this unpublished work, distributed occasionally in communication courses at New York University, Nystrom provides an overview of this second intellectual tradition of studying environments as media:

> In the sense that studies of communication environments take as their focus questions about the structure and effects of social setting, symbolic systems, and cultural contexts on meaning-making and its human consequences, they may with some felicity be labeled *media ecology*. For ecology is the study of the structure of environments. And "media," as I am using the term here, are the social, symbolic, and cultural environments of which communication—the structuring of human meaning—is a product. (1979, Chapter 1, p. 20)

Nystrom elaborates on the notion of environments as media, and stresses the significance of studying social settings as communication environments:

> A medium of communication is an ordered social and symbolic environment—a particular organization of people and objects, using certain symbols and communication technologies, having a certain organization in time and space, and operating within a given culture—that structures the meaning-responses and consequently the thoughts, feelings, expectations, and transactions of its participants in particular ways. In this view, a school is a medium of communication. And a library. And a movie theatre, a coffee shop, a livingroom in which a family gathers to watch TV, an airplane, a teachers' conference, a

study where a solitary man simply sits and reads. What distinguishes these as environments, as media, is not that they are different *places*. For the same place may become a different medium of communication—that is, structure things differently—by changing its organization of space and time, its use of symbols, its use of communication technologies, or any one of a number of other variables. What those variables may be, and how they structure the meanings, not only of individuals in different social settings but, at the broader level, the patterns of thought and response, the habits of mind, of a culture, is the subject matter of media ecology. (1979, Chapter 1, pp. 22–23)

The second intellectual tradition in media ecology of studying environments as media draws heavily on what is often referred to as the symbolic interactionist approach to human affairs, originating in the field of sociology. Symbolic interactionists view social relations as transactional phenomena involving active meaning-making by participants, and social psychologist George Herbert Mead is the leading figure identified with the symbolic interactionist approach (see, e.g., Lofland, 1998, p. xvi; Surratt, 1996, pp. 4–5; West & Turner, 2000, pp. 74–76). Describing himself as a social behaviorist, Mead focuses on the psychology of the self in the context of group behavior, and his most important work, *Mind, Self, and Society* (1934), has influenced generations of scholars in various fields.

The symbolic interactionist approach to social relations provides the foundations for the perspective Meyrowitz refers to as situationism (1985, pp. 23–33; see also Cutler, 1996). Meyrowitz indicates social anthropologist Erving Goffman as the major situationist of relevance to the study of media (1985, p. 28), and summarizes his perspective as follows: "Goffman describes social life as a kind of multi-staged drama in which we each perform different roles in different social arenas, depending on the nature of the situation, our particular role in it, and the makeup of the audience" (1985, p. 2). Addressing social relations from a transactional point of view, Goffman deals with "the ways in which people—both alone and in 'teams'—constantly structure their appearance and behavior to convey socially meaningful messages and impressions" (Meyrowitz, 1979/1986, p. 254).

Among Goffman's many ethnographic investigations of the structure and dynamics of social situations, two books stand out as especially significant for the study of environments as media. In *The Presentation of Self in Everyday Life* (1959), probably his most often cited work, Goffman uses metaphors of theatrical performance to analyze social relations, focusing on how individuals present themselves to others. And in a later book, *Behavior in Public Places* (1963), less frequently mentioned but equally worthy of attention, Goffman examines the social organization of gatherings, with particular emphasis on rules of interaction in face-to-face encounters. That Goffman's ideas are of great import to media ecologists is confirmed by Nystrom, who singles out his work as furnishing one of the fundamental paradigms for media ecology research:

Goffman's model is also compatible with the assumptions, needs, and perspectives of media ecologists. Goffman is always concerned to describe the setting (or environment) in which the play takes place; the media ecologist places similar stress on the communication environment, whether it is a room in a university or a television set. Goffman is also concerned with the "masks" people wear, and, of course, the kinds of performances their situation compels them to give. Translated into media ecology terms, the Goffman model focuses attention on the states of mind media environments compel people to assume. (1973, p. 214)

The ethnographic approach used by Goffman to analyze everyday situations brings to mind a related discipline which also informs the second intellectual tradition in media ecology of studying environments as media: anthropology. From this field, the second intellectual tradition draws most notably on the work of Edward T. Hall, an anthropologist investigating cultural environments as media of communication. In *The Silent Language* (1959), Hall proposes a theory of culture as consisting of shared sets of "primary message systems." He identifies ten such message systems which form what he calls the "vocabulary of culture" (pp. 38–59), including temporality and territoriality, and addresses elements such as time and space in relation to different patterns of human activity and interaction. Hall underscores the importance of examining "unspoken, but very real patterns of behavior—what he calls *silent languages*—which serve to organize action and thought in any given culture" (Meyrowitz, 1979/1986, p. 255). Expanding on his notion that "space speaks" (Hall, 1959, pp. 162–185), in *The Hidden Dimension* (1966), Hall introduces a theory of "proxemics," the study of spatial aspects of behavior, devoting special emphasis to distinguishing different types of space (e.g., visual, auditory, olfactory) in discussing "the ways in which people use space and adjust interaction distances to suit different types of relationships" (Meyrowitz, 1979/1986, p. 254).

What Hall's anthropological research has in common with Goffman's sociological investigations, as Meyrowitz points out, is that both scholars suggest "an observable structure to interpersonal behavior—a structure that encompasses 'elements' or 'variables' which are commonly manipulated by people to create specific meanings and effects" (1979/1986, p. 254). By focusing on behavioral structures and elements from which people make meaning as well as the social impact of the meanings people make, Hall and Goffman shed light on areas of interpersonal communication that are critical for the study of environments as media. Meyrowitz explains the significance of their contribution as follows:

> Hall and Goffman present the kind of ethnographic data normally found in the work of anthropologists studying strange or primitive societies. Their observations, however, illuminate our own culture and behavior. Hall and Goffman try to make us aware of perceptions and actions which are normally intuitive and unconscious. Their work, therefore, does not tell us about behavior patterns which are foreign to us, but about patterns we know but do not usually know we know. (1979/1986, p. 254; see also Meyrowitz, 1985, p. 2)

But Hall and Goffman are not the only scholars to provide insight into aspects of communication environments that lie, for the most part, out of the realm of conscious awareness. The more subtle, hidden aspects of communication which are key factors in social interaction, and therefore of utmost importance to the study of environments as media, have stimulated various other researchers as well. Related areas of inquiry are illustrated by Nystrom in the following passage:

> Such students of culture and communication as Edward Sapir, Benjamin Lee Whorf, Dorothy Lee, Claude Levi-Strauss, Mary Douglas, Clifford Geertz, Edward Hall, Edmund Carpenter, Gregory Bateson, Paul Watzlawick, Erving Goffman, Eric Havelock, Walter Ong, Harold Innis, and Marshall McLuhan— to name only a few—have argued persuasively, each in his own way, that it is those aspects of language, of situations, of communications technologies which we least consciously recognize that most firmly regulate our meaning-making. Hall calls these the "covert" aspects of communication, the "hidden dimensions" of culture. Douglas refers to the hidden "rules" that regulate cultural meanings. McLuhan and others talk of the "invisible environments" created by communication technologies, and of the hidden ways in which these environments structure our meanings. Whatever the labels they use to describe the nonconscious, the unintended, the largely unrecognized aspects of human communication, such writers seem firmly agreed on one point: in shaping the meaning-making, not only of individuals but of entire cultures, that which is outside of our awareness plays a far more important role than the overt content of "messages." (1979, Chapter 1, p. 11)

Moreover, as Nystrom's summary reveals, connections exist between scholarship in the second intellectual tradition in media ecology, which addresses environments as media, and research in the first intellectual tradition, which deals with media as environments, the two traditions being complementary in nature rather than mutually exclusive. McLuhan provides a prime example of someone who transcends distinctions between the two intellectual traditions: despite his identification as the epitome of "medium theory" (Meyrowitz, 1985, pp. 3–4), McLuhan nevertheless ventures occasionally into subject matter more typical of situationists. In *Understanding Media* (1964), for instance, McLuhan highlights several structural elements of situations such as time in discussing clocks (pp. 135–144); and space in discussing roads and paper routes (pp. 90–104), housing (pp. 117–123), and transportation (pp. 162–169). In addition, the anthology edited by Carpenter and McLuhan, *Explorations in Communication* (1960b), contains several articles that take structural elements of situations into account, including the editors' collaboration on acoustic space (Carpenter & McLuhan, 1960a), Frank's essay on the role of skin and touch in tactile communication (1960), and Birdwhistell's piece on body motion or kinesics, "the study of non-verbal interpersonal communications" (1960, p. 54; see also Birdwhistell, 1970). Similarly, Postman transcends the distinction between the two intellectual traditions as well: his contributions to the study of media as environments mentioned previously (e.g., 1982, 1985, 1992) are complemented by certain areas of his work which advance the second intellectual tradition in media ecology of studying environments as media. For instance, Postman's books on education, such as *Teaching as a Subversive Activity* (Postman & Weingartner, 1969), *Teaching as a Conserving Activity* (1979), and *The End of Education* (1996a), demonstrate the second intellectual tradition by considering schools as environments. Likewise, Postman's *Crazy Talk, Stupid Talk* (1976) provides insight into various social aspects of face-to-face interpersonal communication.

Finally, it must be noted that the second intellectual tradition in media ecology of studying environments as media is also informed by other lines of inquiry, as well as those mentioned above. Strate suggests additional scholarship associated with the second intellectual tradition in media ecology:

> The other theoretical underpinning for environments as media, which begins with Shannon and Weaver's information theory, and Wiener's cybernetics, connects to systems theory as pioneered by Laszlo and Bertalanffy, and to the Palo Alto School started by Gregory Bateson, and including Paul Watzlawick with his relational approach to communication, Edward T. Hall's work on culture and nonverbal communication, Ray Birdwhistell's emphasis on context in the study of kinesics, and yes Goffman who obviously bridges both situationism and systems. This other stream is important because it then becomes a focus of Nystrom's dissertation comparing media ecology to systems theory, and is implicit in Meyrowitz, in that information systems is the common ground he establishes between the situations of symbolic interactionism and media ecology's media. (Strate, personal communication, August 9, 2001)

No doubt, the study of environments as media includes additional lines of inquiry such as these (and perhaps others yet to be recognized), and their contributions to the second intellectual tradition in media ecology deserve to be explored more fully in future research. But among these related perspectives, for this study, symbolic interactionist and situationist approaches appear the most relevant.

These, then, are the general outlines of the second intellectual tradition in media ecology, the study of environments as media, focusing on interpersonal modes of communication in face-to-face situations. Having described this second tradition, as well as the first tradition of studying media as environments, it will be argued further ahead that an integrated perspective which combines these two traditions is essential for the study of mediated interpersonal communication. But before proceeding to the subject of mediated interpersonal communication, and the relative scarcity of media ecology research in this area, especially with respect to online CMC, certain key concerns of the second tradition of studying environments as media require elaboration.

Prominent among the concerns of those who study environments as media are conceptions of space and place, as well as the significance of situations, rules, and rule-breaking in social affairs. These five key areas of concern in the second intellectual tradition merit summary discussions in their own right because they are highly germane to the present study of misbehavior in online environments but less familiar to many media ecologists. Therefore, conceptions of space and place in relation to communication environments are surveyed next, followed by a review of situations, rules, and rule-breaking and their significance in social interaction.

SPACE AND PLACE

The fundamental importance of space in social interaction cannot be overstated. As Hall explains in his seminal work on this "hidden dimension" of human affairs:

> Virtually everything that man is and does is associated with the experience of space. Man's sense of space is a synthesis of many sensory inputs: visual, auditory, kinesthetic, olfactory, and thermal. Not only does each of these constitute a complex system—as, for example, the dozen different ways of experiencing depth visually—but each is molded and patterned by culture.... The study of culture in the proxemic sense is therefore the study of people's use of their sensory apparatus in different emotional states during different activities, in different relationships, and in different settings and contexts. (1966, p. 181)

A similar sentiment is expressed by Nystrom, who asserts that "of all the factors that shape human meaning and response, that define situations, that tell us who and what we are, none is more compelling than space. . . . there is no aspect of human behavior that is not grounded in space" (1979, Chapter 3, p. 1). Like Hall before her, Nystrom argues that space is a powerful determinant of "public and private behavior, our feelings of group belonging, our social roles, our positions in the drama of hierarchy, our sense of potency or impotence, dependence or autonomy" (Chapter 3, p. 44). And in highlighting the dominant role space plays in social situations, Nystrom points to space as a concept linking the ideas of Goffman to those of Hall:

> It is space—how it is bounded and who has access to it—that tells us in large measure how we are to behave and how others may be expected to behave in a situation. It is space that tells us what is the relative status and power of different persons within a situation, and space that reveals how people in a situation are, to use Erving Goffman's term, "teamed." The space between persons shapes our feelings—of allegiance, intimacy, solidarity, security, hostility, even our sense of humor—and the orientation of people *in* space structures the kinds of transactions they are likely to have. Space even tells us what are the purposes to be accomplished in situations, and what attitudes or "mind sets" are appropriate. It is for these reasons that Edward Hall—who, more than any other contemporary writer, has brought space to the conscious attention of students of communication—calls space and its uses a "primary message system" of culture. (1979, Chapter 3, p. 3)

The relationship between space and media has not gone unexplored in the field of media ecology, as Strate observes in surveying this area of research (1996a; 1999, pp. 386, 396–397). Other scholars besides Hall address space in relation to media, although for the most part, they focus on mass and intrapersonal modes of communication rather than interpersonal communication. Among the earliest to present the basic notion of media altering conceptions of space is Innis, who distinguishes between space-biased media and time-biased media, and the space-binding and time-binding cultures to which they give rise, in *The Bias of Communication* (1951; see also Meyrowitz, 1985, pp. 16–17; Strate, 1996a). Another influential figure in media ecology, Mumford, considers space and communication in relation to architecture, cities, and urban planning in *Technics and Civilization* (1934; see also Strate, 1996a; Strate & Lum, 2000). Several articles in the Carpenter and McLuhan anthology, *Explorations in Communication* (1960b), also deal with space: for example, the piece by Carpenter and McLuhan contrasting acoustic space in oral cultures with visual space in literate cultures (1960a); and Giedion's essay on conceptions of visual space in prehistoric art (1960). As noted above, McLuhan's *Understanding Media* (1964) contains discussions of space in relation to transportation and housing, as well as his claim that electronic media have altered space to the extent of creating a "global village." Carpenter also tackles cultural conceptions of space in *They Became What They Beheld* (1970), a collaborative effort with Heyman which juxtaposes commentary about media analysis with multi-cultural photographs. In *The Responsive Chord* (1973), Schwartz discusses acoustic space with respect to psychological aspects of advertising. And Ong examines acoustic and visual space in *Orality and Literacy* (1982), while Eisenstein takes space into account in connecting the introduction of print to the rise of nationalism in *The Printing Revolution in Early Modern Europe* (1983).

Yet because scholars such as these study media as environments, in line with the first intellectual tradition in media ecology, they tend to concentrate on cultural and psychological aspects of space in relation to mass communication and intrapersonal communication, rather than social aspects of space in relation to interpersonal communication. For guidance on the role of space in face-to-face interpersonal communication, the second tradition of studying environments as media relies primarily on the core ideas of Hall (1959, 1966) and other situationists like Goffman (1959, 1963), augmented by interpretations and extensions of their work by subsequent generations of media ecologists such as Nystrom (1973, 1978, 1979) and Meyrowitz (1979/1986, 1985). In addition, as will be discussed further ahead, several other researchers besides Meyrowitz combine ideas from both the first and second intellectual traditions in media ecology in addressing the relationship between space and interpersonal communication in mediated environments (e.g., Drucker & Gumpert, 1997; Gumpert, 1987; Gumpert & Cathcart, 1986c; Gumpert & Drucker, 1996; Strate, 1982/1986, 1999).

Building on the chapter about territoriality in *The Silent Language*, in which he suggests that "space speaks" (1959, pp. 162–185), the theory of proxemics that Hall presents in *The Hidden Dimension* (1966) includes several central ideas about space and human affairs, which can be summarized as follows. Perception of space is multi-sensory, involving eyes, ears, nose, skin, and muscles (pp. 41–75). Based on sensory perception, Hall identifies six kinds of space: visual (sight); auditory (hearing); olfactory (smell); thermal (heat); tactile (touch); and kinesthetic (body movement). Furthermore, spatial perception is relative, Hall argues, depending on what sensory information is attended to and what is screened out; and perception of space is influenced by cultural context as well (pp. 1–6, 131–164). Hall also proposes three categories of space: "fixed feature" space, involving unmovable spatial characteristics, such as internal layouts of rooms and buildings and external groupings of villages and cities; "semi-fixed" space, involving movable positions and arrangements of objects and people; and "informal" space, involving interpersonal distances between people in face-to-face interaction (pp. 101–112). In the latter category, Hall distinguishes four zones of interpersonal space appropriate for different social situations: intimate distance, involving physical closeness often unsuitable in public; personal distance, the norm for separating people in general, a sort of invisible bubble around individuals; social distance, appropriate for impersonal business and casual gatherings; and finally, public distance, amplified or exaggerated spacing typical of formal occasions and large gatherings (pp. 113–129; see also Meyrowitz, 1979/1986, pp. 255–256).

A like-minded approach to space and interpersonal communication is found in Nystrom's unpublished manuscript (1979), which consists of three chapters dealing in general with the study of environments as media, and in particular, with social situations and space. Although no bibliographical information is included, Nystrom's discussion of space refers not only to Hall's work, but also to the ideas of sociologists such as Mead and Goffman. Thus, Nystrom focuses more on social aspects of space than on physical or cultural aspects as Hall does. In discussing spatial environments, Nystrom emphasizes four characteristics of space as most significant for social interaction (1979, Chapter 2, pp. 6–9, 24–25). First is the space itself: its size, shape, configuration, and boundaries. Second is what a space contains: people, furnishings, and other objects, as well as their arrangements within that space. Third are limitations on access to space, such as entry and exit, as well as access to people and objects within a particular space. Such limitations on who has access to a space under what circumstances, as well as the degree to which they have access to the animate and inanimate contents of that space, generally depend on the authority controlling the space. And the fourth characteristic pertains to the types of activities that go on inside a space, the sorts of situations and transactions which may occur in given spatial environments.

The issue of access to space involves two related factors, as Nystrom points out: "the first is *who* may have access to a space, and the second is the conditions under which access may be obtained" (1979, Chapter 3, p. 10). Based on these factors, Nystrom distinguishes three types of space: public, private, and semi-public (pp. 9–10). She defines public space in relation to access as follows:

A "public" space is a space to which any and all members of a community have access; and there are no conditions which one must meet to gain access to it. To put it somewhat differently, a public space is a space in which no individual may control the entry, exit, or behavior of others. (1979, Chapter 3, p. 10)

Access to private space, on the other hand, is quite limited: as Nystrom explains, "the individual determines who may enter, and under what conditions; how long and under what conditions others may stay" (p. 17), the most important consequence being that in private space, "we are not compelled to transact with strangers" (p. 18). Nystrom also proposes that limitations on access to space contribute to feelings of group identity (pp. 21–22), and that one of the primary means of defining a group's identity is to deny outsiders access to shared spaces occupied by that group (p. 26). Similar observations about the connections between group identity and group territory are made by Meyrowitz as well (1985, pp. 56–57).

The distinction between public and private space that Nystrom bases on levels of access reflects Goffman's definitions of public places as "any regions in a community freely accessible to members of that community" versus private places as "soundproof regions where only members or invitees gather" (1963, p. 9). Goffman's definitions are also cited by Samarajiva and Shields, two telecommunications researchers outside the field of media ecology, who suggest that "public environments are those not designated as private. . . . characterized by a relative openness to initiation of communication by others, and private spaces are characterized by a relative closedness to initiation of communication" (1997, pp. 541–542). And like Nystrom, media ecologists Gumpert and Drucker as well distinguish between public and private spaces on the basis of access (1996, p. 30; see also their discussion of public and private space in relation to gender and media in Gumpert & Drucker, 1997, pp. 3–9).

But public space and private space are merely the extremes on a spectrum of discriminatory access. Nystrom identifies a third intermediate category which she refers to as semi-public space:

Ranged between those most private spaces to which none but ourselves have access and those most public spaces to which any and all have access is a vast continuum of spaces and situations neither fully public nor fully private, but semi-public. These are spaces to which we do not personally control the access of others, but to which access is limited by certain conditions, established jointly by the state and the individuals to whom the space "belongs." A movie theatre is such a space, and a college, a business office, a museum. How we feel and behave in such spaces depends on their relative position in the continuum between "private" and "public." And that depends on the complexity of the conditions that permit and deny access to strangers. (1979, Chapter 3, pp. 19–20)

An intriguing class of semi-public space where strangers interact is illustrated in Nystrom's essay on transitional space, those territories like elevators and waiting rooms that lie between well-defined social systems (1978, p. 246). Transitional space is described by Strate as "something of a no one's land or interzone; for example an airport or train or bus station, or one of the vehicles themselves," as opposed to permanent space which is "regularly occupied and consistently cared for" (1999, p. 406).

Similar characterizations of space according to levels of access are provided by Lofland, a sociologist whose work on cities and urban settings is influenced by situationists such as Goffman and Hall. In *A World of Strangers* (1973), Lofland defines public space as "those areas of a city to which, in the main, all persons have *legal access*," as opposed to private space, where access may be legally restricted, noting also that "the line between public and private space, like the line between strangers and personally-known others, is a fluid one" (pp. 19–20; see also 1998, p. 8). In her later book, *The Public Realm* (1998), Lofland presents a three-part categorization of space reminiscent of Nystrom's (1979) differentiation of public, semi-public, and private space discussed above. However, Lofland refers to social territories as "realms" and distinguishes among private, parochial, and public realms based on the dominant type of relations occurring therein:

> A private realm exists when the dominating relational form found in some physical space is intimate. A parochial realm exists when the dominating relational form found in some physical space is communal. A public realm exists when the dominating relational form found in some physical space is stranger or categorical. (1998, p. 14)

And, like Nystrom, Lofland emphasizes the significance of transacting with strangers in defining the public realm as:

> Those areas of urban settlements in which individuals in copresence tend to be personally unknown or only categorically known to one another. . . . spaces in a city which tend to be inhabited by persons who are strangers to one another or who "know" each other only in terms of occupational or other nonpersonal identity categories (for example, bus driver-customer). (1998, p. 9)

The kinds of communal territories identified by Lofland as parochial realms and by Nystrom as semi-public spaces bring to mind the notion of "third places" proposed by Oldenburg, another urban sociologist. Often cited in the literature on computer-mediated communication (e.g., Cheung, 1995; Danet et al., 1998; Doheny-Farina, 1996; Rheingold, 1993; Sproull & Faraj, 1995/1997; Surratt, 1996; Turkle, 1995), in *The Great Good Place: Cafés, Coffee Shops, Community Centers, Beauty Parlors, General Stores, Bars, Hangouts, and How They Get You Through the Day*, Oldenburg writes about the crucial role played in people's lives by "those happy gathering places that a community may contain, those 'homes away from home' where unrelated people relate" (1989/1997,

p. ix). Third places where people congregate for social interaction serve as key settings for informal public life, as Oldenburg explains:

> The third place is a generic designation for a great variety of public places that host the regular, voluntary, informal and happily anticipated gatherings of individuals beyond the realm of home and work. . . . the first place is the home. . . . the second place is the work setting. (1989/1997, p. 16)

Such third places constitute parochial realms, according to Lofland (1998, p. 93), who cites Oldenburg's work in connection with "the beneficial functions of settings in which nonintimate relationships abound" (p. 62). The value of communal activities in public spaces outside the home is also stressed by Gumpert and Drucker:

> We learned about events and people. We played and watched others play. We escaped the tyranny of those we love for a moment or two by watching others whom we had not yet met. We conversed with strangers we might not meet again and old companions who were recurring supporting characters in our lives. (1996, p. 30; see also Gumpert, 1987, pp. 167–189; Gumpert & Fish, 1990a, pp. 3–4)

In surveying such discussions of social territory as those provided by Hall and Nystrom about space, by Lofland about realms, and by Goffman and Oldenburg about place, it becomes evident that the terms "space" and "place" are not always clearly differentiated and often used interchangeably. For example "place" is obviously a central concept in Meyrowitz's *No Sense of Place*, yet he omits it from an appendix discussing key terms, content merely to state that he uses "place" to mean "both social position and physical location" (1985, p. 308). And the lone entry under "space" in Meyrowitz's index simply refers the reader to "place" (p. 412).

Nevertheless, several scholars do distinguish place as a more subjective social construct than space. For instance, Gumpert and Drucker propose that "a *place* is a *space* with 'psychological or symbolic meaning' . . . *space* refers to the abstract geographical qualities of environment, which become transformed into meaningful places as people use, modify, or attribute symbolic value to specific settings" (1997, p. 2). Similarly, Strate notes that "space is associated with the natural, the chaotic, the unnamed and the untamed; place is associated with the cultural and rhetorical, with order and familiarity" (1999, p. 395). Strate goes on to quote geographer Yi-Fu Tuan's distinction between place and space: "'place is security, space is freedom: we are attached to the one and long for the other.'" Referring to Tuan's distinction, Healy adds that "we long for place as well as space" (1997, pp. 57, 65–66). Also citing Tuan's distinction, Lofland concludes that "places are *especially meaningful spaces*, rich in associations and steeped in sentiment" (1998, p. 64), and further, that "the critical component of 'place' is sentiment" (p. 75, n. 18).

Such distinctions between place and space adequately reflect the transactional nature of human meaning-making with respect to spatial environments, and the difference between the two concepts can be summarized as follows: places are particular spaces (or categories of spaces) that people invest with extra meanings. These extra meanings arise through repeated transactions people have with the same (or similar) spaces, singling out certain spaces as special in some way, such as giving them names or addresses. It is essential to note, however, that conceptions of place do not necessarily depend on specific geographic or physical locations. As Nystrom remarks in discussing transitional spaces such as airports, elevators, and waiting rooms, "a place may remain the same from a physical point of view and yet be the setting for many different roles and situations" (1978, p. 247; see also 1979, Chapter 1, p. 22). Or, as Goffman puts it, "multiple social realities can occur in the same place. . . . the same physical space can come to be used as a setting for more than one social occasion" (1963, pp. 20–21). And the reverse is true as well: different locations may be classified as the same type of place if similar roles and situations are enacted within them. Nystrom offers a simple yet perceptive illustration of the independence of place from location:

> It is tempting to say . . . that home is a *place* that has a particular relation to other places and spaces—that "home" is the first apartment to the left of the elevator on the fourth floor of the building across the street from the church . . . and so on. But this explanation—that "home" is a specific location—raises some problems. If I move, for example, that place will still be where it was. But I will no longer call it "home." Moreover, I can recognize at once that I am in someone else's "home," even though I arrive in the dead of night and have no idea of its location. And so it is with other situations as well. Most of us would recognize at once the situation called "a coffee shop" or "a classroom," without reference to signs or specific locations. (1979, Chapter 2, pp. 2–3)

That we recognize categories of space and place independent of specific locations suggests that the activities and transactions occurring within spaces and places are crucial factors in shaping the meanings people make of social territories. This is why Nystrom identifies the situations and behavior that occur within a given spatial environment as among its most important defining characteristics (Chapter 2, p. 3). In addition to space and place, what Nystrom describes as "the social situations that structure human meanings" (p. 1), as well as the "transactional patterns—who says what to whom, through what symbol system, and how, and when, and under what conditions" (pp. 24–25), are also prominent concerns for those who study environments as media. Therefore, having surveyed conceptions of space and place of relevance to the intellectual tradition of studying environments as media, the areas reviewed next involve the significance of situations, rules, and rule-breaking in social affairs.

SITUATIONS, RULES, AND RULE-BREAKING

If the second intellectual tradition in media ecology, the study of environments as media, has roots in Hall's anthropological approach to space, then it is equally grounded in Goffman's sociological approach to situations and rules of behavior. Beginning with the metaphor of theatrical performance for analyzing social relations introduced in *The Presentation of Self in Everyday Life* (1959), perhaps his best-known work, and continuing with *Behavior in Public Places* (1963), his classic on the social organization of gatherings in face-to-face environments, Goffman stands out as one of the most influential situationists for scholars studying environments as media. As noted above, subsequent generations of media ecologists such as Nystrom (1973, 1979) and Meyrowitz (1979/1986, 1985) explicitly acknowledge their intellectual debt to Goffman. And in Goffman's own field, urban sociologist Lofland commends the scope and insight of his contributions:

> Goffman almost inadvertently focused his enormous talent for microanalysis on numerous instances of public realm interaction. . . . Goffman demonstrated eloquently and persuasively that what occurs between two strangers passing on the street is as thoroughly social as what occurs in a conversation between two lovers, that the same concerns for the fragility of selves that is operating among participants in a family gathering is also operating among strangers on an urban beach. (1998, p. 4).

While Goffman's earlier study of the presentation of self highlights the ways individuals manage the performances they enact in group situations (1959), his later work brings group behavior into the foreground, focusing on the patterns of interaction themselves, "that aspect of public order pertaining to the conduct of individuals by virtue of their presence among others" (1963, p. 242). Suggesting that the significance of behavioral patterns in group interaction has been underestimated, Goffman describes the target of his research as:

> An important area of social life—that of behavior in public and semipublic places. Although this area has not been recognized as a special domain for sociological inquiry, it perhaps should be, for rules of conduct in streets, parks, restaurants, theaters, shops, dance floors, meeting halls, and other gathering places of any community tell us a great deal about its most diffuse forms of social organization. . . . the study of ordinary human traffic and the patterning of ordinary social contacts has been little considered. (1963, pp. 3–4)

Clearly, Goffman's subject matter involves behavior in the same range of social territories referred to as public and semi-public spaces by Nystrom (1979) and as public and parochial realms by Lofland (1998), as well as those Oldenburg considers third places (1989/1997). But Goffman is one of those scholars who, as noted above, never quite explains precisely what he means by place or space. Place and space are concepts which Goffman often mentions, and certainly takes into account; however, he addresses these concepts indirectly as part of his discussion. Instead, concerned primarily with the structure of *what* goes on and only secondarily with *where*, Goffman concentrates on scrutinizing the social transactions in which people engage.

In analyzing how people behave when they interact in public, Goffman emphasizes the notion of gathering rather than place, as Lofland astutely observes (1973, p. 185, n. 21; 1998, p. 20, n. 7). Goffman himself states his focus as "the study of *gatherings*, all occasions when two or more persons are present to one another" (1963, p. 9). Goffman further defines "gathering" in relation to two other key concepts, "situation" and "occasion":

> I shall use the term gathering to refer to any set of two or more individuals whose members include all and only those who are at the moment in one another's immediate presence. By the term situation I shall refer to the full spatial environment anywhere within which an entering person becomes a member of the gathering that is (or does then become) present. . . .
>
> Along with "gathering" and "situation," another basic concept must be tentatively defined. When persons come into each other's immediate presence they tend to do so as participants of what I shall call a *social occasion*. This is a wider social affair, undertaking, or event, bounded in regard to place and time and typically facilitated by fixed equipment; a social occasion provides the structuring social context in which many situations and their gatherings are likely to form, dissolve, and re-form, while a pattern of conduct tends to be recognized as the appropriate and (often) official or intended one—a "standing behavior pattern." . . . Examples of social occasions are a social party, a workday in an office, a picnic, or a night at the opera. (1963, pp. 17–18)

Thus, Goffman seems to propose a continuum of related concepts, with "gathering" as the narrowest or most specific, "occasion" as the broadest or most general, and "situation" in the middle range between the two. And in claiming that "the regulations of conduct characteristic in situations and their gatherings are largely traceable to the social occasion in which they occur" (p. 20), Goffman suggests that to some degree, all three concepts are relevant for understanding patterns of group behavior. Nonetheless, Goffman restricts his investigations to the narrower range of "situations and their gatherings, not social occasions" (p. 21). Given that Goffman's approach is usually referred to as "situationism," and based on common usage in the related literature, it appears that of the three concepts, "situation" has become the most widely accepted.

In the decades since Goffman first called attention to the study of behavioral patterns in social situations, this line of inquiry has continued to evolve, albeit slowly. According to Meyrowitz, "because of the lack of full awareness of situations, situations have remained a minor part of social inquiry until recently. . . . in recent years there has been a dramatic increase in the examination of social 'episodes,' 'settings,' and 'contexts'" (1985, p. 27). As noted above, in *No Sense of Place* Meyrowitz reviews the situationist perspective in relation to the study of information-systems or environments (pp. 23–33). In so doing, Meyrowitz summarizes what he calls "the elusive variable of 'social situation'" (p. 23) as:

> The social environments, or "contexts," in which certain types of behaviors are socially expected and exhibited. They are the complexly determined and often elusive settings in which we play out and witness social roles. . . . People consciously and unconsciously vary their behavior to match the definition of social situations and the "audience" for their performances. (1985, pp. 332–333)

Meyrowitz further observes that social situations are generally characterized by a number of structural elements, including "*where* one is, who else is *there*, the date and time, and the overall definition of the event taking place in that particular time/space frame ('party' vs. 'meeting,' for example)" (p. 333).

Among the structural elements that characterize situations, perhaps the most commonly addressed relate to conceptions of place. Meyrowitz explains that "situations are usually defined in terms of behaviors in physical locations" (p. 35), and underscores how conspicuously conceptions related to place figure in several situationist approaches:

> Goffman, for example, describes a behavioral region as "any *place* that is bounded to some degree by barriers to perception." Roger Barker sees "behavioral settings" as "bounded, *physical-temporal locales*." Lawrence Pervin defines a situation as "a specific *place*, in most cases involving specific people, a specific time and specific activities." . . . Situationists also consider many other characteristics of situations, including: tasks, goals, rules, roles, traditions, temporal factors (season, month, day, time, and length of encounter), the characteristics of the people present (number of people, their age, sex, status, nationality, race, religion, degree of intimacy with each other), and the subjective perceptions of participants. But place often figures as an implicit part or explicit part of the definition of situation, perhaps because situationists realize that so many of the other factors would be affected by a major change in the physical setting or its boundaries. (1985, p. 35)

One illustration of the power of place in orienting social behavior, as well as the awareness some researchers have of this power, comes from an anecdote recounted by Oldenburg. He tells of an environmental psychologist who, when asked how to explain human behavior, suggested that "he merely needed to know where the individual in question was located—if the person is in church, he 'acts church.' If he's in a post office, he 'acts post office'" (Oldenburg, 1989/1997, p. 295). A less simplistic and more revealing portrayal of how location shapes human meaning-making is furnished by Nystrom:

> Knowing *where* we are tells us *who* we are, and who are the others around us. . . . In a very real sense, we do not now *how* to speak, to move, dress, think, feel—how to respond to the people, objects, and events around us—unless we know where we are. Imagine, if you can, awakening out of a profound

unconsciousness, such as only deep anaesthetic or traumatic head injury can produce, to utter darkness, unplaceable sounds, and the touch of *something* against your skin. How would you respond? Most likely, with panic. Not just *fear*—that you might be ill, injured, captive. But the panic of meaninglessness—of not knowing *how* to respond, *how* to feel, *what* to make of your sensations. This is why ambulance attendants and recovery room personnel make it a practice to tell patients returning to consciousness, at once, where they are. "You're in the hospital" reassures, not because it's not frightening to be injured or ill, but because it allows one to make meaning of one's experience—makes certain things, even unpleasant things like pain, predictable. . . . doctors do not tell reviving patients *who* they are. And no soap opera amnesiac, on first regaining consciousness, demands at once to know "Who am I?" We may manage things—shakily—it seems, without knowing who we are. But without knowing where we are, we cannot manage things at all. (1979, Chapter 2, pp. 4–5)

But if where we are tells us how to behave, this brings up another question: how do we know where we are to begin with? The short answer is: it depends on the situation in which we find ourselves. Among media ecologists, it is perhaps Nystrom who most carefully addresses this issue. Analyzing situations as communication environments, Nystrom explains the structure of a situation as a set of conditions that orients how people respond to events, objects, and behaviors around them:

If we do not recognize situations by their labels, locations, or functions, how then do we know where we are? And what does it matter, anyway? We know where we are, I think, because we recognize, all unawares, a set of *conditions*: conditions involving space, conditions involving time, conditions involving objects, symbols, and the transactions between people. And it matters because those conditions allow us not only to label a situation, but to predict how others will behave and what expectations they will have of us. (1979, Chapter 2, p. 3)

Nystrom goes on to provide a brief but thorough microanalytic view of the conditions and variables of situations in which people transact. Similar to the structural elements described by Meyrowitz as characteristic of social situations (1985, p. 35), Nystrom considers a set of structural conditions which she summarizes as follows:

The structure of a situation, then, is a set of conditions that limits the responses of people to specific events, objects, behaviors within it. . . . And these conditions, the variables that define a situation and make a difference in response, involve space—its boundaries and internal arrangements; objects—their type and arrangement in space; time—its boundaries and organization; access—to other persons, to space, to objects, to sensory information; dress; personal demeanor; and transactional patterns—who says what to whom, through what symbol systems, and how, and when, and under what conditions. . . . [and] two other characteristics of situations . . . roles and purposes. Indeed, no analysis of situations can be complete without reference to these two factors. (1979, Chapter 2, pp. 24–25)

So where we are tells us who we are, and who we are depends, in large part, on the roles we perform in social interaction. It is therefore no coincidence that Nystrom stresses how influential roles are in guiding transactional patterns of situational behavior. The term "role," according to Cutler, "comes from George Herbert Mead (1934), who defined it as 'a socially prescribed way of behaving in particular situations for any person occupying a given cultural or social organizational position'" (1996, p. 321, n. 3). In Goffman's work on the presentation of self, he defines social roles as "the enactment of rights and duties attached to a given status," and suggests that a role follows a part or a routine, a "pre-established pattern of action which is unfolded during a performance and which may be presented or played through on other occasions" (1959, p. 16). Nystrom similarly refers to "parts" and "roles" in describing situational behavior:

> By a "part" or a "role" I mean a pattern of behavior that differs in identifiable ways from other patterns of behavior in the situation, no matter who is performing it. To put it somewhat differently, a role is those aspects of behavior that remain the same in a given situation, irrespective of the personalities of the individuals enacting the role. (1979, Chapter 2, pp. 26–27)

Nystrom also observes that role structure—how many roles are involved and the extent to which those roles are fixed or flexible—is an important ingredient in the meanings participants make of situations (p. 30). And two additional points to bear in mind, according to Nystrom, are that roles are "*relative*—based on relationships with others" and that they are "*behaviorally* defined" (p. 32). The idea that roles are relative to behavior in situations is also apparent in Meyrowitz's definition:

> A social role is a *selected* display of behaviors that, when taken as a whole, is perceived by members of the social community or group to be appropriate for an individual in a given social situation. As one sociologist notes, "Crying as such is a behavior which cannot be described as a 'role'; crying at a funeral is behavior which can be so described—it is expected, appropriate, specific to the situation." The performance of a social role is determined not only by the situation, but also by the relative status or position of those engaged in the situation. Thus the priest at a funeral is expected to enact a different set of behaviors from the widow. (1985, p. 335)

How particular roles should be performed depends on another powerful factor involved in situational behavior: rules. Someone enacting a role or playing a part in a situation must do certain things and must not do other things; such behavioral requirements and limitations constitute the rules of a given role.

Meyrowitz effectively describes how roles and rules are implicated in the definition of particular situations:

> Each defined situation has specific roles and rules. A funeral demands behaviors different from those at a wedding, a party has rules different from those of a classroom, a job interview entails roles that are distinct from those in a psychiatric counseling session. Anyone who believes that situational definitions and situationally defined roles have no "reality" should attempt to behave in the first of each of these pairs of situations as they would normally do for the second.
>
> Each situational definition also prescribes and proscribes different roles for the different participants. When a patient goes to speak to a psychiatrist, the situation determines the range of behaviors for each person. Only one of the two participants, for example, is "allowed" to cry. Similarly, a minister at a funeral must behave differently from the relatives of the deceased.
>
> When people enter any given interaction, therefore, the first thing they need to know is "what is going on here?" They need to know the "definition of the situation." The definition of the situation is a simple concept that is used to describe the complex dynamics of encounters and the rules that govern them. (1985, p. 24)

As Goffman explains, "when in the presence of others, the individual is guided by a special set of rules . . . situational proprieties" (1963, p. 243). These situational proprieties or rules of "proper conduct" are "the regulations of conduct characteristic in . . . gatherings (pp. 20, 24). In examining the structure and function of such "social norms regulating behavior" (p. 17), Goffman distinguishes codes of situational proprieties—i.e., rules of conduct appropriate for various situations—from other sorts of social regulations:

> When persons are present to one another they can function not merely as physical instruments but also as communicative ones. This possibility, no less than the physical one, is fateful for everyone concerned and in every society appears to come under strict normative regulation, giving rise to a kind of communication traffic order. . . . The rules pertaining to this area of conduct I shall call *situational proprieties*. The code derived therefrom is to be distinguished from other moral codes regulating other aspects of life (even if these sometimes apply at the same time as the situational code): for example, codes of honor, regulating relationships; codes of law, regulating economic and political matters; and codes of ethics, regulating professional life. (1963, pp. 23–24)

Various sorts of situational rules come into play in group behavior. In his study of the presentation of self, for instance, Goffman discusses a panoply of rules that guide individual and team performances in group situations (1959; see also Meyrowitz, 1979/1986). But it is Goffman's research on public behavior that best displays his talent for discerning the most subtle rules that operate in situations where people socialize in groups. Goffman summarizes the comprehensive range of situational rules examined in his study of public behavior as follows:

> Rules about access to a bounded region, and the regard that is to be shown its boundaries, are patently rules of respect for the gathering itself. Regulations against external preoccupation, "occult" involvements, and certain forms of "away" ensure that the individual will not give himself up to matters that fall outside of the situation. Regulations against unoccasioned main involvements or overtaxing side involvements (especially when either of these represents an auto-involvement) seem to ensure that the individual will not become embroiled divisively in matters that incorporate only himself; regulations against intense mutual-involvement provide the same assurances about the conduct of a subset of those present. In short, interests that are larger or smaller than the ones sustainable by everyone in the gathering as a whole are curtailed. (1963, p. 194)

The rules encapsulated by Goffman in this passage are rather abstract and somewhat hard to imagine without the benefit of his accompanying discussion. A more concrete depiction of the kinds of situational rules of behavior appropriate for particular roles comes from Meyrowitz, who states in plain terms some of the rules governing a waiter's public behavior:

> He is polite and respectful. He does not enter into the dinner conversation of his patrons. He does not comment on their eating habits or table manners. He rarely, if ever, eats while in their sight. In the dining hall, setting, appearance, and manner are carefully controlled. (1979/1986, pp. 264–265)

A key idea suggested by the sorts of situational proprieties Goffman and Meyrowitz describe is that many such rules of group behavior are implicit rather than explicit, covert as opposed to overt. This notion is also evident in Meyrowitz's observation that "when we chastise someone for acting 'inappropriately,' we are implicitly paying homage to a set of unwritten rules of behavior matched to the situation we are in" (1985, p. 23). In contrast to the numerous explicit laws and regulations that govern public behavior in a judicial sense, the basic rules that operate in social situations are, for the most part, implicit, internalized, and unconscious, as Nystrom explains:

> Such controls on behavior "in public" as do exist are exerted through only two channels: by the state and its representatives and by the internalized set of shared social rules—norms—that regulate behavior from within the individual. The state, of course, regulates public behavior through its laws and the agents delegated to enforce them. . . . far more powerful, pervasive, and rigid than the controls exercised by the state are the internalized social norms that regulate behavior in public. (1979, Chapter 3, pp. 10–11)

The differences between formalized codes of conduct involved in legal systems and the lower-level, hidden sorts of rules guiding social behavior are reminiscent of Hall's distinctions among formal, technical, and informal levels of culture in *The Silent Language* (1959, pp. 60–96). In the realms Hall identifies as formal and technical are overt and consciously-known rules, often stated explicitly or written down; in the informal realm are covert and unconscious rules that remain implicit, unstated, and out-of-awareness.

Among the situational rules orienting group behavior, there is none more fundamental than the imperative to conform to the situation, or as Goffman puts it, to "fit in." Goffman describes how this overarching rule of "fitting in" is a theme encountered throughout the range of situations covered in his study of group interaction:

> The rule of behavior that seems to be common to all situations and exclusive to them is the rule obliging participants to "fit in." The words one applies to a child on his first trip to a restaurant presumably hold for everyone all the time: the individual must be "good" and not cause a scene or a disturbance; he must not attract undue attention to himself, either by thrusting himself on the assembled company or by attempting to withdraw too much from their presence. He must keep within the spirit or ethos of the situation; he must not be *de trop* or out of place. Occasions may even arise when the individual will be called upon to act as if he fitted into the situation when in fact he and some of the others present know this is not the case; out of regard for harmony in the scene he is required to compromise and endanger himself further by putting on an air of one who belongs when it can be shown that he doesn't. . . . No doubt different social groupings vary in the explicitness with which their members think in such terms, as well as in the phrases selected for doing so, but all groupings presumably have some concern for such "fitting in." (1963, p. 11)

An enlightening lesson on this social imperative to conform to the situation that Goffman identifies as the rule of "fitting in" comes from one of the most infamous social science experiments of the twentieth century: the research performed by social psychologist Milgram and reported in his book, *Obedience to Authority* (1974). Milgram's study furnishes a fascinating illustration of how structural elements of situations can be manipulated to influence the social meanings people make and the ways they behave in contexts of group interaction. An excellent summary of what Milgram's findings imply about the power of social situations to mold people's behavior is provided by Postman:

> A piece of work that is greatly admired as social science, at least from a technical if not an ethical point of view, is the set of experiments (so called) supervised by Stanley Milgram, the account of which was published under the title *Obedience to Authority*. In this notorious study, Milgram sought to entice people to give electric shocks to "innocent victims" who were in fact conspirators in the experiment and did not actually receive the shocks. Nonetheless, most of Milgram's subjects *believed* that the victims were receiving the shocks, and many of them, under pressure, gave shocks that, were they real, might have killed the victim. Milgram took great care in designing the environment in which all this took place, and his book is filled with statistics that indicate how

many did or did not do what the experimenters told them to do. As I recall, somewhere in the neighborhood of 65 percent of his subjects were rather more compliant than would have been good for the health of their victims. Milgram drew the following conclusion from his research: In the face of what they construe to be legitimate authority, most people will do what they are told. Or, to put it another way, the social context in which people find themselves will be a controlling factor in how they behave. (Postman, 1988, p. 10)

The extremes to which people will go to "fit in" are demonstrated rather conclusively by Milgram's findings. In his experimental design, Milgram manipulated various situational elements and conditions such as those mentioned by Meyrowitz (1985, p. 35) and Nystrom (1979, Chapter 2, pp. 24–25), including space, time, roles, participants, dress, personal demeanor, objects, symbol systems, and access. Using variables like these, Milgram's experimental situation was structured so as to generate impressions of authority and to pressure people into defining the situation in a certain way and acting accordingly. In the design and interpretation of his research, Milgram draws on situationist approaches such as Hall's proxemics (1996) and Goffman's study of the presentation of self, particularly the concepts of performance teams and frontstage and backstage behavioral regions (1959; for interpretations and extensions of Goffman's work in this area, see also Meyrowitz 1979/1986, 1985; Nystrom, 1973, 1979). Clearly, one of the key factors on which Milgram's experiment depends is the tendency of people to conform to the definition of a situation established by its various structural characteristics and conditions. Explaining the nature of this social urge to conform to the situation, Milgram also indicates some of the consequences of breaking the rule of "fitting in":

Goffman (1959) points out that every social situation is built upon a working consensus among the participants. One of the chief premises is that once a definition of the situation has been projected and agreed upon by participants, there shall be no challenge to it. Indeed, disruption of the accepted definition by one participant has the character of moral transgression. Under no circumstance is open conflict about the definition of the situation compatible with polite social exchange. . . .

Social occasions, the very elements out of which society is built, are held together, therefore, by the operation of a certain situational etiquette, whereby each person respects the definition of the situation presented by another and in this way avoids conflict, embarrassment, and awkward disruption of social exchange. The most basic aspect of that etiquette does not concern the content of what transpires from one person to the next but rather the maintenance of the structural relations between them. (Milgram, 1974, pp. 150–152)

What Milgram's remarks only hint at is that his study of obedience can also be viewed as an investigation of *disobedience*, or *rule-breaking*. Perhaps more revealing than the majority of subjects who "fit in" and complied with the demands of the experimental situation are those cases where subjects refused to obey and broke the rule of "fitting in." The incidents Milgram reports where people challenged authority and deviated from conventional behavior by disobeying are, in large part, what make visible the patterns of conformity of those who did obey. Thus, not only does Milgram's experiment elucidate the rule of "fitting in," it also demonstrates the fruitfulness of looking beyond rules and behavior to rule-breaking and misbehavior.

The question then arises as to how productive it might be to investigate rule-breaking and misbehavior directly instead of considering them simply as negative counterparts of rules and appropriate behavior. Indeed, several scholars answer that the study of rule-breaking and misbehavior can unveil and illuminate patterns in regular behavior which might not otherwise penetrate our awareness or catch our attention. For instance, Goffman discusses "discrepant" roles and performances (1959) and emphasizes the social significance of "inappropriate behavior," "misconduct," and "situational impropriety" in revealing what constitutes "proper public conduct" (1963, pp. 3–25, 193–197). Hall notes that it is often easier to discern what rules exist, especially informal, unstated, or implicit rules, when they are violated (1959, p. 127). Meyrowitz observes that "the sense of 'appropriateness' is generally unconscious and becomes visible only when people behave 'improperly'" (1985, p. 335). In fact, Meyrowitz refers to one researcher developing "a method of making situational conventions visible by breaking the rules of situations and then observing the resulting confusion and the process of reconstruction that follows" (p. 28). More recently, a sociologist studying computer-mediated communication asserts that "it is quite often the case that a researcher's best understandings of the particular social order under consideration stem from the observance of the violation of that order, social deviance" (Surratt, 1996, p. 363; for detailed discussions of social deviance, see Becker, 1963/1973; Pfuhl & Henry, 1993). And one participant in an online symposium sums up the relevance of misbehavior as well as anybody:

> It is only [through] deviant behavior that we can in fact define what is normative. [Deviant behavior] is an essential component of culture without which we'd have difficulty defining what is normative. Durkheim said that, not me. So a bit of deviance in all communities is essential. ("Cilla," as cited in Bruckman, 1999).

In short, looking at misbehavior and rule-breaking is like using a lens for sharpening our perceptions of behavior that does conform to rules.

At this point, it should be apparent that situations, rules, and rule-breaking are extraordinarily significant in shaping social interaction, and that conceptions of space and place are intricately tied up with the meanings people make of the situations in which they find themselves. The survey of these five key areas completes the review of the lesser known of the two intellectual traditions informing the field of media ecology, the study of environments as media. So far, discussion has revolved around social situations in face-to-face environments. But what about social situations in environments that involve mediated communication? The subject addressed next, therefore, is mediated interpersonal communication, an area in which both the study of media as environments and the study of environments as media contribute as equally indispensable traditions.

MEDIATED INTERPERSONAL COMMUNICATION

The preceding review of the two intellectual traditions in media ecology suggests that media ecologists tend to concentrate on issues related to mass communication and *intra*personal communication, in line with the first tradition of studying media as environments that prevails in the field. As a result, the second tradition, the study of environments as media, has been relegated to a more obscure position, and in general, researchers in the field do not often contemplate matters associated with *inter*personal communication. In particular, media ecologists have made few excursions into the realm of mediated interpersonal communication.

For the most part, the relatively scarce research that applies both intellectual traditions in media ecology to the investigation of mediated interpersonal communication grows out of work carried out in each tradition related to space and place. The relationship between space and media has not gone unexplored in the field of media ecology, as discussed above. In surveying this area of research (1996a; 1999, pp. 386, 396–397), Strate points to contributions from foundational scholars such as Carpenter, Eisenstein, Innis, McLuhan, Mumford, Ong, and Schwartz, as well as to more recent work on mediated space and place by researchers such as Drucker, Gumpert, and Meyrowitz.

Scholars such as these consider interpersonal communication in conjunction with a wide range of media, including speech, writing, and print. However, interpersonal communication in computer-mediated environments is of greatest relevance to the present study; therefore, the discussion in this section is confined to media ecology research in the areas of electronically-mediated and computer-mediated interpersonal communication. The first area reviewed below encompasses media ecology research published primarily during the 1980s on interpersonal communication involving electronic media such as telephone, radio, and television. Computers are occasionally mentioned in this area, but to a limited degree, which is understandable given that interpersonal communication in computer-mediated environments was still emerging at the time such literature was published. The second area surveyed concerns media ecology research published since 1990 on computer-mediated communication, particularly related to social interaction in online environments.

Some of the earliest media ecology approaches to electronically-mediated interpersonal communication appear in a series of anthologies edited by Gumpert and Cathcart entitled *Inter/Media: Interpersonal Communication in a Media World* (1979, 1982, 1986a). The three editions contain articles reprinted from other sources as well as pieces written especially for the series. One of the most noteworthy selections is an article by the editors themselves, originally published in the *Quarterly Journal of Speech*, in which they propose a typology of mediated interpersonal communication (Cathcart & Gumpert, 1983/1986, also reprinted in Gumpert & Fish, 1990b). Grounded in the ideas of important figures in the second media ecology tradition such as Mead and Hall, the typology presented by Cathcart and Gumpert includes useful definitions of mass, intrapersonal, interpersonal, and mediated interpersonal modes of communication. They define *mass communication* as "a circumstance of communication in which a medium replicates, duplicates, and disseminates identical content to a geographically wide spread population" (1983/1986, p. 27); *intrapersonal communication* consists of "non-observable internalized dialogue which occurs in all humans" (p. 28); and *interpersonal communication* involves "dyadic interaction which takes the form of verbal and nonverbal exchanges between two or more individuals, consciously aware of each other, usually interacting in the same time and space, performing interchangeable sender-receiver roles" (p. 29). And they define *mediated interpersonal communication* as "a general category referring to any situation where a technological medium is introduced into face to face interaction. . . . any person-to-person interaction where a medium has been interposed to transcend the limitations of time and space" (p. 30). Cathcart and Gumpert consider even written messages such as letters and artifacts bearing text (e.g., bumper stickers or T-shirts) to constitute mediated interpersonal communication, although they devote more attention to electronically-mediated communication, including telephone conversations, CB and ham radio, audio and video recordings, and even electronic mail (pp. 30–31).

Other salient articles in the Gumpert and Cathcart anthologies also deal with the impact of electronic media on interpersonal communication. The editors' own piece on non-physical intimacy addresses media-based relationships conducted exclusively through various electronic technologies (Gumpert & Cathcart, 1986c). In an article on talk radio as an example of a medium which provides interpersonal as well as mass communication, Avery and McCain review some of the differences between mass and interpersonal communication, making the vital point that in mass communication individuals are typically passive receivers whereas in interpersonal communication they are active senders as well as receivers (1982/1986). Schafer brings up the idea of "sound walls" in his essay on acoustic space with respect to electronic technologies such as telephone, phonograph, and radio (1977/1986). Also included in the anthologies is Aronson's classic article from the *International Journal of Comparative Sociology* about the impact of the telephone on social relationships (1971/1986). A piece by Meyrowitz combines Goffman's work on impression management with Hall's ideas about proxemics in comparing space as experienced interpersonally with space as portrayed through television cameras (1979/1986). Finally, in an imaginative essay about media and the sense of smell that extends Hall's work on proxemics and olfactory space in admirable fashion, Strate considers the lack of olfactory space in electronic environments, though focusing on products such as perfume rather than on electronic media (1982/1986).

Two additional collections of short pieces tackle various aspects of electronically-mediated interpersonal communication from media ecology points of view. One is Gumpert's *Talking Tombstones* (1987), a set of his own essays including several related to social interaction and mediated space and place: "Walls of Sound" about the effects on acoustic space of electronic technologies for playing recorded sound, ranging from portable devices such as personal stereos (with and without headphones) to the institutional systems known as "Muzak" (pp. 76–100); "Talking to Someone Who Isn't There" about the social implications of telephone sex (pp. 121–139); and the "The Limits of Community," about the influence of various electronic media on group socialization (pp. 167–189). The second relevant collection is *Talking to Strangers*, an anthology on mediated therapeutic communication edited by Gumpert and Fish (1990b), which contains articles exploring "the various ways in which media of communication serve the therapeutic needs of contemporary society" (1990a, pp. 6–7), and includes material on electronic media used for social interaction such as telephone, radio, and television.

But the big fish in the little pond of media ecology research on mediated interpersonal communication is unquestionably Meyrowitz. As opposed to the short pieces mentioned above in the anthologies edited by Gumpert and his various collaborators, with *No Sense of Place* (1985) Meyrowitz contributes a full-length treatment of mediated interpersonal communication, perhaps the most significant book in this area so far in the media ecology canon. Despite the book's age and the fact that computers are barely mentioned (not surprising given the 1985 publication date), the scholarship displayed in this work continues to stand out for its scope and depth, evident in the rich theoretical framework Meyrowitz provides as well as the ingenuity with which he uses this framework to analyze the impact of electronic media, principally television, on social interaction. One media ecologist writing in later years who applauds Meyrowitz for extending Goffman's ideas to the medium of television summarizes his research as follows:

> In his discussion of roles, Meyrowitz (1985) builds on the work of Erving Goffman (1959), who uses analogies between roles played on the dramatic stage and those played in social life. Goffman proffers the idea of stages to distinguish between role behaviors in public (front stage) and private (backstage). Meyrowitz applies Goffman's analogy to mediated behavior and makes the point that television publicly portrays for all ages and sectors of society behavior that was once private, thus blurring the distinction between the two stages and the roles played there. (Cutler, 1996, p. 324)

Among the many virtues of Meyrowitz's work is that the discussion in *No Sense of Place* suggests a reason why there are relatively few studies of mediated interpersonal communication in the discipline of media ecology. The scarcity of research in this area can be attributed to an underlying lack of integration between the two intellectual traditions informing the field: the study of media as environments tends to be divorced from the study of environments as media. Nobody complains more vehemently or more lucidly than Meyrowitz about the lack of integration of the approaches informing the two intellectual traditions in media ecology, approaches he refers to as "medium theory" and "situationism" (1985, pp. 16–34). In surveying the differences between these two approaches, as noted above, Meyrowitz argues that medium theorists tend to concentrate on mediated environments, with scant consideration of social interaction in face-to-face communication environments; whereas situationists tend to concentrate on face-to-face environments, with little attention to social interaction in mediated communication environments (p. 33). Based on such deficiencies, Meyrowitz criticizes the two leading scholars identified with these approaches:

> Goffman and McLuhan have complementary strengths and weaknesses: Goffman focuses only on the study of face-to-face interaction and ignores the influence and effects of media on the variables he describes; McLuhan focuses on the effects of media and ignores the structural aspects of face-to-face inter-action. These oversights may stem from the traditional view that face-to-face behavior and mediated communications are completely different types of inter-action—real life *vs.* media. (1985, p. 4)

In fact, Meyrowitz takes Goffman to task not only for restricting his research solely to situations of co-presence, but also for neglecting media overall:

> Goffman's emphasis on face-to-face rather than mediated interaction, for example, is clear throughout his work. He explicitly focuses on information received through the "naked senses," not through sensory augmenters. . . . defining situations in terms of "immediate physical presence." . . . Even when Goffman mentions electronic or other media (often as literal footnotes to his work), he seems to view their effects as unusual or amusing and, in most cases, as peripheral to the core of social action he describes. (1985, p. 345, n. 53)

There can be no doubt that Goffman confines his work to face-to-face encounters where people are physically co-present. As he states in discussing the limitations of his research on "behavior of persons immediately present to each other" (1963, p. 17), Goffman is concerned exclusively with:

> One type of regulation only, the kind that governs a person's handling of himself and others during, and by virtue of, his immediate physical presence among them; what is called face-to-face or immediate interaction will be involved. . . . the component of behavior that plays a role in the physical traffic among people. (1963, pp. 8–9)

Face-to-face interaction is defined in Goffman's earlier work as "the reciprocal influence of individuals upon one another's actions when in one another's immediate physical presence" (1959, p. 15). Further stressing the role of physical presence in his later work, Goffman asserts that to meet "the full conditions of *copresence*," people must "sense that they are close enough to be perceived in whatever they are doing, including their experiencing of others, and close enough to be perceived in this sensing of being perceived" (1963, p. 17). And co-presence is significant, Goffman claims, because it "renders persons uniquely accessible, available, and subject to one another. Public order, in its face-to-face aspects, has to do with the normative regulation of this accessibility" (p. 22). Like Goffman, Nystrom also emphasizes the significance of co-presence in discussing conditions of situations (1979). She defines situations of full co-presence as those in which "all have access to the same information within the temporal and spatial boundaries of the meeting" (Chapter 2, p. 15). However, Nystrom acknowledges that situations in technologically-mediated environments differ with respect to degrees of co-presence:

> The extent to which others are co-present defines situations and shapes our meanings. To be "fully co-present," as I am using the term, means that each person in a situation is accessible to the others through sight, sound, smell, and, in particular, touch. Persons accessible to each other only through sound (as in telephone conversations), or only through sight and sound (as in two-way interactive television hookups) are not fully co-present. And this fact accounts for important differences in behavior—a point critical to our understanding of the impact of modern communication technologies on human meaning-making. (1979, Chapter 2, pp. 13–14).

And as a consequence of isolating themselves from the role played by communication technologies in shaping social behavior, situationists tend to overlook the impact of media change. Meyrowitz finds fault with situationists like Goffman for this reason: "situationists are more concerned with describing situations and situational behaviors as they exist in a society rather than in analyzing how and why situations evolve. Such a static, descriptive approach is not very useful in analyzing or predicting social change" (1985, p. 33). And even situationists acquainted with electronic media seem unaware that changes in communication technologies imply concomitant changes in social interaction, as Meyrowitz observes:

> Ironically, the development of electronic media has been cited by situationists as one possible cause of the recent interest in the study of situations. . . . these media have generally been seen only as lenses to look through in order to examine face-to-face behaviors more closely. The study of the *transformation* of situations through new media . . . has gone largely unexplored. (1985, p. 345, n. 53)

This is where the first intellectual tradition in media ecology of studying media as environments becomes relevant in advancing situationist perspectives beyond their deficits with respect to media change.

Besides the unfortunate lack of integration between medium theory and situationism about which Meyrowitz complains, a related reason for the scarcity

of work on mediated interpersonal communication from media ecology perspectives can be deduced from arguments made by Gumpert and Cathcart. Criticizing underlying divisions in mainstream communication research, Gumpert
and Cathcart identify a detrimental schism separating the study of interpersonal
communication from the study of mediated communication. In their typology of
mediated interpersonal communication, for example, Gumpert and Cathcart
claim that "it is difficult to find an interpersonal communication text or resource
book which treats the subject of media as a significant factor. The role of media
in personal communication has, by and large, been overlooked" (Cathcart &
Gumpert, 1983/1986, p. 26). And in the preface to one edition of their
Inter/Media series (1986a), Gumpert and Cathcart protest against splitting communication studies into separate categories like mediated communication versus
interpersonal communication because such compartmentalized thinking ignores
both the pervasiveness of media technologies in human affairs and the symbiotic
relationship between mediated and interpersonal communication. Gumpert and
Cathcart underscore "the inextricable relationship between media and interpersonal communication" (1986b, p. 9) which calls for the sort of integrated
research included in their anthologies:

> It is our intention, through this collection of readings and original essays, to
> begin to bridge the gap that has existed in the study of mediated communica-
> tion and interpersonal communication. We have tended in the past to treat the
> mass media as isolated phenomena having little to do directly with interper-
> sonal communication, and we have dealt with interpersonal communication as
> though mass media did not exist. . . . To a large extent, the study of interper-
> sonal communication has concentrated on the relationship between two persons
> without regard for the media environment which contains that relation. . . . the
> nexus of media and interpersonal communication has been overlooked. . . .
> What has been underemphasized is the whole of the communication process: a
> process in which each part affects the other part and no one part can be fully
> understood apart from the whole. It is our intent in this book to emphasize the
> connections; to restore a perspective that has been overlooked in the accelera-
> tion of technology and the collision with face-to-face communication. (1986b,
> pp. 10–11)

Like the lack of integration between medium theory and situationism, this gap
between the study of mediated communication and the study of interpersonal
communication also accounts for the limited research media ecologists have
conducted in the area of mediated interpersonal communication. Other than
media ecology studies of CMC discussed further ahead, only occasionally in the
past decade have media ecologists taken up the challenge of combining medium
theory and situationism in approaching electronically-mediated interpersonal
communication (see, e.g., Lum's 1996 study of karaoke music technology and
the construction of identity in Chinese America).

The power of applying an integrated perspective combining medium theory
and situationist approaches to the investigation of interpersonal communication

in mediated environments is best demonstrated by Meyrowitz's work on changes in social interaction due to the advent of electronic media, especially television (1985). In developing an analytical framework grounded in sociological and anthropological theory as well as media and communication theory, the key to Meyrowitz's effectiveness is that he identifies the structure of social situations as "a common denominator that links the study of face-to-face behavior with the study of media" (1985, p. 4). Meyrowitz explains how the idea of focusing on situations guides his approach to mediated interpersonal communication:

> To examine the effects of new patterns of social communication, this book takes a "situational approach" to the study of media and behavior. . . . situations are usually defined in relation to *physical* settings: places, rooms, buildings, and so forth. The theory developed here . . . extends the analysis of physically defined settings to the analysis of the social environments created by media of communication. (1985, pp. viii–ix)

What allows Meyrowitz to link interpersonal communication in face-to-face situations and in mediated situations is that he views both physical place and media as information-systems and therefore as functional equivalents. This approach enables Meyrowitz to extend "the study of situations beyond those interactions that occur in place-bound settings" (p. 37; see also Strate, 1996a; 1999, p. 402), and overcome the schism between research on mediated and interpersonal communication identified by Gumpert and Cathcart (1986b; Cathcart & Gumpert, 1983/1986). According to Meyrowitz, mediated as well as interpersonal situations involve patterns of access to social information and to the behavior of others, which is why they both function as information-systems:

> The notion of situations as information-systems allows for the breakdown of the arbitrary distinction often made between studies of face-to-face interaction and studies of mediated communications. The concept of information-systems suggests that physical settings and media "settings" are part of a continuum rather than a dichotomy. Place and media both foster set patterns of interaction among people, set patterns of social information flow.
>
> Thus, while places create one type of information-system—the live encounter—there are many other types of situations created by other channels of communication. The wider view of situations as information-systems, rather than as places, is especially relevant to the study of *electronic* media because electronic media have tended to diminish the differences between live and mediated interaction. The speech and appearance of others are now accessible without being in the same physical location. The widespread use of electronic media leads to many new social situations. (1985, pp. 37–38)

Not only does Meyrowitz's integrated approach link "the discussion of media with the discussion of place-bound situations," it also expands "the description of relatively fixed role behaviors in static situations into an analysis of situational and behavioral *change*" (p. 34). The introduction of electronic media alters the structure of information-systems, generating new kinds of social situations and, as Meyrowitz observes, "changes in the notion of 'appropriate' roles and behaviors . . . can often be traced back to structural changes in social situations" (p. 174). Meyrowitz explains the potential of new media to change the structure of situations:

> Media are types of social settings that include or exclude, unite or divide people in particular ways. . . . a new type of medium may restructure social situations in the same way that building or breaking down walls or physically relocating people may either isolate people in different situations or unite them in the same situation. (1985, p. 70)

By structurally reorganizing situations and promoting new ways for people to interact in environments that transcend or affect physical co-presence, as Meyrowitz points out, "electronic media have changed the rules that were once particular to specific social situations" (p. 143). Basically, electronic media have provoked profound transformations in the most fundamental aspects of social affairs related to space, place, situations, and behavioral patterns. Meyrowitz summarizes the impact of electronic media on these significant areas related to social interaction as follows:

> The relationship between situations and behavior provides one key to an analy-sis of the impact of new media of communication on social behavior. For when the boundaries of situations change to include or exclude participants in new ways, situational definitions and behavior must change as well. Yet the tradi-tional linking of social situations to physical places has made the impact of media on social settings and behavior difficult to see. For changes in media do not visibly change the structure of places. . . . electronic media create new types of social situations that transcend physically defined social settings and have their own rules and role expectations. (1985, p. 333; see also Cutler, 1996, p. 318)

From the preceding survey of the first wave of media ecology research from the 1980s concerning electronically-mediated interpersonal communication, it can be concluded that the separation of social place from physical space lies at the heart of the impact of electronic media on interpersonal communication. As Gumpert explains, electronic media enable us to "reach beyond the physical limits imposed by the body and interact without the restraints of propinquity" (1987, p. 189). Electronic media have "weakened the relationship between social situations and physical places," according to Meyrowitz (1985, p. 308). In so doing, he notes, "electronic media begin to override group identities based on 'co-presence,' and they create many new forms of access and 'association' that have little to do with physical location" (p. 144). Gumpert and Cathcart also point to the separation of physical place from interpersonal communication initiated by earlier media forms and intensified with the introduction of electronic media:

> The media relationships made possible by the interposition of typographical, iconic, and electronic media are distinctly different from the face-to-face relationship in several ways: by the elimination of the need for contiguity, by the shifting emphasis of sensory modes, and by the development of unique relationships that are media based—that is, without the medium the relationship would not exist. . . . Obviously, it is possible for relationships to be established with individuals who have never shared a contiguous place. . . . The evolution of media technology has brought about the extraordinary separation of place from communication. Where formerly communication could occur only within the context of a place, place has become irrelevant as space has been bridged by the media. (1986c, p. 166)

And Gumpert and Fish as well observe that modern technologies alter the role of space and place in communication: "human beings have been emancipated from the boundaries of place. . . . Contemporary dialogue is not restricted to *a* place since the media of communication have dispersed or expanded the possibilities through the reallocation of space" (1990a, p. 3; see also Gumpert, 1987, pp. 167–189). Of course, media ecologists are not the only scholars to notice that electronic media provide new opportunities for interpersonal communication by reshaping social space. To cite just one example, in an analysis that extends Goffman's ideas about social interaction in physical settings to the impact of telephone caller identification services on conceptions of public and private space, telecommunications researchers Samarajiva and Shields concur that:

> Until the advent of electronic media, most social interactions occurred in proximate space, but virtual space is rapidly emerging as a significant terrain of human interaction. In virtual space, actors currently achieve rudimentary forms of co-presence via electronic communication media ranging from two-way video to the ubiquitous telephone. (1997, p. 539)

Thus, because electronic media permit social interaction in locations other than traditional physical spaces, it is quite clear that electronic media radically alter the nature of behavior in gatherings and public places. As Meyrowitz explains, "the computer and other new technologies certainly enhance the most significant difference between electronic and all previous modes of communication—the undermining of the relationship between social place and physical place" (1985, p. 328). And because "electronic technologies and computing [present] us with a space that is not a space," as Strate puts it (1999, p. 407), we no longer can be sure which behavioral patterns are appropriate in the new sorts of electronically-mediated social situations we encounter. After all, where we are tells us who we are and how to behave, Nystrom reminds us (1979, Chapter 2, pp. 3–5); but if we are not sure where we are, we cannot be sure what roles to play or what rules of behavior to follow. Meyrowitz sums up the behavioral predicament engendered by electronically-mediated interpersonal communication as follows:

> Electronic media . . . eat away at the very meaning of distinct places. . . . electronic media create new placeless situations that have no traditional patterns of behavior. . . . a "location" that is not defined by walls, or streets, or neighborhoods, but by evanescent "experience." How does one behave in such "places"? (1985, p. 146)

In short, when we interact in spaces vastly different from those to which we are accustomed, our conceptions of social places, situations, and appropriate behavior must differ as well: new types of places bring forth new types of situations and new behavioral patterns. And social issues raised by electronic media such as telephone, radio, and television become more even more acute in the context of computer-mediated interpersonal communication, a subject taken up in the 1990s by a second wave of media ecology studies.

Research on the social consequences and interpersonal aspects of online CMC from media ecology perspectives has begun to emerge mostly in the last decade or so. Yet during the same period, computers have amplified exponentially the trend initiated by earlier electronic media to separate social interaction from physical location. Physical space and place have become less relevant to interpersonal communication than ever before as people gather in the computer-mediated environments of cyberspace to socialize in ways unimaginable with previous electronic media such as telephone, radio, and television. Nevertheless, media ecologists are just starting to explore the realm of interpersonal CMC in online environments, and the relatively few studies in this area consist mostly of short pieces appearing in anthologies and journals. To date, extended treatments of online CMC from media ecology perspectives appear primarily in doctoral dissertations. The literature comprising this second wave of media ecology research on interpersonal communication in computer-mediated environments is reviewed next.

The bulk of media ecology research on interpersonal CMC is found mostly in anthologies and occasionally in journals. Among of the earliest media ecology studies to focus directly on interpersonal CMC are several articles in the collection on mediated therapeutic communication edited by Gumpert and Fish, *Talking to Strangers* (1990b). For example, Gumpert compares telephone sex with computer sex (1990; see also Gumpert, 1987, pp. 121–139); Fleming discusses computer-mediated therapeutic interaction (1990); and the volume also includes an often cited 1985 magazine article by Van Gelder about identity deception online, "The Strange Case of the Electronic Lover" (reprinted in several mainstream CMC anthologies as well; for a summary of this case, see Barnes, 1996a, p. 212). More significant, however, is the array of articles about social interaction in CMC environments presented in *Communication and Cyberspace*, the anthology edited by Strate, Jacobson, and Gibson (1996a). Despite a certain negative prejudice against CMC in some media ecology circles evident, for example, in the volume's rather deprecatory epilogue entitled "Cyberspace, Shmyberspace" (Postman, 1996b), the selections in the Strate et al. anthology cover a wide range of topics related to communication in digital environments. Not all the selections address mediated interpersonal communication: some are more in line with the first tradition in media ecology, approaching media as environments. For example, Beniger emphasizes economic, legal, and political factors in examining who owns and controls cyberspace, concluding that cyberspace is vulnerable to exploitation by commercial and government institutions (1996). And Kleinman provides a historical discussion of legal issues related to ownership of intellectual property rights, comparing copyright in contexts of print and electronic publishing (1996). But the Strate et al. anthology does include various pieces on computer-mediated interpersonal communication; the most relevant selections are highlighted next, with the remainder discussed further ahead in conjunction with mainstream research on CMC in online environments and on virtual communities.

Perhaps the most generally informative piece in the Strate et al. anthology is the editors' introduction, "Surveying the Electronic Landscape" (1996b). They offer a well-balanced review of major topics in cyberspace research, including a commendable effort to summarize conceptions and definitions of cyberspace, a subject which Strate pursues in more depth in a subsequent journal article (1999; see also Strate, 1996a). In their introduction, the editors explain how broad a spectrum of meanings the term "cyberspace" encompasses:

> We have many different definitions of cyberspace, some viewing it as a fictional construct, others as imaginary but in development, others as real and present. Some equate cyberspace with virtual reality, others with the electronic storage and transmission of information, or with computer-mediated communication, or with communication over computer networks. Some see cyberspace as an individual conceptual space, others as a product of social interaction. Part of the ambiguity surrounding this word may be related to its novelty, but it is also true that the term acts as a nexus for a variety of different phenomena, such as telecommunications, cybernetics and computer technology, computer-mediated communication, virtual reality and telepresence, hypertext and hypermedia, and cyberculture. (Strate et al., 1996b, p. 4)

The editors as well as many of the anthology's contributors are certainly cognizant of changes in space, place, situations, and behavioral patterns that accompany the advent of computer-mediated interpersonal communication. As the editors observe in one of their chapter introductions:

> Face-to-face interaction in real, physical space is the primary mode of human communication. The technologies of telecommunication and computer-mediated communication are meant to function as substitutes and extensions of the primary mode, providing new ways of disseminating information, sharing meaning, and congregating and communing. Used as a functional alternative to

a place or a set of places, these technologies give rise to the electronic equivalent to space. (Strate et al., 1996a, p. 121)

And making explicit their intellectual debt to Meyrowitz's "sociological elaborations of media ecology theory," the editors suggest that "cyberspace technologies further contribute to the fact that we have 'no sense of place'" (Strate et al., 1996b, pp. 13–14).

Influences from the second tradition in media ecology, the study of environments as media, are also clear in several other articles on interpersonal CMC in the Strate et al. anthology. Building on the work of scholars such as Gumpert, Hall, Innis, and Meyrowitz, Strate offers a trenchant analysis of the neglected counterpart of cyberspace—cyber*time*, the *when* as opposed to the where of computer-mediated environments—less often studied but no less important, Strate argues convincingly in this rare treatment of a topic deserving additional investigation (1996b; see also Sternberg, 1998; Strate, 1996b; Zerubavel, 1981). There is Barnes's well-rounded piece on the ecology of the self online, providing summaries both of definitions of cyberspace (1996a, p. 194) and of theories of self based on the work of Mead (pp. 203–204), as well as overviews of artificial intelligence (pp. 198–202), virtual reality technologies (pp. 204–208), and cyberculture genres like cyberpunk (pp. 195–202). Barnes also discusses related topics such as online communities and support groups, as well as CMC addiction (1996b, pp. 34–37), in a parallel journal article that effectively combines ideas about the presentation of self from Goffman and about electronically-mediated social interaction from Meyrowitz and extends them to online relationships in various cyberspace contexts. In a similar vein, Cutler's provocative contribution to the Strate et al. anthology addresses identity, relationships, and selves in online environments. Applying ideas from Goffman, Mead, and Meyrowitz to the realm of cyberspace, and in particular, endorsing Meyrowitz's revival of situationist perspectives, Cutler discusses "new senses of self and group identity" (1996, pp. 318–319); he reviews definitions of cyberspace as well (p. 320). And in considering the nature of online relationships, Cutler emphasizes a tremendously important point: "the interactive quality of communication contents and processes found in cyberspace. Interaction is the characteristic of cyberspace technology that differentiates it from other public electronic media such as television" (1996, p. 325; see also Strate, 1999, p. 405). The high degree of interactivity that socializing in online environments entails, according to Cutler, has a positive effect on participants' sense of self (1996, p. 332).

Finally, the Strate et al. cyberspace anthology contains a pertinent article by Gumpert and Drucker contrasting social interaction in physical environments with social activities in computer-mediated environments, mentioned above in the discussion of media ecology approaches to space and place. As Gumpert and Drucker explain, CMC continues the tendency of a new medium to alter patterns and places of social interaction:

> Face-to-face communication in physical space and mediated communication may serve the same purposes but are experienced in very different ways. Every media development alters the availability and nature of traditional private and public places. The newspaper influenced and defined, in part, the barbershop, the village green, and the café. The telephone shaped the nature of courtship. Radio altered the experiences of the living room, the car, and the doctor's office. The computer keyboard opens up distant retrievable visits. (1996, p. 31)

Taking a dim view of computer-mediated options which complement and even replace physical locations, Gumpert and Drucker claim that cyberspace "not only co-opts but devalues the domain of public space," undermining the traditional sorts of places where people gather to socialize face to face (1996, p. 35). "It is the electronic highway (and what it symbolizes) that threatens to dismantle the traditional streets, squares, highways, and communities that once were so important to us," Gumpert and Drucker argue (p. 36). Their rather wistful lament over the loss of traditional gathering places is a recurring theme throughout Gumpert's work (see, e.g., Gumpert, 1987, pp. 167–189; Gumpert & Fish, 1990a, pp. 3–4). Here, Gumpert and Drucker conclude that both the decreasing availability of traditional gathering places in everyday urban life as well as the rising frequency of electronic interaction are connected to issues of safety and risk:

> There is something seductive about electronic communication with others, and we in the United States have begun to rely on mediated communication and even to prefer that mode to the old, particularly because it is safe, forgetting that there are qualitative differences between the two. The mediated functional alternatives that we choose generally occur inside controlled private space. So we retreat inward where we can control at least some of the threats. (1996, p. 36; see also 1997, pp. 5–6)

The idea that mediated interaction in general poses less physical risk than face-to-face interaction is noted by Meyrowitz as well: "in live settings, we also often ask 'Who can touch or hurt me?' Indeed, one of the things that distinguishes mediated communication from live communication is the lack of risk of physical harm or involvement" (1985, p. 39). But what Gumpert and Drucker stress is that traditional physical places are become more dangerous and problematic at the same time that CMC presents increasing opportunities for social interaction in spaces that transcend the need for physical contact. CMC environments that dispense with physical co-presence, therefore, appear safer and hence more appealing. So, as Gumpert and Drucker put it, we choose telecommunication over locomotion and opt for "paths of safety" rather than "streets of gore" (1996, p. 31). But this tradeoff, they emphasize, has repercussions for the balance of public and private space in social affairs.

Besides the pieces from the Strate et al. cyberspace anthology and the related journal articles described above, there is some additional material on interpersonal CMC from media ecology perspectives. Another source of articles is the collection edited by Drucker and Gumpert, *Voices in the Street* (1997), addressing the relationships among gender, public space, and media. But the Drucker and Gumpert anthology focuses more on gender and space than on media, with prominence given to face-to-face environments like Oldenburg's third places (1989/1997); in fact, the collection includes an extract about gender and third places reprinted from Oldenburg's book. However, many of the articles do refer to leading figures from the second intellectual tradition in media ecology, such as Goffman and Meyrowitz. Though the volume incorporates the second tradition of studying environments as media, other than the editors' introduction, only a few articles refer specifically to electronically-mediated interpersonal communication. These few selections all concentrate on the role of women in relation to electronic technologies such as the telephone (Rakow, 1997), shortwave radio (Luther, 1997), and cable television (Tankel & Banks, 1997). In the entire collection, only Hunkele and Cornwell address interpersonal CMC in their article on gender issues in cyberspace (1997). Of some interest is the editors' preface and introductory article, but they mostly reiterate observations made by Gumpert and Drucker on previous occasions (e.g., Gumpert & Drucker, 1996). For example, they point out once again that electronic media provide alternatives to face-to-face interpersonal communication:

> Sites of public interaction where two or more people link via telephone, radio, television, or computer. . . . an electronic medium is viewed as it functions to provide an alternative, aspatial loci for communication once reserved for physical public space. . . . as a supplement to or substitute for social contact that was once reserved for face-to-face contact (Gumpert & Drucker, 1997, p. 10; see also Gumpert & Drucker, 1996, pp. 30–31)

As for full-length treatments addressing interpersonal CMC, in contrast to articles or collections of shorter pieces, the offerings are typified by a pair of dissertations in media ecology, both case studies. Mineo (1998) explores the use of asynchronous online computer conferencing as an alternative setting for adult higher education. And Conforti (2001) examines the role that computer-mediated relationships play in the personal experiences and self-development of women. The paucity of extended investigations of interpersonal CMC in online environments from media ecology perspectives is one symptom of the need for further in-depth research in this area, such as undertaken in the present study.

A review of media ecology research on CMC would be incomplete without a closer look at Strate's work in this area. Having collaborated with co-editors Jacobson and Gibson on their 1996 cyberspace anthology, and with Barnes in an article on educational implications of computers (Barnes & Strate, 1996), Strate's own publications on CMC include the article mentioned above on cybertime (1996b), as well as "Containers, Computers, and the Media Ecology of the City" (1996a), a piece in an online media ecology journal. In the latter, Strate summarizes relevant media ecology research on space from scholars such as Mumford, Innis, McLuhan, Ong, Gumpert, and Meyrowitz in applying the spatial metaphor of containers to compare computers and cities as information systems or environments.

But the item in Strate's CMC repertoire most germane to the present study is a journal article, "The Varieties of Cyberspace" (1999; see also Strate, 2011). Building on the survey of definitions provided in the editors' introduction to the Strate et al. anthology (1996b, p. 4), in this comprehensive article Strate offers a rigorous analysis of numerous definitions and categories of cyberspace. Remarks from this piece were cited above in connection with the discussion of space and place: for example, Strate is among those few scholars who take the trouble to distinguish between space and place (1999, pp. 394–395), concluding that "cyberplaces are the figures to cyberspace's ground" (p. 395). In addressing the definitional problems involved in conceptions of cyberspace, Strate refers to the most significant work on space in the second media ecology intellectual tradition including Gumpert, Hall, and Meyrowitz, as well as Goffman's concepts of front and back region behavior (1959; see also Cutler, 1996; Meyrowitz, 1979/1986, 1985; Nystrom, 1973, 1979).

Strate argues that cyberspace is "heterogeneous and multiple, better understood as the *cyberspaces*" (1999, p. 406), elaborating on this idea as follows:

> The phenomena in question is better understood as a plurality rather than a singularity. As a collective concept, cyberspace can then be defined as the diverse experiences of space associated with computing and related technologies. Thus, it would follow that we can refer to the varieties of cyberspace. (1999, p. 383)

The categories of cyberspace which Strate therefore distinguishes include physical, conceptual, perceptual, and aesthetic space, as well as data or information space and interactive or relational space, among others. Strate develops an astonishingly thorough taxonomy of cyberspace, which he condenses into a single-page summary table that furnishes definitions as well as relevant authors for each category of cyberspace identified (p. 385). In addition, Strate considers related issues including virtual communities (pp. 394, 404), public versus private space (pp. 405–406), and even sacred versus profane space (p. 406). Like Cutler (1996, p. 325), Strate also notes that CMC encourages active participation: "cyberspace diverges from media such as television, which generally relegate us to the role of viewer" (1999, p. 405). And expanding on ideas about transitional space introduced by Nystrom (1978), Strate astutely observes that the chaotic nature of cyberspace seems to encourage rule-breaking behavior:

> Transitional cyberspace, like its physical counterpart, is characterized by a breakdown of social rules, as the space does not seem to belong to anyone. It is an anomalous region in which anything goes, and this perhaps accounts for much of the carnival-like behavior on the Internet, from gender-switching and false identities to flaming and spamming. (1999, p. 406)

Overall, this article on cyberspace in tandem with the piece on cybertime (Strate, 1996b) rank among the most meticulous and perceptive theoretical analyses of these topics to date, not only within the field of media ecology but also in communication research at large. Abundant in fertile ideas that await further contemplation and application, should these articles someday be showcased in publications of wider circulation, they may well become required reading for those interested in grasping the complexity and multi-dimensionality of the online environments afforded by CMC.

It seems, then, that Strate and others in the most recent wave of media ecology research on interpersonal communication in computer-mediated environments have begun to build on the foundations laid by Meyrowitz and others in the earlier wave of research on electronically-mediated environments. Nevertheless, despite the admirable accomplishments of media ecologists such as these, Meyrowitz's plea for integrating medium theory and situationism (1985), as well as Gumpert and Cathcart's appeal for integrating research on mediated and interpersonal communication (Gumpert & Cathcart, 1986b; Cathcart & Gumpert, 1983/1986), have gone largely unheeded. A comparable lack of integration in media ecology research exists with respect to the two intellectual traditions informing the field: scholars working in the first intellectual tradition, the study of media as environments focusing on mass communication and *intra*personal communication, tend to ignore the second intellectual tradition, the study of environments as media focusing on *inter*personal communication. And vice versa. Thus, with the exceptions duly noted in the preceding review, approaches which apply a combination of both intellectual traditions in media ecology to the investigation of mediated interpersonal communication, especially in the realm of online CMC, are relatively rare. Furthermore, the second intellectual tradition in media ecology continues to be comparatively under-represented in the field, overshadowed by the first intellectual tradition, leading to a general state of imbalance in the discipline itself.

The lack of integration between the two intellectual traditions in media ecology and the resulting imbalance in the field can be elucidated with a metaphor from Chinese philosophy: the equilibrium between the forces of yin and yang. This metaphor is often expressed graphically in the traditional yin/yang symbol: a circle divided into two matched shapes, one a dark shape corresponding to yin and the other a light shape corresponding to yang, each shape containing a small spot of the other one's color. This design symbolizes the relationship between the forces of yin and yang, a relationship effectively described in the following summary:

> The original meaning of "yin and yang" is representative of the mountains—both the dark side and the bright side, or the contrasting shaded and sunlight slopes of the mountain. The "Yin" represents the female or the shaded aspect, the earth, darkness, the moon, and passivity. The "Yang" represents the male, light, sun, heaven, the active principle in nature. . . . This symbol shows the perfect balance between opposites, or the great forces of universe. This portrays

that there is no "real" masculine or feminine nature, but that each contains a part of the other. The two are contained in one circle thus showing that both powers are in one cycle. Instead of these two being held in antagonism, they are held together to show [that] they are mutually interdependent partners. One cannot exist without the other. (Ehmen, 1996)

Thus, the symbolism of the yin/yang image and metaphor involves an ecological outlook which strives for balance, proportion, and harmony between two distinct but complementary elements that fit closely together, each element intertwined with and bearing traces of the other, forming an integrated, unified whole.

In the case of media ecology, the yin/yang metaphor applies in the following sense. The first intellectual tradition which dominates in the discipline is the yang of media ecology: the more prominent and better illuminated study of media as environments, involving the cultural and psychological consequences of technologies and techniques of mass communication and *intra*personal communication. The second intellectual tradition is the yin of media ecology, the more obscure and less familiar study of environments as media, involving the social impact of the mysterious silent languages and hidden dimensions of *inter*personal communication. What the yin/yang metaphor demonstrates is that these two intellectual traditions in media ecology complement one another and that elements of both traditions are integrally necessary for a fully balanced approach to the study of communication.

By applying the yin/yang metaphor to the two intellectual traditions in media ecology, an argument can be made which runs parallel to other complaints about a lack of integration in the field, such as those proffered by Meyrowitz about medium theory versus situationism (1985), as well as Gumpert and Cathcart about mediated communication versus interpersonal communication (1986b; Cathcart & Gumpert, 1983/1986). Presented initially in a convention paper (Sternberg, 2000a; see also Sternberg, 2002), the yin/yang argument suggests that the current state of affairs in media ecology involves a serious imbalance resulting from a lack of integration between the two intellectual traditions, with the yang tradition of studying media as environments eclipsing from view the yin tradition of studying environments as media, to the detriment of the field as a whole. Yet the philosophy of yin and yang calls for equilibrium between the two, stemming from mutual interdependence and requiring partnership and cooperation. It is just this sort of integration and balance between yin and yang that the discipline of media ecology needs with respect to its two underlying intellectual traditions.

The preceding review of media ecology research attempts to demonstrate the propensity of media ecologists to follow the first yang intellectual tradition in the field rather than the second yin intellectual tradition, by documenting the relative paucity of integrated approaches to the study of mediated interpersonal communication. But to emphasize how media ecologists favor the yang over the yin in current approaches, it is helpful to examine some additional evidence from an instructive exercise: comparing the degree to which leading scholars from the two intellectual traditions in media ecology have been represented in the field.

Revealing clues about the imbalance between the two intellectual traditions can be uncovered by scrutinizing recent media ecology literature. For example, the index of the Strate et al. anthology on communication and cyberspace (1996a) fails to provide a single entry for scholars of the yin intellectual tradition, such as Goffman, Hall, Mead, or Meyrowitz, although bibliographies of several individual articles in the volume do mention these authors. Yet the index does list an abundance of scholars working primarily in the yang intellectual tradition such as Innis, Langer, McLuhan, Mumford, and Postman. A production error may be responsible for omissions in the anthology's index, but even individual articles show surprising bibliographic deficiencies. Both the editors' introduction (Strate et al., 1996b) and Strate's piece on cybertime (1996b) cite Gumpert, Hall, and Meyrowitz as well as McLuhan, but neither mentions Goffman. Likewise, in tackling the ecology of self (1996a), Barnes refers to Mead and Meyrowitz but not to Goffman. Fortunately, at least a couple of contributors do mention relevant figures from the yin intellectual tradition: in Cutler's study of online selves and relationships (1996), he explicitly builds on the work of Goffman, Mead, and Meyrowitz; and references to Goffman and Meyrowitz also appear in Lee's article on the rhetoric of email (1996). Nonetheless, considering the subject matter of many of the selections, the collection overall displays a remarkable lack of acknowledgement of the yin intellectual tradition in media ecology.

More telling than the Strate et al. cyberspace anthology is the special issue of the *New Jersey Journal of Communication* edited by Lum (2000b), celebrating the intellectual roots of media ecology. In the entire issue, no mention whatsoever is made of Goffman, Hall, or Mead; and Meyrowitz is referred to only once in an article on Mumford by Strate and Lum (2000). Even Nystrom, among the most enthusiastic proponents of the second intellectual tradition in media ecology, whose work as a whole has a strong yin component (e.g., 1973, 1978, 1979), makes no mention of Goffman, Hall, or Mead in her contribution to this journal issue, an article on Whorf and Langer in which she refers instead to yang scholars such as McLuhan, Ong, and Postman (Nystrom, 2000). That the bulk of this set of reflections on the intellectual roots of media ecology is devoted to scholarship from the first yang tradition of studying media as environments lends credence to the claim that current generations of media ecologists are not attending sufficiently to the second yin tradition of studying environments as media.

Other hints about the dearth of yin vis-à-vis the wealth of yang in media ecology affairs come from conference and lecture activities in the discipline. In recent years, the spotlight at media ecology events has shone almost exclusively on scholars from the yang intellectual tradition. For instance, there was the 1998 McLuhan symposium at Fordham University, as well as the McLuhan lecture series co-sponsored by Fordham and the Canadian government. And the inaugural convention of the Media Ecology Association led off with a featured paper on McLuhan and media ecology (Levinson, 2000). Similarly, at the September 2000 conference of the New York State Communication Association, to which many media ecologists belong, a panel was devoted to the intellectual legacy of McLuhan. At the annual convention of the National Communication Association in November 2000, there were showcased sessions praising the contributions to media ecology of Mumford and Ong. Even Meyrowitz, champion of the yin, invoked yang scholarship (namely McLuhan) in his keynote address at the second annual convention of the Media Ecology Association (2001), as a point of departure for encouraging media ecologists to broaden their theoretical perspectives by morphing McLuhan with yin scholars such as Birdwhistell and Goffman. In contrast, leading figures from the yin intellectual tradition in media ecology such as Goffman, Hall, and Mead have been conspicuously absent from these sorts of professional commemorations of scholarship in the field. Few occasions in recent years come to mind where representatives of the yin intellectual tradition in media ecology take center stage.

Thus, rather ironically, the field of media ecology seems to suffer from an internal ecological imbalance due to the disproportionate amount of work done on the yang side of the intellectual equation, with a resulting lack of research on the yin side. Despite promising efforts in the yin intellectual tradition of studying environments as media such as those described above, limited in quantity but not in quality, two gaps remain to be filled as a consequence of the yin/yang disparity in media ecology research. In general, the field needs more yin-oriented studies of mediated interpersonal communication, due to the relative scarcity of research in this area compared to the volume of work done on yang-oriented mass communication and intrapersonal communication. In particular, the field needs more studies of interpersonal CMC, due to the lack of research in this area from media ecology points of view. So far, media ecology investigations have merely scratched the surface of interpersonal CMC.

To date, with respect to interpersonal CMC, media ecology is rich in relevant theory but poor in related applications. Yet media ecology provides a productive theoretical framework for understanding CMC, especially in online environments. The subject of online misbehavior, largely untouched within the field until the present study, provides a suitable opportunity to apply a unified media ecology approach to the realm of computer-mediated interpersonal communication. This study, therefore, aims for an integrated and balanced perspective based on both intellectual traditions in media ecology, blending medium theory and situationism as Meyrowitz recommends, and also combining research on mediated communication and interpersonal communication as Gumpert and Cathcart advise.

Like the CMC research of Strate, Barnes, Cutler and other contemporary media ecologists, this report on misbehavior in online environments builds not only on foundations laid by yang scholars such as McLuhan and Postman, but also on yin ideas drawn from Mead's symbolic interactionist standpoint, Goffman's situationist explorations, and Hall's anthropological inquiries, as further developed by Nystrom, Meyrowitz, and others such as Gumpert,

Cathcart, and Drucker. In this way, the theoretical underpinnings of the present investigation incorporate elements of both intellectual traditions which contribute in equal measure to the analytical framework: the yang tradition of studying media as environments as well as the yin tradition of studying environments as media. Studies such as this one which strive for a balanced approach, especially by attempting to boost the yin factor to similar levels of prominence as the yang already enjoys, contribute to better equilibrating the field of media ecology itself, because both intellectual traditions are indispensable components for understanding communication environments.

But the present study of misbehavior is also informed by research outside the field of media ecology, from which there is a great deal to learn about CMC in online environments as well as virtual communities. For example, various scholars other than media ecologists have already applied Goffman's ideas about face-to-face encounters to social gatherings in online environments (e.g., Aycock & Buchignani, 1995; Cheung, 1995; Donath, 1999; Gotved, 2000; Hiltz & Turoff, 1978/1993; H. Miller, 1995; Rheingold, 1993; Rintel & Pittam, 1997a, 1997b; Rutter & G. Smith, 1999a, 1999b; Samarajiva & Shields, 1997; Surratt, 1996; Tapscott, 1998). So, having clarified the significance of this investigation of online misbehavior within the larger theoretical context of media ecology by surveying the two intellectual traditions in the field, as well as pertinent ideas from the second tradition about space, place, situations, rules, and rule-breaking, it is also necessary to situate the present study in the context of mainstream research on CMC in online environments and on virtual communities, the two areas reviewed next.

COMPUTER-MEDIATED COMMUNICATION
IN ONLINE ENVIRONMENTS

Since the foundation of the U.S. government-sponsored ARPANET in the late 1960s, through the introduction of the TCP/IP standard Internet protocol in the 1970s, computer networks of various types have developed around the world, eventually coalescing into the "network of networks" known today as the Internet (e.g., Beniger, 1996, p. 50; Chen & Gaines, 1998, p. 222; Danet et al., 1998, p. 42; P. J. Denning, 1998b, pp. 15–19; Giese, 1996, pp. 125–140; Gumpert & Drucker, 1996, p. 28; S. G. Jones, 1998b, pp. xiii–xv; Morris & Ogan, 1996, p. 39; Rheingold, 1993, pp. 67–89; Schnurr, 2000, p. 22; Sproull & Faraj, 1995/1997, p. 35; Strate 1996a; Strate et al., 1996b, p. 8; Surratt, 1996, pp. 24–27). As these networks evolved, scholars interested in CMC began to investigate various social aspects of online CMC, that is, CMC in networked as opposed to non-networked environments. Reviewers of online CMC research generally identify Hiltz and Turoff as pioneers in this area, with their book, *The Network Nation: Human Communication Via Computer* (published in 1978 and revised in 1993), universally cited as a landmark in the field (e.g., December, 1995, 1996; Gurak, 1996; Herring, 1996a, pp. 2–3). It is also worth noting that

Hiltz and Turoff are among the earliest to apply Goffman's ideas to interpersonal communication in cyberspace, devoting a section of their classic volume to "Computerized Conferencing as a Goffmanesque Establishment" (1978/1993, pp. 83–103). By 1996, when the International Communication Association dedicated the winter issue of its official publication, *Journal of Communication*, to "The Net," what one contributor refers to as "Internet CMC" (December, 1996, p. 6) had clearly become a well-established area of communication and media research.

In the twenty years since Hiltz and Turoff launched the study of interpersonal CMC in online environments, a number of major research themes have emerged. Most of these themes turn out to have little, if any, direct bearing on the present study of misbehavior, and therefore do not require much consideration. However, to provide a richer background for discussing other relevant material further ahead, particularly literature on virtual communities, it is helpful first to review in brief some of the main themes in online CMC research, although they prove largely inconsequential in this study of misbehavior.

Among the most popular themes in online CMC research are conceptions of identity and self. Perhaps the best-known and most comprehensive investigation of this subject is *Life on the Screen: Identity in the Age of the Internet* (1995) by Turkle, but many others discuss identity and self in connection with online environments as well (e.g., Barnes, 1996a; Bolter, 1996; Donath, 1999; Goertzel, 1998; Holmes, 1997a, 1997b; Poster, 1998; Reid, 1998; Rutter & G. Smith, 1999a, 1999b; Waskul & Douglass, 1997; Wilbur, 1997). There is also abundant literature on several themes related to identity and self in cyberspace, such as gender (e.g., Broadhurst, 1997; Danet, 1998; Herring, 1996b; Hunkele & Cornwell, 1997; Kramarae, 1998; Morahan-Martin, 1998; Rodino, 1997), sexuality (e.g., Gumpert, 1990; Lipton, 1996; Noonan, 1998; Shaw, 1997), embodiment (e.g., Baym, 1997a; Biocca, 1997; Ito, 1997), and language (e.g., Condon & Cech, 1996; Gackenbach et al., 1998; Lee, 1996; Perrolle, 1991; Savicki et al., 1996; Yates, 1996).

Another set of themes in CMC research involves online relationships. Chesebro and Bonsall's collaboration, *Computer-Mediated Communication: Human Relationships in a Computerized World* (1989), offers the earliest and broadest treatment of relationships conducted in online environments, a subject which has since been approached from various angles. Some scholars compare online and offline relationships (e.g., Chenault, 1998; S. G. Jones, 1996), while others discuss virtual friendship (e.g., Barnes, 1996b; Parks & Floyd, 1996) and online relationships in particular social contexts (e.g., Clark, 1998; Kling, 1996b; Wellman, 1997). The interplay of relationships, identity, and self in cyberspace is also subject to investigation (e.g., Conforti, 2001; Cutler, 1996; Deuel, 1996; Gergen, 1997). Other associated topics include therapeutic relationships in CMC environments (e.g., Fleming, 1990; Grohol, 1998; King & Moreggi, 1998), as well as CMC addiction (e.g., Griffiths, 1998; S. G. Jones, 1996).

Several research themes can be identified which relate to organizational CMC. One of the first and most frequently-mentioned examinations of online CMC in organizational settings, *Connections: New Ways of Working in the Networked Organization* (1991), comes from Sproull and Kiesler; others pursue this type of inquiry as well (e.g., Coltman & Romm, 1997; Garton & Wellman, 1995; Kraut et al., 1998). Along similar lines are reports relating to computer-supported collaborative work in online contexts (e.g., B. Anderson, 1996; T. Anderson & Kanuka, 1997; Chen & Gaines, 1998; Haythornthwaite et al., 1998; Kupst et al., 1997; Mynatt et al., 1997; Patkin, 1996). Also in this realm lies research concerning online arbitration and dispute resolution (e.g., Katsh, 1996; Perritt, 1996). It must be noted that although phrases like "online dispute resolution" or "online conflict mediation" suggest a possible relevance to the study of misbehavior in cyberspace, closer inspection reveals the adjective "online" in these phrases to be misleading, referring not to conflicts which take place online, but instead to mediation processes occurring online which pertain to disputes originating in the offline world.

A few other clusters of themes recur in online CMC research. Studies of community networks (not to be confused with virtual communities, discussed below) deal with the use of network technologies and digital environments by members of traditional communities for offline community-building purposes (e.g., Cisler, 1995; Foster, 1997; M. Hauben, 1997; Igbaria et al., 1998; Shapiro, 1999; Uncapher, 1999; Wellman, 1999). Similarly, some scholars investigate civic and political uses of networks (e.g., Burrows, 1997; Jacobson, 1996; Lockard, 1997; Nguyen & Alexander, 1996; Shade, 1997), as well as cyberdemocracy (e.g., S. E. Miller, 1996; Poster, 1997; Riley et al., 1998). An additional group of CMC themes can be found in studies involving virtual reality (e.g., Heim, 1993; Schroeder, 1996; Slouka, 1995; Zettl, 1996) and virtual worlds (e.g., Doyle & Hayes-Roth, 1998; Ostwald, 1997; Schroeder, 1997), as well as research on interface design for online environments (e.g., Agre, 1998; Donath, 1996; Gibson, 1996; S. Johnson, 1997; Preston, 1998), and architectural approaches to cyberspace (e.g., Cicognani, 2003; Mitchell, 1995).

Research on major themes like these related to online CMC has unquestionably broadened our general understanding of social interaction in cyberspace. Books and articles such as those cited above contribute valuable information and insights about many different aspects of interpersonal communication in computer-mediated environments. But of all the main themes in online CMC research, it is the topic of virtual communities that stands out as most significant for the study of misbehavior in online environments. If "cyberplaces are the figures to cyberspace's ground," as Strate suggests (1999, p. 395), then perhaps the figures to a cyber place's ground are its virtual communities, the area of online CMC research reviewed next.

VIRTUAL COMMUNITIES

Among the ideas and forms of social life that have changed most rapidly and dramatically in the past few decades, primarily as a consequence of computer-mediated interpersonal communication, is the conception of "community." Conceptions of community have shifted throughout human history, of course, along with changes in communications technology. Changes in conceptions of community grow out of the sorts of altered patterns of social interaction discussed above in connection with changes in conceptions of space and place due to the introduction of new media. For example, as Ong (1982) points out, in oral cultures, communities are based on physical co-presence, that is, people being able to see and hear each other; literacy and electronic media, however, permit wider conceptions of community that transcend space and time. According to Eisenstein, the introduction of the printing press and the spread of typography broadened conceptions of community and reduced the role of physical co-presence by creating a "commonwealth of learning" and a "republic of letters" among widely-dispersed authors and readers in seventeenth-century Europe; somewhat paradoxically, print and mass literacy fostered the spread of nationalism as well (1983; see also Ong, 1982; Strate, 1996a). And by the twentieth century, electronic media have surpassed the limitations of physical co-presence to the extent of engendering conceptions of community as broad as McLuhan's "global village" (1964).

Several researchers connect media with evolving conceptions of community, as Strate observes: "beyond a basic interest in the role of media in communities, media ecology is also concerned with how media serve as communities.... In this sense, it becomes possible to speak of media communities (Gumpert), symbolic communities (Gergen), or virtual communities (Rheingold)" (Strate, 1996a). One explanation of how modern media have expanded conceptions of community by transforming social space comes from Gumpert and Fish:

> The traditional concept of community is linked to place and territory.... Community which was linked to the sharp demarcation of territory dissolves. The identification between self and neighborhood, village, or town recedes into the background as the contact and identification with myriad other points on the globe becomes a reality. Community which was rooted in face-to-face dialogue between two or more persons in the same place has been replaced by the "media community." Contemporary dialogue is not restricted to place since the media of communication have dispersed or expanded the possibilities through the reallocation of space. (1990a, pp. 2–3; see also Gumpert, 1987, pp. 171–187)

And even Meyrowitz, writing in the dawn of the online CMC era, notes presciently that "electronic media begin to override group identities based on 'co-presence,' and they create many new forms of access and 'association' that have little to do with physical location. . . . Media create new 'communities'" (1985, p. 144). The rise of computer-mediated social gatherings in online environments, then, presents the latest set of challenges to conceptions of community.

Conceptions of community have come under increasing scrutiny in light of the evolution of online CMC in recent years, but sociologists have been debating exactly what constitutes community for several centuries, according to some scholars (e.g., Surratt, 1996; Wellman & Gulia, 1999). And other scholars observe that such debates still continue (e.g., Lazar, 1999), and that the term remains ambiguous (e.g., Gumpert, 1987, p. 168; M. A. Smith, 1992; Williams, 2000). Nevertheless, some patterns in recent conceptions of community can be discerned. Mynatt et al. identify a "loose consensus around community as referring to a multi-dimensional, cohesive social grouping that includes, in varying degrees: shared spatial relations, social conventions, a sense of membership and boundaries, and an ongoing rhythm of social interaction" (1997). Riley et al. report a number of historical uses of the term, such as "developing a place with boundaries that identifies a neighborhood and thus marking who lives inside and who lives outside; or more ideologically, a coming together in social communion," but they claim that "the most common notion seems to be that communities are identified groups of interdependent people who discuss actions and share certain practices and have a concern for the common good" (1998).

Yet, as S. G. Jones observes, "definitions of community largely have centered around the unproblematized notion of place, a 'where' that social scientists can observe, visit, stay and go, engage in participant observation" (1998a, p. 15). However, according to Surratt, who provides a thorough overview of conceptions of community in the field of sociology, "there are definitions of community which attempt to alter the definition of space, and thereby allow for reconceptualization of the possible forms community may take" (1996, p. 62). Wellman and Gulia elaborate on the movement away from defining communities primarily in terms of space:

> Sociologists have discovered that . . . neighborhood and kinship ties are only a portion of people's overall community because cars, planes, and phones can maintain relationships over long distances. . . . communities do not have to be solidary groups of densely knit neighbors but could also exist as social networks of kin, friends, and workmates who do not necessarily live in the same neighborhoods. It is not that the world is a global village, but as McLuhan originally said, one's "village" could span the globe. This conceptual revolution moved from defining community in terms of space—neighborhoods—to defining it in terms of social networks. . . . community can stretch well beyond the neighborhood. (1999, p. 169)

Thus, current conceptions of community tend to focus on social relations rather than space or place. For example, M. A. Smith suggests that "generically, a community can be understood as a set of on-going social relations bound together by a common interest or shared circumstance" (1992). Foster describes the term as embodying "a set of voluntary, social, and reciprocal relations that are bound together by an immutable 'we-feeling'" (1997, p. 25). And as Surratt observes, "the important points to note are, first, that community is not a place, it is the set of social identifications that emerge from interaction, and second, that out of such interaction, both cooperation and conflict can and do result" (1996, p. 64).

The interplay between changing conceptions of community and new media technologies is amply illustrated in the realm of CMC by what have come to be known as "virtual communities." As early as 1978, when the use of computers for interpersonal communication was just developing and the Internet was still in its infancy, the idea of virtual communities began to appear in both scholarly and popular accounts of computer use (e.g., Hiltz & Turoff, 1978/1993; M. A. Smith, 1992; Stone, 1991). Undoubtedly, the seminal work in this area is Rheingold's *The Virtual Community: Homesteading on the Electronic Frontier* (1993), characterized by one scholar as "the most comprehensive and sustained discussion of community in cyberspace" (Healy, 1997, p. 61), and by another as "the current benchmark for any study of virtual community" (Wilbur, 1997, p. 7). Rheingold defines virtual communities as "social aggregations that emerge from the Net when enough people carry on those public discussions long enough, with sufficient human feeling, to form webs of personal relationships in cyberspace" (1993, p. 5; see also Strate, 1999, p. 404). Other phrases sometimes used to describe virtual communities include "electronic gathering" (Sproull & Faraj, 1995/1997), "digital gathering place" (S. Johnson, 1997, p. 70), "electronic group meeting" (Mitra, 1997a, p. 161), "virtual settlement" (Q. Jones, 1997), and "cybercommunity" (e.g., Branscomb, 1996; MacKinnon, 1997; Maltz, 1996; A. D. Smith, 1999). A common alternative phrase is "online community," for which Lazar provides the following explanation, adequately supplementing Rheingold's original definition:

> Online communities are any group of people who communicate with each other via computers. Online communities are supported by listservs, bulletin boards, chats, MUDs, MOOs or combinations of these software programs along with web pages. Some communities are complex with highly integrated sites, others comprise just a single bulletin board or listserv, some support geographical communities, others are purely virtual, some have real concerns while others are fantasy worlds. There are a wide variety of communities focusing on many topics including health, religion, education, culture, community, sports, pets, children, old age, professional issues, games and so on. Thousands of online communities exist and more come online everyday. (Lazar, 1999; see also Lazar & Preece, 1998; Preece & Ghozati, 1998)

Over the past decade, a significant amount of literature on virtual communities has accumulated, not all of it relevant to the present study of online misbehavior. Yet a brief overview of virtual community research in general is helpful in order to situate more fully the discussion further ahead of pertinent material that directly addresses online misbehavior in particular. For purposes of this study, the literature on virtual communities falls into three categories, each of which is reviewed in turn: first, debates about the nature of virtual communities; second, surveys of various communities; and third, case studies of specific communities.

As virtual communities have spread, increased, and diversified, scholarly and popular debate has intensified around questions such as, "How are conceptions of community being transformed by our engagement with virtual communities and their functions, structures, and practices?" and "How are virtual communities like—and unlike—traditional offline communities, particularly those communities where participants engage in face-to-face communication, co-present in shared physical space?" For example, as Lazar (1999) notes, what exactly constitutes a virtual or online community continues to be disputed. And summaries of such discussions are plentiful (e.g., Foster, 1997; Holmes, 1997a, 1997b; Q. Jones, 1997; S. G. Jones, 1995, 1998a; Mynatt et al., 1997; Riley et al., 1998).

Another frequent debate concerns the authenticity of virtual communities, that is, whether they can be considered "real" communities or not (e.g., Bromberg, 1996; Heim, 1995). Reminiscent of Gumpert's recurring lament about the undermining of traditional public gathering places by electronic media (e.g., 1987, pp. 167–189; Gumpert & Drucker, 1996, pp. 35–36; 1997, pp. 5–6; Gumpert & Fish, 1990a, pp. 3–4), some CMC scholars express rather negative views about virtual communities. For instance, Weinreich (1997) argues that virtual communities are not "real," Willson (1997) suggests that participation in virtual communities is detrimental to participation in "real" life, Lockard (1997) claims that the idea of virtual community is a myth, and Lajoie (1996) asserts that virtual communities contribute to the elimination of public space. Generally, though, researchers investigating virtual communities tend to consider them "real" enough (e.g., Barnes, 1996b; December, 1997a, 1997b; Kollock & M. A. Smith, 1999; Lajoie, 1996; Surratt, 1996; Wellman & Gulia, 1999; Williams, 2000, 2001). Worth noting in this connection is the wisdom of eschewing the semantically-loaded opposition of "virtual" versus "real" in favor of the more objective distinction between "online" and "offline."

As for surveys covering various communities, Rheingold's classic may be the most cited, but others have produced similar overviews. For example, one preliminary survey is an Australian master's thesis by Vincent, *Collegiality in Cyberspace* (1992). More recent surveys of virtual communities include Moore's *The Emperor's Virtual Clothes: The Naked Truth about Internet Culture* (1995), Randall's *The Soul of the Internet: Net Gods, Netizens and the Wiring of the World* (1997), and Tapscott's *Growing Up Digital: The Rise of the Net Generation* (1998). Some survey discussions have an "adventures online" flavor. Among the earliest in this vein are Rushkoff's *Cyberia: Life in the Trenches of Hyperspace* (1994) and Herz's *Surfing on the Internet: A Nethead's Adventures On-Line* (1995), followed by others such as *Escape Velocity: Cyberculture at the End of the Century* (1996) by Dery and *The Wired Neighborhood* (1996) by Doheny-Farina. Similar offerings include Dyson's *Release 2.0: A*

Design for Living in the Digital Age (1997), Grossman's *Net Wars* (1997), McGrath's *Hard, Soft & Wet: The Digital Generation Comes of Age* (1997), and Seabrook's *Deeper: My Two-Year Odyssey in Cyberspace* (1997). Surveys of this genre are aptly labeled "popular cyberspace travelogues" by Parks and Floyd (1996, p. 82).

Many case studies of specific virtual communities exist, with researchers often taking an ethnographic or participant-observer approach to their subjects. M. A. Smith's *Voices from the WELL: The Logic of the Virtual Commons* (1992) provides an early account of this famous California-based BBS ("Whole Earth 'Lectronic Link," http://www.well.com). Along similar lines, in *Cyberville: Clicks, Culture, and the Creation of an Online Town* (1998), Horn describes the New York-based equivalent BBS, Echo ("East Coast Hang Out," http://www.echonyc.com). One of the first and best-known ethnographies of virtual communities is Reid's *Electropolis* (1991) about IRC, followed by her similar shorter piece (1996a), but IRC has also been studied by others as well (e.g., Cheung, 1995; Danet et al., 1998; Puterman, 1995; Rintel & Pittam, 1997a, 1997b; Surratt, 1996; Werry, 1996). MUDs and MOOs have been the object of a variety of case studies, such as Dibbell's *My Tiny Life: Crime and Passion in a Virtual World* (1998), among others (e.g., Beaubien, 1996; Bromberg, 1996; Bruckman & Resnick, 1995; Curtis, 1997; Fanderclai, 1995; Reid, 1995, 1996b; M. S. Rosenberg, 1992; Wilbur, 1997). There is also an anthology edited by Haynes and Holmevik, *High Wired* (1998), containing various articles about the design, use, and theory of educational MOOs. Among case studies of Usenet newsgroups, *Netizens: On the History and Impact of Usenet and the Internet* by M. Hauben and R. Hauben (1997) is frequently cited, but there are numerous other investigations of newsgroups as well (e.g., Aycock & Buchignani, 1995; Baym, 1993/1997b, 1994, 1995, 1998, 1999; Giese, 1998; Gotved, 2000; M. Hauben, 1995; Mitra, 1997b; Rintel, 1995; Rutter & G. Smith, 1999a, 1999b; Watson, 1997). And reports about communities on the Web are beginning to appear, such as Figallo's *Hosting Web Communities* (1998), and Kim's *Community-Building on the Web* (2000), as well as others (e.g., H. Miller, 1995; Mitra, 1997a).

Among the many topics and themes which have captured the attention of virtual community researchers is misbehavior in online environments. However, investigations which directly address this subject are still relatively scarce. For the most part, the literature on virtual communities reviewed above and the online CMC literature described previously offer basic information about life in specific virtual communities, as well as about life online in a general sense. Some of this literature mentions misbehavior merely in passing, suggesting simply that people misbehave. Some surveys and case studies of virtual communities provide more concrete albeit fleeting glimpses of misbehavior, scattered examples and random insights that can serve as data for other investigations such as this one. But from the perspective of the present study, the most pertinent material about misbehavior is found in three bodies of literature related to online CMC and virtual communities.

The three bodies of literature which offer the most fertile and provocative ideas and information relevant to this study of misbehavior in online environments represent the following areas of inquiry: first, trouble brewing in cyberspace; second, cybercrime and law-breaking on the Internet; and third, misbehavior and rule-breaking in virtual communities. Sources from these three bodies of literature were used to provide data for the present study of misbehavior and the regulation of online conduct in virtual communities on the Internet. Each of these three bodies of literature is discussed in a separate chapter of this report.

The first body of literature (reviewed in Chapter Three) concerns trouble brewing in cyberspace. Often anecdotal or journalistic as well as scholarly, sources in this group report in varying degrees of detail on the emergence of troublesome online behavior, in particular, an infamous triad of activities referred to as flaming, spamming, and virtual rape. Sources in this body of literature also tell of an ensuing frontier mentality in cyberspace, driving a desire to develop ways of handling such troublesome online behavior. Finally, this group of sources includes material on the evolution of two kinds of approaches for dealing with troublesome behavior in online environments: on the one hand, externally-oriented approaches focusing on cybercrime and law-breaking throughout the Internet; and on the other hand, internally-oriented approaches, focusing on misbehavior and rule-breaking within virtual communities.

The second body of literature (reviewed in Chapter Four) includes research on cybercrime and law-breaking on the Internet, primarily from computer science and jurisprudence perspectives, representing approaches which focus on technological and legal dimensions of troublesome online behavior. The literature on cybercrime and lawbreaking is extensive as well as mature, no doubt because crime in the offline world has existed far longer than misbehavior in the online world. Computer science and jurisprudence literature on cybercrime and law-breaking concerns problems of legal applications, definitions, and jurisdictions, offering ideas and information worth examining and bearing in mind when analyzing misbehavior in virtual communities. Among the contributions to this study derived from cybercrime and law-breaking literature, for example, is a series of themes involved in electronic abuse such as: anonymity, attacks, censorship, deception, defamation, dissent, eavesdropping, fraud, harassment, hijacking, liability, monitoring, obscenity, piracy, pornography, privacy, sabotage, surveillance, terrorism, theft, trespassing, vandalism, and violence. Because global Internet-wide abusive behavior is often mimicked and reproduced at the local level, consideration of themes like these from cybercrime and law-breaking literature helps furnish background and context for analyzing misbehavior and rule-breaking in virtual communities.

The third and most pertinent body of literature (reviewed in Chapter Five) encompasses investigations which directly address misbehavior and rule-breaking in virtual communities, primarily from communication and media theory perspectives, representing approaches which focus on sociological and psychological dimensions of troublesome online behavior. This literature directly related to misbehavior and rule-breaking in virtual communities is limited in quantity, and in this sense is comparatively immature: a reasonable start has been made, but not enough is known yet. Only recently has online misbehavior begun to capture the attention of scholars to any significant degree and to gain recognition as a subject meriting study in its own right. As discussed in Chapter Five, such research on misbehavior and rule-breaking in virtual communities consists mostly of shorter reports on issues related to behavior management and social control, which examine either specific aspects of online misbehavior, or misbehavior in specific virtual communities. To date, no overview, general survey, or book-length treatment appears to have been published about misbehavior in online environments; the present study may be the first such endeavor. However, existing research on misbehavior in virtual communities offers valuable ideas and information concerning rule-breaking, as well as rule-making and rule-enforcement. This body of literature also reveals major relevant themes beyond flaming, spamming, and rape. In the literature on misbehavior in virtual communities, it is possible to discern distinct areas and issues for further investigation, among them: how people establish, revise, disseminate, apply, and implement rules of online conduct; the roles of offenders and enforcers, and their possible motivations and personality profiles; and the technical mechanisms and sociological measures for sanctioning those who misbehave.

Throughout these three bodies of literature, there is unanimous agreement that additional inquiry is needed into misbehavior in online environments. For example, D. E. Denning and Lin emphasize that "how to determine the appropriate, acceptable, and effective sanctions to control miscreant behavior is an area that still needs careful analysis and development" (1994, p. 54). Dutton agrees that regulation of electronic communities is "a serious issue that merits more sustained debate and systematic analysis," and notes that "relatively few studies have looked at the norms governing this new medium. Norms have been identified as a critical factor shaping communication on networks . . . but rarely studied" (1996, pp. 270, 288, n. 3). Sproull and Faraj, too, claim that more research is necessary, particularly comparing different online environments: "we also need research that documents implicit codes of behavior and social influence mechanisms across a wide variety of group types" (1995/1997, p. 49). MacKinnon also highlights the importance of investigating online misbehavior:

> Sociopathy has been a major part of our virtual interaction from the beginning, despite our inability or failure to comprehensively document and research it. It is abundantly clear that the "darker side" of virtual life merits considerable study. (1997, p. 207)

And Kollock and M. A. Smith argue that "given the new possibilities that emerge in computer-mediated interaction, cyberspace provides an important research site to explore this fundamental question of social order" (1996, p. 110).

Moreover, the need for research on the social organization of cyberspace is growing increasingly urgent. According to Kollock and M. A. Smith, "as computer-mediated interaction becomes the medium through which public discourse takes place, the ways in which that discourse is socially organized become more consequential" (1996, p. 125). Perhaps the most telling assessment of the state of research in this area comes from MacKinnon, who astutely observes that "the literature on virtual communities and cyberspace is increasing at a phenomenal rate and thereby boasts a plethora of competing theories and analyses in search of a paradigm" (1998, p. 148). Thus, a comprehensive study of misbehavior and the regulation of online conduct in virtual communities on the Internet, grounded in a coherent media ecology theoretical framework, provides a promising way to shed light on social issues of importance in online environments that may well bear on social relations in the offline world.

This, then, is the theoretical context of the present study of misbehavior and the regulation of online conduct in virtual communities on the Internet. The preceding review of literature supports the two premises on which this study is based. The first premise is that the field of media ecology lacks applications of existing theory to the analysis of interpersonal communication in mediated environments, especially those involving online CMC. Support for this first premise was provided by situating this investigation within the larger context of the field of media ecology. The second premise on which this study is based is that significant research and data exist, related to online CMC in general and to virtual communities in particular, suggesting the need for a more thorough and substantive investigation of misbehavior than has been undertaken so far. Support for this second premise was provided by situating this study in the context of mainstream research related to online CMC and to virtual communities. Having reviewed the theoretical context of this investigation, it is appropriate at this point to start examining the literature related to misbehavior in online environments used as source material for the present study. The discussion which follows in the next three chapters begins with the earliest body of source material, addressing the genesis of misbehavior in online environments: trouble brewing in cyberspace.

Chapter Three
Trouble Brewing in Cyberspace

AN INFAMOUS TRIAD OF TROUBLESOME ONLINE BEHAVIOR

Throughout the rise of interpersonal computer-mediated communication ("CMC"), one aspect of life in cyberspace which has received considerable attention is how to deal with troublesome online behavior. Initially, troublesome online behavior mostly preoccupied participants. Subsequently, scholars and professionals in various fields joined the growing ranks of those concerned with developing approaches for handling online troublemakers and the problems they cause in cyberspace.

As group interaction in online environments has evolved, constant attempts are made to minimize the likelihood of trouble by promoting appropriate behavior. Participants themselves have developed a rich tradition of producing electronic documentation pertaining to appropriate online behavior, for the convenience and edification of their fellow users. Available on the Internet in diverse forms, and varying in degree of formality and authority, such documents typically set forth rules of conduct applicable in different online environments, stipulating policies for enforcing rules as well as sanctions for breaking them. Some documents are informal primers on proper network etiquette, often referred to as "netiquette." Some are compilations called Frequently Asked Questions ("FAQs"). Still others are more formal agreements known as Acceptable Use Policies ("AUPs") and Terms of Service ("TOSs"), as well as Network Working Group Requests for Comments ("RFCs"), a numbered series of Internet-wide proclamations. Additionally, guidelines for appropriate conduct often appear in the help features and manuals of software used to access online environments, as well as on electronic mailing lists, message boards, newsgroups, and Web sites related to particular virtual communities. Such an abundance of user-oriented documentation demonstrates how concerned participants are to keep troublesome behavior under control in a wide range of online environments.

Among the earliest scholars to notice and comment on troublesome behavior in cyberspace are Hiltz and Turoff, the pioneers of online CMC studies. Writing originally in 1978, in their classic, *The Network Nation: Human Communication Via Computer*, Hiltz and Turoff mention inevitable "difficulties with users. . . . [who] exhibit certain undesirable behavior. . . . Users will do the unexpected, the unanticipated, and the forbidden. Users will disregard or forget instructions" (1978/1993, p. 322). Because of such troublesome behavior, Hiltz and Turoff suggest, online groups "can form and develop norms and sanction deviants" (p. 96). According to Hiltz and Turoff, problematic behavior online is largely due to lack of familiarity with CMC environments:

> For most forms of communication, societies have had decades or even centuries to develop cultural guidelines on appropriate use. These are enforced as norms, taught to children by their parents, and embodied in codes of law. There has not been time, however, for an adequate ethical and legal framework to emerge to regulate the use of CMC. Lacking this, groups must explicitly formulate policies and socialize new members about appropriate and inappropriate behavior. Some groups or systems go so far as to require prospective members to read and sign a networkers' creed before they are allowed access. . . . Generations hence, it could very well be that future networkers will look back at our society and ask, "How could they have acted that way?" There may very well be scholarly studies on how ethics and behavior on networks evolved out of their primitive roots. (1978/1993, p. 509)

Norms and guidelines for appropriate online behavior, therefore, are still developing, as Hiltz and Turoff explain:

> The "norms," or expected rules for participation, have not fully emerged. When users feel a great deal of confusion about . . . what is socially correct or likely to be considered in poor taste or deviant, then the communication behavior observed is likely to show some irregularities. With time, it can be expected that users both individually and as a kind of collective "subculture" will develop much more skill as well as some shared norms and understanding about etiquette and level of participation. (1978/1993, p. 91)

Roughly a decade later, in another early collaborative work, *Computer-Mediated Communication: Human Relationships in a Computerized World* (1989), Chesebro and Bonsall agree that in online environments, "the circumstances of the interactions lack any predetermined social customs and rules, and users must create their own sense of what is appropriate for such interactions" and that participants "must create the social norms and rules that govern these new social contexts" (pp. 58, 124). In addition to such observations, Hiltz and Turoff identify the following issues as "high priority research areas" in CMC: "What sorts of norms and rituals evolve? . . . What are the supportive human roles, such as facilitation and gatekeeping? What are the characteristics that enhance leadership? What are the mechanisms of group control?" (1978/1993, pp. 253–254).

Nevertheless, despite early insights like these about the importance of studying troublesome online behavior, it would be several years before scholars investigated such questions in any depth. In the meantime, from the early 1990s until the present, certain types of troublesome online behavior began to capture the attention of numerous writers, in both scholarly and popular publications. In particular, attention has focused on a triad of disturbing activities known as flaming, spamming, and virtual rape. These three types of virtual offenses have been the subject of many reports, and even today, this infamous triad of troublesome online behavior continues to receive substantial consideration. Relevant research on flaming, spamming, and virtual rape is reviewed next.

FLAMING:
DIGITAL DEBATES AND VIRTUAL VITRIOL

Flaming is the first kind of troublesome online behavior to taken up in the literature, perhaps because it was noticed early in the development of online environments. As MacKinnon asserts,

> Although the first studies of flaming or the general equivalent of virtual violence were not concluded until 1992, there is no doubt that the first flames were felt not long after the first virtual salutations were exchanged way back in the "ancient" Usenet year of 1979. (1997, p. 207, references omitted)

Initial studies of flaming are summarized by both M. Collins (1992) and Dery (1993). More recently, Dsilva et al. survey various definitions of flaming, settling on the following general description: flames are "critical comments directed toward another participant in online discussion" (1998, p. 181). Similarly, Kollock and M. A. Smith succinctly define a flame as "a hostile, provocative post" (1996, p. 116). Two slightly more elaborate definitions come from Herring: flaming is "the practice of sending hostile or insulting electronic messages, usually in response to a message posted by someone else" (1996a, p. 10); and flames are "personal put-downs . . . generally characterized by a challenging, adversarial, or superior stance vis à vis the intended addressee(s)" (1996b, p. 118). Chenault (1998) gives a brief summary of research on flaming, but Thompsen (1996) provides a far more thorough overview. Thompsen lists no less than thirteen definitions of flaming collected from the literature (pp. 299–300), and also mentions "flaming-like behavior in other media, such as complaint letters, prank phone calls, and televised debates" (p. 309).

Many studies deal with flaming in particular online settings. For example, Baym (1993/1997b, 1995) and D. J. Phillips (1996) consider flaming in Usenet newsgroups, Danet et al. (1998) tackle flaming on IRC, and Machado (1996) examines flaming in post systems. Bunn (1999) and Millard (1997) take on flaming in mailing lists. Sempsey (1995) presents a psychological approach to flaming in MUDs, while King (1995) offers a psychological perspective on flaming in general. Gurak (1997) and Holland (1996) discuss flaming in general as well. Mabry (1998) provides statistical research on flaming in newsgroups, mailing lists, and post systems on BBSs and CompuServe. And in a study of IRC and newsgroups, Shade (1996) links flaming to issues involving censorship and free speech. Finally, anecdotal mention of flaming can be found in the CMC and virtual community literature surveyed in Chapter Two (e.g., Barnes, 1996b; Cutler, 1996; Garton & Wellman, 1995; Grossman, 1997; Herz, 1995; Moore, 1995; Morris & Ogan, 1996; Randall, 1997; Savicki et al., 1996; Seabrook, 1997; Tapscott, 1998, Wellman & Gulia, 1999).

SPAMMING:
ELECTRONIC JUNK MAIL AND OTHER CYBER DEBRIS

Spamming is the second activity in the triad of troublesome online behavior frequently discussed in the literature. The origins of the term are explained by Sempsey as follows:

> This term is derived from a famous Monty Python [British television comedy] sketch and refers to the flooding of appropriate media with information (such as repeated very long sentences). Intentional spamming is considered very rude or a form of aggression and is akin to filibustering. (1995)

Marvin (1995) defines spam most succinctly as any "excess of words," but spam is widely acknowledged to contain a high degree of repetitiveness. Wisebrod (1995), for example, cites a definition of spamming in Usenet newsgroups as "posting identical or nearly-identical ads to a lot of newsgroups, one right after the other." In addition to repetitiveness, Q. Jones (1997) invokes the element of advertising in defining spamming as "posting the same article to many electronic forums, usually . . . as a form of advertising." Herring similarly notes a commercial motivation for spam: "the practice of sending multiple copies of the same message to different electronic destinations . . . is often associated with unsolicited commercial advertising" (1996a, p. 10). An elegant and generally-applicable definition of spam, as well as an overview of this phenomenon, are provided by Stivale (1996/1997), who confirms the origins of the term in a Monty Python comedy skit about the eponymous canned meat product (see also Randall, 1997, pp. 102–103). According to Stivale, spam "refers to that unnecessary data transmission that one participant deliberately produces often simply to fill lines on the recipients' screens, but sometimes to communicate aggressive messages as well" (1996/1997, p. 133). Besides such definitions and discussions, anecdotal mention of spamming in various online environments can be found in the CMC and virtual community literature surveyed in Chapter Two (e.g., Grossman, 1997; Tapscott, 1998; Wellman & Gulia, 1999).

One of the earliest famous cases of spamming involved advertisements posted to Usenet newsgroups by Laurence Canter and Martha Siegel, recounted in detail by Moore:

> The lawyers, a married couple, posted an advertisement in April 1994 to thousands of Usenet newsgroups, everything from misc.fitness to rec.arts.disney. Sending a post to more than one group in this way is known as crossposting. Sending to a multitude of groups is known as a spam, after a famously repetitious Monty Python comedy sketch. Canter and Siegel, as their notoriety increases on the Internet, are often simply referred to as Crosspost & Spam by their detractors. (1995, p. 111)

Moore himself posted to alt.current-events.net-abuse asking "what was so onerous about the Canter and Siegel green card incident, and received numerous replies within hours, many of them pages long" (pp. 113–114). Moore explains the strong negative reactions inspired by this case as follows:

> The crossposting to literally thousands of unrelated Usenet groups was seen as a new form of electronic junk mail: it was not related to any topic normally discussed on the newsgroups, nobody had apparently asked for the information, yet it filled countless electronic mailboxes.
>
> What really bothered people was not that Canter and Siegel did this once (or even that they went on to repeat it again), but the thought of what would happen if other people started to do it, too, if the firm's innovative electronic advertising strategy worked out and innumerable companies, large and small, jumped on the bandwagon.
>
> You see, this ability to spam, to reach millions of readers sitting in front of millions of machines, is, unlike conventional junk mail, basically free, aside from the cost of an access account. Name another way to reach millions of potential customers at such a price. Short of jumping off a tall building with advertising on your T-shirt, there aren't many. With a little technical knowledge, I could spam, you could spam, every charity and mail-order shoe company on the planet could spam, and what would that do to the Internet itself? Would it change the basic character of the Net—the hopeful, forward-looking, free-speech frontier mentality? Would it drive people away? Would the whole thing just explode?
>
> People went to a lot of trouble to make sure that Canter and Siegel's crossposting strategy did not work, everything from filling the firm's return electronic mailbox with flames and junk so that no legitimate replies could get through, to notifying various state bar associations of the firm's conduct and alleging that it was improper, to writing complicated programs called cancel-bots that automatically erased subsequent Canter and Siegel postings moments after they appeared.
>
> Others took thousands of those little subscription cards that fall out of magazines and filled them out with Martha Siegel's name and address.

Following the green card lottery post. Ms. Siegel told The Wall Street Journal
that she received "carloads" of magazines to which she had never subscribed.
  And others simply took to the Net: denouncing the pair, calling for retalia-
tion or legislation, protecting their home turf. The argument has been going on
for over a year now, and shows no sign of stopping. (1995, pp. 112–113)

The subject of spamming turns up often in the popular press, especially in
relation to the particularly odious type of spam polluting the Internet landscape
since the Canter and Siegel incident, the virtual equivalent of traditional postal
junk mail which has come to be known as Unsolicited Commercial Email
("UCE"). Writing for the online magazine *Salon* (http://salon.com), Leonard
(1997a, 1998) discusses anti-spam grassroots organizations ranging from "vigilantes" to non-profit organizations such as the Coalition Against Unsolicited
Commercial Email (*http://www.cauce.org*) and the Internet Mail Consortium
(*http://www.imc.org*), which lobby for anti-spam legislation; the Campaign to
Boycott Internet Spam (http://spam.abuse.net), whose goal is to stem the tide of
UCE; and the Mail Abuse Protection System (http://mail-abuse.org) and the
Open Relay Behavior-modification System (http://www.orbs.org), which generate prominent blacklists of notorious spammers. Scoblionkov (1999) also considers the use of blacklists in discussing anti-spam activism and spamming by
political candidates. But another news writer criticizes the efforts of such
"watchdog" organizations, suggesting that they "smack of McCarthyism"
(Kobelius, March 15, 1999). Nevertheless, the race is underway to criminalize
spam of the UCE genre, and several lawsuits have been brought successfully in
the United States: for example, America Online won cases against spammers in
three different states (Fusaro, December 23, 1998). As for other discussions of
spam in the popular press, Brown has informative articles about spamming in
Usenet newsgroups (1998), post systems and the Web (1999a), and electronic
mailing lists (1999b).

Virtual Rape:
Sexual Harassment in Online Gathering Places

The last and most nefarious of the troika of troublesome online behavior often
discussed in the literature is referred to as virtual rape, involving online episodes
of what participants perceive to be extreme sexual harassment. The term "rape"
was perhaps first applied in print to online sexual harassment by Dibbell, in "A
Rape in Cyberspace," a piece originally published in *The Village Voice* (1993).
Rarely does one article see as many incarnations as Dibbell's account of the
activities of a certain character named Mr. Bungle in a virtual community called
LambdaMOO. Reprinted under the same title in several anthologies (e.g.,
Ludlow, 1996; Stefik, 1996), the identical article also appears in one collection
under a different title (Dibbell, 1996); furthermore, the same piece serves as the
basis for a significant portion of *My Tiny Life*, Dibbell's 1998 book about his
experiences in LambdaMOO.

To make a long story short, Bungle (a participant apparently logged into LambdaMOO from New York University) used special software later known as a "voodoo doll" to make it appear to all the MOO participants online at the time as if their characters were communicating and behaving in sexually perverse and sadistic ways. Actually, it was Bungle manipulating what seemed to be the other participants' characters by remote control, while the participants (themselves inactive) could only observe helplessly. The chaos continued until a veteran user stopped Bungle by means of another software routine called a "gun," which trapped Bungle and rendered him unable to continue the attack. Subsequently, LambdaMOO participants debated what to do about Bungle, and although no group consensus was reached, a system administrator or "wizard" acted independently and "toaded" Bungle's account. In this instance, "toading" meant deleting Bungle's entire existence from the LambdaMOO database, the virtual equivalent of a death penalty.

Besides the multiple iterations of Dibbell's account of the Bungle virtual rape, others have written about it as well. For example, Beaubien distills the essential facts of the Bungle affair into a concise handful of paragraphs (1996, pp. 184–185), while MacKinnon (1998) provides a thoughtful and thorough critique of the Bungle episode, including a historical and cross-cultural overview of the social construction of rape in the offline world. Stivale, on the other hand, characterizes the LambdaMOO incident as "pernicious spam" because Bungle flooded his victims with unwanted and excessive "sexually explicit verbiage" (1996/1997, pp. 139–140). In addition, Stivale presents a definition of virtual rape suggested by some members of LambdaMOO in the aftermath of the Bungle rampage: "'any act which explicitly references the non-consensual, involuntary exposure, manipulation, or touching of sexual organs of or by a character'" (as cited in Stivale, 1996/1997, p. 141; the same definition is also cited in other sources, e.g., MacKinnon, 1997, p. 228; Mnookin, 1996; Williams, 2000). Not only is the Bungle affair the most often reprinted tale of virtual rape, it is certainly the most famous, almost always mentioned when this genre of troublesome online behavior is discussed (e.g., Bartle, 1996; Maltz, 1996; Reid, 1999). MacKinnon calls the Bungle case "the incident known as the first widely publicized rape in cyberspace" (1998, p. 147), but elsewhere notes that "while 1993 may be the year of the first *reported* incident of virtual rape, it is doubtfully the year of the first incidence of 'net.rape'" (1997, p. 207).

Since the Bungle story first appeared in 1993, virtual rape has become a recurrent theme in relation to cyberspace, according to MacKinnon (1997, p. 211), and other cases have surfaced. MacKinnon compares the Bungle affair in LambdaMOO with a second virtual rape, this time in Usenet newsgroups. As MacKinnon tells it, Jake Baker, a student at the University of Michigan, was expelled and arrested in 1995 for posting a story on alt.sex.stories, a newsgroup dedicated to the sharing of sexually-explicit textual fantasies. Baker's posted story involved the fictional rape, torture, and murder by his persona of a female character held captive in her own apartment, this woman representing a fellow student with whom the live, corporeal Baker apparently had minimal contact in the offline world (pp. 214, 226). The Baker newsgroup rape is also compared with the Bungle MOO rape by Stivale (1996/1997), although in less detail than MacKinnon provides. Another researcher who examines virtual rape, including the Bungle and Baker cases, is Williams (2000, 2001). Taking a linguistic perspective, Williams views virtual rape as online sexual harassment conducted by means of textual messages, describing this variety of troublesome behavior as "derisory discourse" and "words that wound," almost as if such "derisory and harmful textual performances" were flaming taken to a salacious extreme (2000). In a subsequent article (2001), Williams continues this line of inquiry into virtual rape by considering forms of redress for the harms inflicted by the abusive discourse he characterizes as "injurious illocutions within a textual environment."

Bad things come in threes, the saying goes, and so it is with virtual rape cases in the literature. Reid reports on a third, lesser-known rape in a virtual community called JennyMUSH, "a social MUD used as a virtual support center by survivors of sexual assault" (1999, p. 111). Reid's account of this incident is worth citing as an illuminating example of just how strongly participants feel about sexual harassment in their online gathering places.

> A single user of JennyMUSH was able to subvert the delicate social balance of the system by using both technical and social means to enact anonymously what amounted to virtual rape. Two weeks after being assigned a character, a user of the system used the MUD's commands to transform him or herself into a virtual manifestation of every other user's fears. This user changed "her" initial virtual gender to male, "his" virtual name to "Daddy," and then used the special "shout" command to send messages to every other user connected to the MUD. He described virtual assaults in graphic and violent terms. At the time at which this began, none of the MUD's administrators, or Wizards, were connected to the system, a fact that may well have been taken into account by the user. For almost half an hour, the user continued to send obscene messages to others. (1999, p. 115).

The tables turned on the abuser after a wizard logged on, took control of the situation using technical measures available exclusively to wizards, and subsequently led other participants in a virtual equivalent of lynching the perpetrator. Reid describes the vehemence with which participants took their vengeful retribution on the troublemaker:

> At the end of that half hour, one of the Wizards connected to the system. He found twelve users connected to the system, all congregated in one place. On transporting himself to that place, he found eleven of those users being obscenely taunted by the twelfth. Quickly realizing what was going on, the Wizard took a kind of vengeance upon the erring user that is possible only in virtual reality. He took control of the user's virtual manifestation, took away from him the ability to communicate, changed his name to "Vermin" and changed his description to the following: "This is the lowest scum, the most pathetic dismal object which a human being can become." What had preceded

had been painful and ugly—what ensued has been described to me as "virtual carnage." The eleven users who had been victimized by this now impotent one turned upon him and took dreadful virtual revenge. They described all the most violent punishments they would like to enact on this and all other attackers. (1999, pp. 115–116)

Studies such as these by Reid (1999), MacKinnon (1997, 1998), and Williams (2000, 2001) feature virtual rape as a dominant theme, but there is also anecdotal mention of virtual rape in some of the CMC and virtual community literature surveyed in Chapter Two (e.g., Chenault, 1998; Dery, 1996; Deuel, 1996; Morris & Ogan, 1996; Mynatt et al., 1997; Turkle, 1995).

A FRONTIER MENTALITY: THE INTERNET BESIEGED

If activities such as the infamous triad of flaming, spamming, and virtual rape were the earliest to draw attention to troublesome behavior in online environments, there certainly has been no lack of trouble in cyberspace ever since. In the preface to an anthology about online security, revealingly entitled *Internet Besieged: Countering Cyberspace Scofflaws*, editors D. E. and P. J. Denning offer a vivid description of the sorts of troublesome behavior found in cyberspace nowadays. The Dennings summarize various online security perils and the atmosphere created thereby as follows:

> The Internet is a risky place. . . . Hackers, crackers, snoops, spoofers, spammers, scammers, shammers, jammers, intruders, thieves, purloiners, conspirators, vandals, Trojan horse dealers, virus launchers, and rogue program purveyors run loose, plying regularly their nasty crafts and dirty deeds. Many do so shamelessly, enjoying near perfect anonymity—using forged addresses, untraceable links, and unbreakable codes. Analogies to the Old American West, populated by unruly cowboys and a shoot-first-ask-later-mentality, are more appropriate than the coiners of the phrase "electronic frontier" ever imagined. Many law-abiding citizens, who simply want to conduct their business in peace, are demanding that the marshal come to cyberspace. (1998a, p. vii)

With troublesome behavior such as the Dennings depict casting ominous shadows on the Internet horizon, it comes as no surprise that metaphors related to a Wild West or frontier mentality are often applied to life online (Strate, 1999, pp. 392–394; Strate et al., 1996b, pp. 3–4). As Strate observes, the "electronic frontier" metaphor is usually attributed to John Perry Barlow, co-founder (together with Mitchell Kapor) of the Electronic Frontier Foundation (http://eff.org), a non-profit organization concerned with issues such as freedom of expression and digital privacy in cyberspace. Strate quotes one account of Barlow's initial conception of cyberspace as uncharted territory:

> Barlow was the first commentator to adopt novelist William Gibson's striking science-fictional term "cyberspace" as a synonym for the present-day nexus of

computer and telecommunications networks. Barlow was insistent that cyberspace should be regarded as a qualitatively new world, a "frontier." According to Barlow, the world of electronic communications, now made visible through the computer screen, could no longer be usefully regarded as just a tangle of high-tech wiring. Instead, it had become a *place*, cyberspace, which demanded a new set of metaphors, a new set of rules and behaviors. (Sterling, 1992, p. 236, as cited in Strate, 1999, p. 392)

The frontier metaphor and associated motifs are quite evident in contemporary discussions of cyberspace. For example, one anthology about cyberspace issues bears the evocative title *High Noon on the Electronic Frontier* (Ludlow, 1996). In studying a MUD, A. D. Smith uncovers "a frontier ethic of taking the law into one's own hands. . . . an informal system of frontier justice" (1999, p. 147). McLaughlin et al. identify "outlaw" as a social role online (1995, p. 94), while Kim (1998) reports on an outlaw mindset prevalent in virtual gaming communities such as Ultima Online (http://uo.com). And in relation to flaming, Thompsen introduces the "cyberspace cowboy—someone who may be mild-mannered in person, but dons a flamboyant CMC persona when online" (1996, p. 305). References such as these often focus on negative aspects of Wild West or frontier-oriented attitudes.

However, some researchers portray the electronic frontier in fairly cheerful fashion. For instance, one optimistic assessment of the Internet's potential for expansion comes from Healy, who declares cyberspace to be an "appealing frontier for a new generation of Americans" (1997, p. 57). A similarly sunny vision of cyberspace as "the new frontier" comes from Danet et al., who assert that users "treat the medium as a frontier world" and that "the frontierlike quality of this new world" fosters considerable playfulness (1998, p. 44). Another optimist, Thompsen, claims that troublesome online behavior such as flaming is "part of life on the electronic frontier" and blithely predicts that "as with previous frontiers, law-abiding citizens will eventually displace the outlaws" (1996, p. 311). But the most balanced and sensible evaluation is provided by the doyenne of cyberlaw studies, Branscomb, writing as guest editor of a special issue of the *Journal of Computer-Mediated Communication* entitled "Emerging Law on the Electronic Frontier." In her introductory article, after reviewing the history of legal concerns about rogue and abusive online behavior, Branscomb ultimately concludes that cyberspace offers "both familiar territory and lawless frontiers" (1996).

Nonetheless, despite those who argue against representing cyberspace as a Wild West frontier colonized by outlaws (e.g., Maltz, 1996), this perception still endures, as evidenced by a remark made in 1999 by U.S. Attorney General Janet Reno. Speaking to Department of Justice officials and members of the Information Technology Association of America, in a summit meeting aimed at forging a partnership to fight cybercrime, Reno cautioned that "we cannot allow cyberspace to become the Wild West of the Information Age" (as cited in Associated Press, March 15, 1999; Tillett, March 23, 1999).

TWO APPROACHES: EXTERNAL LAWS VERSUS INTERNAL RULES

In an atmosphere clouded by troublesome online behavior, the perception of the Internet as a lawless and unruly frontier lingers until today, generating significant concern and debate among participants and researchers alike. For researchers, troublesome online behavior has been an especially problematic area, despite early observations about users who engage in undesirable conduct, and ongoing inquiry into particular activities such as flaming, spamming, and virtual rape. No doubt this relates to the tremendous ambiguity and confusion that exist about where to draw the line between cybercrime throughout the Internet, on the one hand, and misbehavior within virtual communities, on the other.

It is helpful, at this point, to reiterate from Chapter One a pair of parallel distinctions drawn in this study: between cybercrime and misbehavior, and between laws and rules. People engage in a broad spectrum of troublesome behavior in cyberspace, ranging from serious and malicious transgressions to playful and mischievous pranks. Cybercrime involves the higher end of the spectrum of troublesome conduct in online environments, situations where law-making and law-enforcement are handled by external authorities and institutions offline. In contrast, misbehavior involves the lower end of the spectrum, situations where rule-making and rule-enforcement are handled internally by participants themselves within their online environments, with appeals to external authorities and institutions offline used only as a last resort.

Thus, cybercrime involves breaking laws, whereas online misbehavior involves breaking rules. In general, laws refer to external, highly formalized legislation, established and enforced outside online environments by offline authorities and institutions. Rules, on the other hand, consist of regulations, principles, guidelines, or customs governing behavior; what a person must or must not do in relation to various elements of a situation. As Goffman describes them, rules are "social norms regulating behavior of persons. . . . the regulations of conduct characteristic in . . . gatherings" (1963, pp. 17, 20). Rules evolve from behavioral norms, norms being the standards, models, and patterns of conduct generally considered to be typical of particular social groups. Rules of online conduct involve internal regulations, expressed in varying degrees of formality, developed and enforced within online environments by participants themselves.

Reflecting this polarization between cybercrime and law-breaking on the one hand, and misbehavior and rule-breaking on the other, over the past decade or so, there has been a gradual bifurcation of the study of troublesome online behavior into two branches of research with divergent approaches. It seems that 1994 was a pivotal point for the study of trouble in cyberspace, for in that year, two ground-breaking publications appeared relating to troublesome online behavior. The first is a short volume edited by D. E. Denning and Lin, *Rights and Responsibilities of Participants in Networked Communities* (1994), which summarizes the proceedings of a workshop and forum sponsored by the

Computer Science and Telecommunications Board of the National Research Council of the United States. The second is a brief abstract edited by Bruckman, "Approaches to Managing Deviant Behavior in Online Communities" (1994), of a panel held at the annual meeting of the Special Interest Group on Computer-Human Interaction of the Association for Computing Machinery.

This pair of 1994 publications constitutes the first literature specifically devoted to troublesome online behavior in general, as opposed to investigations of particular kinds of trouble such as the infamous triad discussed above. But because these two publications and their associated events stress different aspects of trouble in cyberspace, they effectively demonstrate the two divergent branches of inquiry which have emerged in the study of troublesome online behavior. The first approach, exemplified by Denning and Lin's volume, originates in the realms of computer science and jurisprudence, and emphasizes the higher end of the spectrum of troublesome online behavior: cybercrime and law-breaking throughout the Internet. The second approach, illustrated by Bruckman's abstract, comes from the realms of communication and media theory, and focuses on the lower end of the spectrum of troublesome online behavior: misbehavior and rule-breaking within virtual communities. Although they overlap to an extent, these two branches of research, one concentrating on cybercrime and the other on misbehavior, have evolved in different directions, and for purposes of this study are distinguished as follows.

Computer science and jurisprudence approaches to cybercrime and law-breaking offer technical perspectives stressing technological and legal dimensions of troublesome online behavior. These lines of research address Internet-wide cybercrime, situations in which legislation and enforcement are handled externally. The literature related to cybercrime and law-breaking, therefore, concentrates on such areas as legal issues in digital environments, online security, and hackers.

In contrast, communication and media theory approaches to misbehavior and rule-breaking offer humanistic perspectives stressing sociological and psychological dimensions of troublesome online behavior. These lines of research address misbehavior within virtual communities, situations in which regulation and enforcement are handled internally by participants themselves. The literature about misbehavior and rule-breaking, therefore, concentrates on such areas as behavior management and social control in online environments.

Given that this study focuses on misbehavior and rule-breaking in virtual communities, primarily the low rather than the high end of the spectrum of troublesome online behavior, most of the literature on cybercrime and law-breaking lies beyond the scope of this investigation. Nevertheless, several issues raised in this literature do bear on the present study and must be taken into account. Cybercrime literature concerning legal applications, definitions, and jurisdictions offers ideas and information worth considering and keeping in mind when analyzing misbehavior in virtual communities. Thus, to situate and clarify the discussion of misbehavior and rule-breaking in virtual communities from communication and media theory perspectives to be presented further ahead in

Chapter Five, certain issues relating to cybercrime and law-breaking on the Internet from computer science and jurisprudence perspectives are reviewed next in Chapter Four. Or, to frame things according to the Dennings' depiction cited above of the Internet besieged and citizens clamoring for the marshal to take action on the electronic frontier (1998a, p. vii), the discussion which follows in Chapter Four offers a sense of what happens when the marshal attempts to deal with trouble in cyberspace.

Chapter Four
Cybercrime:
Law-Breaking on the Internet

THE 1994 DENNING AND LIN REPORT

Nowadays, cybercrime and law-breaking on the Internet are among the most avidly discussed topics in contemporary society. Consequently, research and literature related to cybercrime and law-breaking cover vast territory, far beyond the scope of the present study of misbehavior in virtual communities. However, as explained in previous chapters of this report, certain relevant issues recur in source material on cybercrime and law-breaking which merit closer review. Such sources originate primarily in the realms of computer science and jurisprudence, and represent approaches which focus on technological and legal dimensions of the higher end of the spectrum of troublesome online behavior. As opposed to misbehavior and rule-breaking, discussed further ahead in Chapter Five, cybercrime involves the breaking of laws, which are highly formalized legislation, established and enforced outside online environments. Studies of cybercrime and law-breaking, therefore, emphasize the higher end of the spectrum of troublesome conduct in online environments, situations where law-making and law-enforcement are handled by external authorities and institutions offline.

To introduce relevant cybercrime and law-breaking issues from computer science and jurisprudence perspectives, nothing is more appropriate than the key 1994 publication mentioned previously in Chapter Three, the slender yet weighty volume edited by D. E. Denning and Lin, *Rights and Responsibilities of Participants in Networked Communities*, the proceedings of a workshop and forum sponsored by the Computer Science and Telecommunications Board of the National Research Council of the United States. The Denning and Lin volume and the meetings about which it reports are best summarized by the editors themselves:

At a workshop held in November 1992 and a public forum in February 1993, technologists, service providers, policy analysts, lawyers, and social scientists from academia, industry, and government met to discuss some of the social issues raised by the emergence of electronic communities. This report is based on the discussions of the workshop and forum, as well as deliberations of the steering committee and material that has appeared in the interim. Its purpose is not to draw conclusions, find definitive answers, or make specific recommendations; rather, its purpose is to illuminate, to question, and to articulate thorny and problematic issues that arise in this domain, thus helping to lay a foundation for more informed public debate and discussion. (1994, pp. 1–2)

Indeed, the seminal Denning and Lin report admirably fulfills its stated goal, examining four major themes which turn up repeatedly in cybercrime and law-breaking literature: free speech, electronic vandalism, intellectual property interests, and privacy. Of particular relevance for the present study of misbehavior is the report's chapter on electronic vandalism, which covers security concerns such as viruses and penetrations by intruders resulting in electronic trespassing or theft (pp. 69–84). Also noteworthy is the chapter on legal considerations, which surveys existing judicial models used to characterize network environments, along with famous relevant court cases from the United States through the early 1990s (pp. 34–49). In addition, although slightly outdated, the report contains a lucid overview of electronic networks (pp. 6–16), as well as a helpful appendix explaining basic network technology and terminology (pp. 123–136).

Acknowledging the controversy over social norms on electronic networks, editors Denning and Lin identify as chronic concerns "the extent to which the government should regulate behavior on electronic networks" and "the need for law that specifically relates to behavior on electronic networks" (pp. 5, 116–117). In elaborating on these concerns, the editors ask "what sanctions should apply when miscreant behavior occurs," noting that "informal sanctions have also been used outside the judicial system. Complaints directed to an offending user by others in the community are a particularly effective sanction" (p. 53). It is through sanctions such as "friendly persuasion, parental admonition, social pressure, contracts, licenses, or informal agreements," Denning and Lin explain, that "codes and standards of acceptable behavior and etiquette are established and enforced. . . . the rules of behavior that the community has come to accept as reasonable" (p. 26).

Alas, informal sanctions do not always suffice to enforce the rules. As Denning and Lin put it, "although making rules for electronic networks is challenging, enforcing the rules may be even more problematic . . . because of technological and economic barriers to enforcement" (pp. 23–24). And while observing that "the means for enforcing behavioral norms in networked communities are as diverse as user values," Denning and Lin point out that "network enforcers basically have three options: disconnect rule breakers, employ peer or social pressures, or apply the law" (pp. 22–23). They suggest that "the law is the forum of last appeal" (p. 24), tending to be "the mechanism invoked by society to shape behavior only after all other avenues have been exhausted and found not to be effective" (p. 26). Finally, in assessing the evolution of values and norms for online environments, they imply a precarious and uneasy balance between external laws and internal rules:

> Networked communities are beginning to grapple with the rules that govern (or should govern) behavior on electronic communities. Less formal rules of conduct and the means to enforce these rules are emerging as people acquire more and more experience with electronic networks. . . . The relevant legal regime is unquestionably changing as new interpretations of existing laws and even new laws are being enacted, but its presence and potential influence on human behavior on electronic networks cannot be denied. . . . Some commentators and analysts believe that the emergence of social norms should be left primarily in the hands of the people who will be affected (i.e., the users of electronic networks) . . . . At the same time, the "natural" evolution of old behaviors into new ones may be problematic and perhaps socially undesirable. A maladapted set of social norms could result. (1994, pp. 113–114)

These, then, are some of the issues summarized in the Denning and Lin volume about the rights and responsibilities of participants in networked communities from computer science and jurisprudence perspectives. In anticipation of discussing misbehavior and rule-breaking in virtual communities from communication and media theory perspectives further ahead in Chapter Five, it is appropriate next to examine several relevant themes that recur in cybercrime and law-breaking literature since the publication of the Denning and Lin report in 1994.

CYBERCRIME AND CYBERLAW

Perhaps the most expedient way to outline the broad array of potential cybercrime offenses is by referring to a text well-known among those involved with computer technologies: the "Ten Commandments of Computer Ethics." These ten commandments are often cited as a baseline for thinking about appropriate and inappropriate computer use in general (e.g., Grabowsky & R. G. Smith, 1998, p. 229; R. S. Rosenberg, 1997, p. 492). Violating any of these commandments in online environments can probably be construed as some form of cybercrime:

1. Thou shalt not use a computer to harm other people.
2. Thou shalt not interfere with other people's computer work.
3. Thou shalt not snoop around in other people's computer files.
4. Thou shalt not use a computer to steal.
5. Thou shalt not use a computer to bear false witness.
6. Thou shalt not use or copy proprietary software for which you have not paid.

7. Thou shalt not use other people's computer resources without authorization or proper compensation.
8. Thou shalt not appropriate other people's intellectual output.
9. Thou shalt think about the social consequences of the program you are writing or the system you are designing.
10. Thou shalt use a computer in ways that insure consideration and respect for your fellow humans.

(Computer Ethics Institute, 1997, pp. 313–314)

The fact that a Computer Ethics Institute exists (http://www.brook.edu/its/cei/cei_hp.htm) to compile and disseminate such a code of appropriate computer behavior is suggestive in and of itself. Also worth noting is the fact that of the ten commandments in the list, eight constitute prohibitions, i.e., rules about what *not* to do, what would be *in*appropriate.

The subject of crimes committed in cyberspace has generated an enormous amount of literature, most of it beyond the scope of this investigation. Nevertheless, here are some representative samples which echo and amplify the major themes reported by Denning and Lin (1994). For example, in a basic overview of computer crime both offline and online, *Morality and Machines: Perspectives on Computer Ethics* (1997), Edgar discusses such issues as property rights, privacy, responsibility, liability, computers in the workplace, computer errors and reliability, government and military computer use, artificial intelligence, and virtual worlds. An excellent and thorough survey, *Fighting Computer Crime: A New Framework for Protecting Information* (1998), comes from Parker, a computer security professional with decades of first-hand field experience, who describes various types of computer abuse, ranging from theft and sabotage to software piracy and information warfare. A textbook by R. S. Rosenberg, *The Social Impact of Computers* (1997), provides a brief but solid overview of computer crime (pp. 229–238). And a volume by Cairncross, *The Death of Distance: How the Communications Revolution Will Change Our Lives* (1997), also refers to cybercrime in relation to security and hacking.

Online environments tending to transcend national boundaries, cybercrime attracts attention abroad as well as in the United States. For instance, *Crime in the Digital Age: Controlling Telecommunications and Cyberspace Illegalities* (1998) by Grabowsky and R. G. Smith offers an Australian point of view, tackling topics such as cryptography, electronic eavesdropping, piracy, electronic fraud, theft of telecommunications services, vandalism and terrorism, criminal conspiracies, and offensive content in pornography and defamatory material. And in *Cyberwars: Espionage on the Internet* (1997), a French writer, Guisnel, covers issues such as free speech and censorship, privacy, cryptology, intellectual property, and information warfare on the Internet in Europe as well as the United States.

Finally, no consideration of crime would be complete without mentioning police. Sterling (1998) discusses "computer cops" with respect to crackdowns on hackers; Tang (1997) contemplates the need for "cybercops" to ferret out copyright violations online; and D. R. Johnson and Post use the term "cybersheriff" (1997). Those who combat cybercrime are described by P. J. Denning as "Internet cowboys and vigilantes" (1998a, p. 381). Guisnel calls cybervigilantes "digital commandos" (1997, pp. 171–174), but van Bakel (1996) labels them "cyberangels." And Whine (1997) offers samples of such vigilante activities on the Internet by far right extremists.

Where there are crime and police, there must be law to break and enforce, and the subject of legality in cyberspace covers an immense expanse of research and literature extending well beyond the scope of the present study. However, the following examples serve to illustrate some of the principal topics addressed in cyberlaw literature. In *Cyberspace and the Law: Your Rights and Duties in the On-Line World* (1994), Cavazos and Morin provide a useful overview aimed at clarifying complex online legal issues for laypersons, such as electronic privacy, electronic transactions, intellectual property rights, First Amendment rights, pornography and obscenity, and cybercrime legislation; and they also include an excellent set of appendices describing applicable state and federal statutes. Another fine summary is *Netlaw: Your Rights in the Online World* (1995) by L. Rose, who discusses free speech, censorship and First Amendment issues; contracts and commercial arrangements; ownership and use of intellectual property; dangers and responsibilities for users; privacy concerns; online crime; searches and seizures; and pornography and obscenity. Rose also offers models for online service agreements, as well as a list of relevant U.S. state legislation and the full text of several important federal statutes, including two pertinent sections of Title 18 of the U.S. Code, the Computer Fraud and Abuse Act (Section 1030) and the Electronic Communications Privacy Act (Section 2510). Related U.S. state and federal legislation is reviewed by Branscomb as well (1995, pp. 99–110).

There are numerous examples of more specific research into online legal issues. For instance, D. R. Johnson tackles due process in cyberspace (1996), and in collaboration with Post, addresses legal concerns related to trademark, defamation, fraud, antitrust, and copyright in cyberspace (1996b). Scheinfeld and Bagley (1997) also consider emerging trademark issues on the Internet, focusing on relevant case law; while Weaver (1996) reviews several U.S. cases concerning responsibilities and liabilities of BBS sysops. International law, obviously of critical magnitude on the Internet, is taken into account by some scholars as well. For instance, Kirsh et al. (1996) examine current U.S. and European legislation and case law with respect to privacy online, while Mashima and Hirose (1996) compare the limitations of U.S. and Japanese attempts to regulate electronic pornography. Gardrat (1997) briefly surveys European Internet case law dealing with intellectual property rights, obscenity, and libel; and Australians Grabowsky and R. G. Smith compile a handy list of significant cyberlaw cases from several countries as part of their volume on digital illegalities (1998, pp. vi–viii).

An especially perspicacious article summarizing legal issues in cyberspace comes from Branscomb (1996), mentioned previously in Chapter Three as the doyenne of cyberlaw studies, not only a lawyer widely published in the field, but also a member of the steering committee behind the 1994 Denning and Lin report. Writing as guest editor of a special issue of the *Journal of Computer-Mediated Communication* devoted to "Emerging Law on the Electronic Frontier," Branscomb gives a history of cyberlaw and the development of concerns regarding security, privacy, defamation, internal sanctions, domain names, obscenity and indecency, and property rights in information. She notes that "the new Networld offers new cybercommunities in which netizens are endeavoring to establish cyberethics, cyberules, and, indeed, cyberlaws." Branscomb also reiterates an important point from the 1994 Denning and Lin report, namely, that people appeal to the law primarily as a last recourse when internal rules and sanctions fail:

> Despite the stated desires of many of the pioneer netizens of the Networld that they would prefer to keep lawyers and laws out of their cyberspaces, this is not always possible. Very simply, the law and lawyers are important because, when something goes wrong, the aggrieved parties turn to their lawyers for help. To determine what they can do to obtain redress for their clients' grievances, lawyers look to existing law for precedent. U.S. citizens are very litigious, so the courts have a vast amount of experience in sorting out their demands for justice. The judges themselves turn to existing law to determine how to seek fair and equitable solutions to the problems presented in court. The policy analysts always use the existing precedents just to see what works and what doesn't. Users also rely upon the existing law, because they carry with them their expectations from one environment to another. Netizens who become frustrated with online procedures often look to the law for guidance or seek redress, if the grievance is substantial, in the courts. (1996)

Finally, Branscomb suggests that "the first legal concerns on the electronic frontier centered around questions of security." In accordance with this observation of Branscomb's, then, several relevant online security issues frequently discussed in cybercrime literature are reviewed next.

ONLINE SECURITY, ATTACKS, AND VIRUSES

A thorough overview of the panoply of security perils lurking online is provided by the collection of articles in *Internet Besieged: Countering Cyberspace Scofflaws* (1998a), the anthology edited by D. E. Denning and P. J. Denning. Cited previously in Chapter Three for their evocative prefatory passage summarizing the various sorts of troublesome online behavior in cyberspace (p. vii), in their introductory article to the anthology, the editors explain how security problems online have proliferated with the evolution of the Internet:

> Attacks against computers have been reported since the earliest days of electronic computing in the 1950s. Since those days, data security mechanisms have been an integral part of computer operating systems. Until the mid-1980s,

however, most such attacks were the work of those who already had an account on a computer or knew someone who did. However, in a short period of time, the inexpensive modem has transformed every personal computer into a potential terminal for any other computer, and the rapidly expanding Internet connected tens of thousands of computers by a high-speed data network. Today, the Internet connects over 20 million computers and 50 million users. New opportunities for electronic mischief and crime have become available to anonymous people in any part of the world. (1998b, p. 2)

Articles in the Denning and Denning anthology cover a wide range of online security problems, noted in the discussion which follows below. And it is also worth observing that D. E. Denning not only co-edited this 1998 security anthology with husband P. J. Denning, but also co-edited with Lin the seminal 1994 report described at the beginning of this chapter. On her own, D. E. Denning has authored numerous other related articles (e.g., 1996 on hackers; 1998 on cyberattacks; 2000a on cyberterrorism; 2000b and 2000c on cyberweapons), as well as a book, *Information Warfare and Security* (1999). A prolific computer science professor renowned for her expertise in this realm, D. E. Denning can certainly be considered the doyenne of cyberspace security scholarship.

Besides articles such as those in the Denning and Denning online security anthology, extended treatments detailing various sorts of network abuse abound in the literature, and only a few examples are warranted here. A comprehensive overview comes from the experienced computer security professional, Parker, who thoroughly surveys information security strategies and techniques in his 1998 book about cybercrime mentioned above. And in a 1997 doctoral dissertation from the field of engineering and public policy, Howard employs quantitative methods to analyze several years' worth of security incidents on the Internet.

Supplementing print publications about security in cyberspace, a myriad of bulletins and advisories can be found online, warning about viruses and other sorts of cyberattacks. In fact, government-sponsored institutions and non-profit organizations exist to monitor such cyberspace emergencies and to counsel the public about appropriate countermeasures. For instance, the Computer Incident Advisory Capability ("CIAC") unit of the U.S. Department of Energy (http://ciac.org) issues bulletins about security problems (e.g., 1996 and 1999a on Internet hoaxes; 1999b on Internet chain letters; Brand, 1990 and Schultz et al., 1990 on responding to security incidents; Rayome, 1998 on IRC security risks). Another such organization producing advisories is the Computer Emergency Response Team ("CERT") at Carnegie Mellon University's Software Engineering Institute (http://www.cert.org) (e.g., 1996a on file transfer abuses; 1996b on email bombing and spamming; 1996c on "spoofed" (forged) email; 1997 and 1998 on "denial-of-service" attacks). According to several scholars, such organizations and their bulletins and advisories play a critical role in formulating effective and timely responses to online security threats (e.g., D. E.

Denning, 1996, p. 162; Wisebrod, 1995). And even universities publish security bulletins (e.g., DelFavero, 1997 and 1998b on abusing educational Internet accounts; 1998a on dealing with spammers; DelFavero & Losco, 1998 on email hoaxes; Tihor, 1998 on electronic attacks).

There are many other security concerns relating to the Internet, among which hoaxes and scams figure prominently. Fraudulent email chain letters particularly preoccupy the U.S. Postal Inspection Service as well as the American Cancer Society (a former target of such fraud), and both organizations have issued online bulletins on their Web sites about chain letters (respectively, http://www.usps.gov/websites/depart/inspect/chainlet.htm and http://www.cancer.org/letter.html). Some individuals maintain Web sites to track online hoaxes (e.g., Hymes at http://www.nonprofit.net/hoax), and similar material is also found in the Urban Legends Archives (http://urbanlegends.com). Financial fraud is a problem online as well (e.g., Zgodzinski, 1999), as are scams involving pornography, especially on the Web (e.g., Leonard, 1997b, 1999b). Pornography scams have generated considerable attention to safety for children in cyberspace: for example, the Office of Crimes Against Children of the U.S. Federal Bureau of Investigation ("FBI") has published an online guide to Internet safety for parents (http://www.fbi.gov/publications/pguide/pguidee.htm). Internet safety for children is also the object of *The Parent's Guide to Protecting Your Children in Cyberspace* (2000) by attorney and free-speech advocate Aftab, executive director of Cyberangels (http://cyberangels.org), a non-profit group calling itself "the largest Internet safety organization since 1995."

Some of the most harrowing security concerns involve online attacks of diverse kinds. A short but comprehensive survey of attacks to which networked computers are vulnerable is provided by D. E. Denning in a 1996 article discussing the history of online attacks as well as measures for preventing, detecting, and recovering from them. She identifies eight major types of attack: eavesdropping (interception of network traffic); snooping (unauthorized acquisition of information); tampering (modifying or deleting information); spoofing (impersonating other users or computers); jamming or flooding (disabling system resources); injecting malicious code (sabotage by means of programs such as viruses); exploiting security holes caused by design, implementation or operation flaws; and last but not least, password cracking. A similar survey comes from Bellovin, who comments on a thought-provoking twist in one common cyberassault: "denial of service attacks are generally the moral equivalent of vandalism. Rather than benefiting the perpetrator, the goal is generally to cause pain to the target, often for no better reason than to cause pain" (1998, p. 131). P. J. Denning (1998a) also summarizes several varieties of cyberattack, with emphasis on those affecting electronic commerce. Other such discussions include Heberlein and Bishop (1998) on address spoofing, offenses involving forged online identification and authentication; P. J. Denning (1998c) on password vulnerabilities; and Dean et al. (1998) on security related to Java programming in Web browsers.

Perhaps the best-known and least-loved online attacks are committed by means of those nasty bits of software generically referred to as viruses. Security issues related to malevolent software online penetrated public consciousness for the first time in 1988 when a so-called "worm" program caused the entire Internet to shut down (see, e.g., Branscomb, 1995; D. E. Denning, 1998, pp. 29, 51; D. E. Denning & P. E. Denning, 1998b, p. 5; L. Rose, 1995, pp. 139, 193; Spafford, 1995). This landmark event, for which perpetrator Robert Tappan Morris was convicted under the Computer Fraud and Abuse Act (18 U.S.C. Section 1030(a)(5)), is summarized by Branscomb as follows:

> The first controversy to attract general public interest came in early November, 1988, when a young computer science student at Cornell tested his wings with a computer program that would, according to his side of the story, demonstrate the vulnerabilities of the Internet. Unfortunately, the student was not quite as skilled as he had hoped nor was the "back door" as unknown as he thought. Robert Morris's "worm" ate up so much space on the Internet that the entire system, primarily of educational networked communities, was brought to a halt within twenty-four hours, and the outside world discovered the Internet. (1996)

A solid history of famous computer viruses, their creators' motivations, and criminal liability under existing U.S. statutes is provided in an earlier article by Branscomb (1995), where she characterizes viruses as "rogue programs." Similarly, Spafford refers to viruses as "vandalware" and "malware" (1994/1998, p. 73; 1995, p. 127). R. S. Rosenberg presents a brief taxonomy of viruses (1997, p. 230), while Edgar offers a lengthier discussion of different virus genres (1997, pp. 188–203).

The Sisyphean task of sorting out and defining different types of computer viruses is undertaken with greatest aplomb by Spafford, a computer science professor highly respected for his expertise in online security matters. Currently director of the Center for Education and Research in Information Assurance and Security (http://www.cerias.purdue.edu), Spafford's books, reports, journal articles, conferences papers and even what his Web site describes as "notable published correspondence" (http://www.cerias.purdue.edu/homes/spaf) related to online security issues are too numerous to list. Certainly one of the foremost authorities on computer viruses, Spafford was the first, according to his Web site, to coin the phrase "software forensics" to describe this line of inquiry.

The article in which Spafford categorizes computer viruses, reprinted in the 1998 Denning and Denning anthology, was originally published a few years earlier as the entry for "virus" in an encyclopedia of software engineering, according to Spafford's Web site. In this influential article, Spafford reviews the etymology of the word "virus" from its biological origins to its metaphorical application to software, attributing definitional difficulties to the fact that so many variations of these wicked software routines exist. But based on differences in "how they behave, how they are triggered, and how they are spread" (1994/1998, p. 73), Spafford identifies major classes of "malicious code," among them: "back doors" or "trapdoors," which involve instructions "written into applications to grant special access without the normal methods of access authentication"; "logic bombs" that execute special, unintended functions when a certain set of conditions is met on the system; "worms" (like Morris's) which "run independently and travel from machine to machine across network connections. . . . [but] do not modify existing programs"; and "Trojan horses," which appear to execute a benign function, while actually performing an entirely different one (pp. 75–77).

Finally, Spafford acknowledges that constant development of new generations of viruses with advanced features renders detection and removal even more problematic (pp. 87–89). As he concludes pessimistically, "if no more computer viruses were written from now on, there would still be a computer virus problem for many years to come," and that "unfortunately, there appears to be no lessening of computer virus activity" (pp. 91–92). The accuracy of Spafford's somber prediction is verified by a cursory examination of news stories starting in late March 1999, when the "Melissa" email virus and its variants erupted worldwide (e.g., Associated Press, March 30, 1999; Reuters, March 31, 1999; see also Cascio, 1999; McIntosh, April 5, 1999; McNamara, April 6, 1999; Ohlson & Harrison, March 30, 1999). And as anybody who uses email nowadays knows quite well, there is no end in sight to virus activity on the Internet.

HACKERS AND OTHER DENIZENS
OF THE CYBERSPACE UNDERGROUND

It would be impossible to discuss online security hazards such as cyberattacks and viruses without referring to those elusive and enigmatic beings known as hackers. Material on hackers and hacking abounds in scholarly publications and in the popular press, approaching the topic from various angles. In the realm of survey treatments, D. E. Denning, ubiquitous in the online security literature, demonstrates her expertise on hackers in a 1996 amended version of a paper originally written around 1990, based on research about hackers, but more significantly, on personal interviews she conducted with many of them (e.g., D. E. Denning & Drake, 1995). Denning applies what she has "learned about hackers from hackers" to answer questions such as "who are they and what is their culture and discourse?" (1996, pp. 139, 158). She distinguishes malicious criminal hackers from non-malicious curious hackers, lucidly setting forth both the characteristics of non-malicious hackers and the issues that concern them:

> The word "hacker" has taken on many different meanings ranging from 1) "a person who enjoys learning the details of computer systems and how to stretch their capabilities" to 2) "a malicious or inquisitive meddler who tries to discover information by poking around . . . possibly by deceptive or illegal means." . . . The hackers described in this paper are both learners and explorers who sometimes perform illegal actions. However, all of the hackers I spoke with said they did not engage in or approve of malicious acts that damage

systems or files. Thus, this paper is not about malicious hackers. Indeed, my research suggests that there are very few malicious hackers. Neither is this paper about career criminals who, for example, defraud businesses, or about people who use stolen credit cards to purchase goods. The characteristics of many of the hackers I am writing about are summed up in the words of one of the hackers: "A hacker is someone who experiments with systems. . . . [Hacking] is playing with systems and making them do what they were never intended to do. Breaking in and making free calls is just a small part of that. Hacking is also about freedom of speech and free access to information—being able to find out anything. There is also the David and Goliath side of it, the underdog vs. the system, and the ethic of being a folk hero, albeit a minor one." (1996, p. 139, references omitted)

Nevertheless, Denning concludes that "hacking is a serious and costly problem. Even when there is no malicious intent, intrusions can be extremely disruptive if not outright damaging" (p. 161).

Thus, in recent years, perceptions of hackers have become less forgiving, and hacking has come to be seen as more threatening than playful. For example, in a survey of law-enforcement responses to hackers, Halbert (1997) claims that the hacker image has evolved "from harmless computer nerd to terrorist," and hacking is perceived now as:

A national security threat. . . . behavior once considered normal and legal becomes abnormal and dangerous, hence the demonization of hackers. The time is long past when hackers are harmless computer geeks. Today, hackers have a new image tainted with a criminal element. (1997, p. 369)

Halbert himself describes the hacker as an "information deviant" (p. 361). Similarly, Branscomb (1995) characterizes hackers as "computer rogues", while Kling (1996a) links hackers to outlaws and pirates. Australians Grabowsky and R. G. Smith distinguish exploratory hacking from electronic vandalism based on malicious intent to disrupt: for them, hacking refers simply to "unauthorised access to computer systems" but vandalism is "intrusion for the primary purpose of hindering a system's operation or functioning, or inflicting damage on the system or its contents" (1998, p. 47). R. S. Rosenberg also reviews relevant definitions and proposes the following distinctions among hackers, crackers, and phreaks: hackers are "the 'wizards' of the computer community; people with a deep understanding of how their computers work"; crackers are "the real-world analogs of the 'console cowboys' of cyberpunk fiction; they break in to other people's computer systems, without their permission, for illicit gain or simply for the pleasure of exercising their skill"; and phreaks are "those who do a similar thing with the telephone system, coming up with ways to circumvent phone companies' calling charges and doing clever things with the phone network" (1997, p. 131).

The experienced security professional, Parker, offers an excellent though perhaps biased survey of what he calls "cyberspace abusers and misusers," in a chapter of his cybercrime book devoted to "the disastrous hacker culture" (1998, pp. 158–187). Parker reviews definitions and popular accounts of hacking, and discusses the motives, skills, and resources of cybercriminals, categorizing them according to seven basic profiles:

> Pranksters. These individuals perpetrate tricks on others. They generally do not intend any particular or long-lasting harm. Juvenile exuberance prevails.
>
> Hackers. These individuals explore others' computer systems for education, out of curiosity, to achieve idealized social justice, or to compete with their peers. . . .
>
> Malicious hackers. Sometimes called crackers, these individuals are intent on causing loss (in contrast to achieving illegal gain) to satisfy some antisocial motives. Many computer virus creators and distributors fall into this category. . . .
>
> Personal problem solvers. By far the most common kind of criminal . . . these individuals often cause serious loss in their pursuit of a solution to their own personal problems. They may turn to crime after conventional problem-solving methods fail, or they may see crime as a quick and easy way to solve their problems. . . .
>
> Career criminals. These individuals earn party of all of their income from crime. . . . In some cases they conspire with others or work within organized gangs. . . .
>
> Extreme advocates. Better known as terrorists, these individuals and groups have strong social, political, and/or religious views and are intent on changing conditions by engaging in crime. . . .
>
> *Malcontents, addicts, and irrational and incompetent people.* These individuals run the gamut from the mentally ill to those addicted to drugs, alcohol, competition, or attention from others, to the criminally negligent. In general, they are the most difficult to describe and the most difficult to protect against. We have no way of determining who is sufficiently irrational to trigger an attack. . . . no way of predicting negligence. (1998, pp. 144–146)

Besides classifications and profiles of hacker types, there are also various popular accounts of notorious hackers. Perhaps the first look at hackers from a less technical perspective comes from Levy, whose book *Hackers* (1984) about engineering mavericks at MIT portrays them as "heroes of the computer revolution." Hafner and Markoff provide another early classic on hacker culture, *Cyberpunk: Outlaws and Hackers on the Computer Frontier* (1991). In *Masters of Deception: The Gang that Ruled Cyberspace* (1995), Slatalla and Quittner report on cyberspace gang wars between hackers in New York and Texas; while in *The Watchman* (1997), Littman writes about "the twisted life and crimes of serial hacker Kevin Paulsen," the latter mentioned by Elias as well (May 6, 1999). There is also *At Large: The Strange Case of the World's Biggest Internet Invasion* (1997) by Freedman and Mann, which sheds light on the obscure case of a disabled hacker known initially as PhantomDialer and later as InfoMaster, who wrought havoc at institutions across the Internet in 1992, and was caught by the FBI but not prosecuted. And Elias (May 6, 1999) has a short report describing how Nicholas Middleton left too clear a trail while hacking in California, and was easily caught and convicted under federal law.

In addition, there are several "hunt-the-hacker" sagas, reminiscent of the cyberspace travelogues mentioned previously in Chapter Two, but with a detective-novel flavor, by computer sleuths who tracked down particular cybervillains, as well as by journalists who followed the chase. One of the best know examples of this genre is *The Cuckoo's Egg: Tracking a Spy Through the Maze of Computer Espionage* (1989), in which Stoll recounts his own stalking of a German intruder who attacked computers at the Lawrence Berkeley Laboratories, a U.S. research institute where Stoll worked. This tale is often cited by others (e.g., Denning & Denning, 1998a, p. ix; L. Rose, 1995, p. 188), and an abbreviated version of this episode also appears as an article by Stoll (1988/1991). In the same vein as Stoll's first-hand account, the Kevin Mitnick chase is detailed by his stalker and a co-writer, Shimomura and Markoff, in *Takedown: The Pursuit and Capture of Kevin Mitnick, America's Most Wanted Computer Outlaw—by the Man Who Did It* (1996). Convicted under federal statutes some years back, Mitnick was sentenced in 1999, bringing the case under scrutiny again. One reporter summarizes as follows the sentencing of the "World's Most Notorious Hacker" (according to the 1999 Guinness Book of World Records):

> Four years, five months and 22 days after it began, *The United States vs. Kevin Mitnick* ended Monday when U.S. District Court Judge Marianna Pfaelzer sentenced the hacker to 46 months in prison. Mitnick was also ordered to pay $4,125 in restitution—a fraction of the $1.5 million federal prosecutors sought. With credit for good behavior, Mitnick could be free by January 2000. (Poulsen, August 9, 1999)

The Mitnick litigation stimulated enough controversy over the years to provoke the establishment of a Web site devoted to the "Free Kevin" cause (http://kevinmitnick.com), housing among other things a timeline of important events in the case as well as copies of court papers and related news items. Mitnick was released in January 2000 (Brunker, January 21, 2000; *CNN*, January 21, 2000; Poulsen, January 20, 2000), but according to his Web site, until January 2003, is restricted by "conditions of supervised release which prohibit him from using a computer and from acting as consultant or advisor in computer-related matters." Many others have also written about Mitnick (e.g., Elias, May 6, 1999; Guisnel, 1997; Littman, 1996; Platt, 1997; Sterling, 1998). And more hacker tracking tales come from Sterling's *The Hacker Crackdown: Law and Disorder on the Electronic Frontier* (1992), which outlines the history of U.S. law-enforcement efforts against hackers and focuses on the 1990 Operation Sundevil search and seizure operation involving the Legion of Doom group.

As for examples of other investigations of hackers and hacking, Spafford (1995) deems hacker break-ins unethical, in an article reworking his own material published earlier and reprinted elsewhere (e.g., in Denning & Denning,

1998a and in Ermann et al., 1997). Edgar reviews the activities of hackers, crackers, and phreaks in his book on computer morality and ethics (1997, pp. 180–186); while Ludlow contemplates responses to such activities in the introduction to a chapter of his cyberspace anthology (1996, pp. 125–129); and Guisnel covers hacker cases in Europe in his volume on cyberwars (1997). A piece by Thieme (1997) reports on an interview with a veteran hacker who revealed himself to the public; and something of a mirror image to Thieme's report is provided in an article about security maven D. E. Denning being interviewed by the editor of a hacker-cyberpunk magazine (Denning & Drake, 1995).

Finally, there are various guides and reference books on hacking. For instance, the well-known *The New Hacker's Dictionary* by Raymond has gone through three editions (1991, 1993, and 1996). Meinel's *The Happy Hacker* (1998) provides a how-to manual for hackers, while a defensive counterpart is offered by Merkle in *The Ultimate Internet Terrorist: How Hackers, Geeks, and Phreaks Can Ruin Your Trip on the Information Superhighway—And What You Can Do to Protect Yourself* (1998). And J. Johnson takes readers on a humorous tour through the hacker underground, complete with do-it-yourself instructions in *Giga Bites: The Hacker Cookbook: Underground Delicacies for the Quick-Crunch, Virtual Reality, Zen-Soaked, Blaster Nineties* (1994).

FIRST AMENDMENT FOLLIES:
DISSENT, FREE SPEECH, AND CENSORSHIP ONLINE

A particularly unsettling variety of hacker is the "hacktivist," a hybrid who employs hacking techniques in pursuit of activist goals, generally expressing political dissent. Whether to classify hacktivists as cybercriminals, terrorist insurgents, net-savvy protesters, or simply rebellious pranksters remains a thorny issue. A negative view of hacktivists is taken by Parker, in elaborating on the profile of "extreme advocates" in his book on computer crime mentioned above, because their actions "usually involve violence against people or property and are calculated to achieve a high level of publicity to bring attention to the terrorists' causes" (1998, p. 145). A positive view comes from an article by Wray (1998), who promotes hacktivism as electronic civil disobedience. While conducting research at New York University on hacktivism, Wray maintained a Web site which apparently transcended its initial scholarly purposes to the point of advocating and fomenting politically-motivated international hacktivism. According to a listserv post by Wray (personal communication, September 10, 1998), the U.S. Department of Defense complained about his site to NYU officials, who diplomatically encouraged Wray to limit his NYU-sponsored Web site activities to research purposes they had previously approved. Wray's involvement with the Electronic Disturbance Theater is discussed by Harmon (October 31, 1998), who also reviews hacktivist incidents worldwide. McKay (September 22, 1998) and Paquin (October 26, 1998) report on global hacktivism as well, while Leonard (1999a) writes of a hacktivist "prank" involving a

Web site about impeaching U.S. President Bill Clinton. There are also non-profit organizations devoted to hacktivist affairs (e.g., http://www.hacktivism.org).

But hacktivism and virtual dissent are not the only areas generating uncertainty about which forms of speech on the Internet are permissible and protected. Cyberspace has inherited problems existing in traditional media "about what people can say to each other, under what circumstances," according to Sterling (1998, p. 487). He argues that "every single one of those problems is applicable to cyberspace. Computers don't make any of these old free-expression problems go away; on the contrary, they intensify them, and they introduce a bunch of new problems." One survey of free speech quandaries online is *Sex, Laws, and Cyberspace: Freedom and Regulation on the Frontiers of the Online Revolution* (1997) by Wallace and Mangan, who review U.S. case law related to censorship and First Amendment issues, focusing on pornography, obscenity, and cryptography. They assert that "free speech is a good thing" and that "new laws are almost never necessary," yet conclude that "indecency has no place on the Net" (pp. 253–255). An article by Fernback (1997) reviews cases involving Internet Service Providers ("ISPs") such as CompuServe and Prodigy with respect to free speech, anarchy, and dissent; while Stamper (1999) reports on Prodigy being absolved in a libel suit. Ludlow briefly discusses censorship and sysop liability (1996, pp. 253–257), as does Godwin (1996a), who offers practical tips for system administrators wishing to reduce their litigation risks. Godwin also has a book on the general topic, *Cyber Rights: Defending Free Speech in the Digital Age* (1998).

As for specific cases involving online censorship, an incident construed by many to have important implications for the free speech debate is the Baker newsgroup rape mentioned previously in Chapter Three, highlighted in this context by Wallace and Mangan (1997, pp. 63–81). The furor raised by the Baker episode with respect to U.S. First Amendment concerns is demonstrated by the archive of case-related documents housed at the Web site of the Electronic Frontier Foundation ("EFF") (http://www.eff.org/pub/Legal/Cases/ Baker_UMich_case; on the history of the EFF, see Branscomb, 1996; Guisnel, 1997, pp. 43–47; note also that EFF co-founder Mitchell Kapor was a member of the steering committee behind the 1994 Denning and Lin report). Other non-profit organizations similar to the EFF keep watch over free speech issues as well, such as the Center for Democracy and Technology (http://www.cdt.org), and the Electronic Frontier Canada (http://efc.ca) (see, e.g., Shallit, 1996, pp. 287–289). A second case involving censorship and First Amendment issues is also considered by Wallace and Mangan (1997, pp. 125–152), that of Carnegie Mellon University's unsuccessful attempt to censor pornography in Usenet newsgroups after one of their students, Martin Rimm, drew the university's attention to his research about the prevalence of sexually-oriented materials online. Elmer-Dewitt (1996) and Platt (1997) also address the CMU-Rimm case, and Shade (1996) looks at censorship in Usenet newsgroups as well. Finally, Shallit, a Canadian librarian, discusses censorship at the University of Waterloo with respect to pornography and obscenity in Usenet newsgroups.

Shallit offers three not-so-facetious "laws of new media" to account for the present confusion about freedom of expression issues in cyberspace:

> Shallit's first Law is the following: Every new medium of expression will be used for sex. . . . Shallit's Second Law: Every new medium of expression will come under attack, usually because of Shallit's First Law. . . . Shallit's Third Law of New Media: Protection afforded for democratic rights and freedoms in traditional media will rarely be understood to apply to new media. (1996, pp. 276–278)

In considering dissent, free speech, and censorship in cyberspace, the question arises as to why online environments seem so different from previous media of communication. After all, the courts have long grappled with freedom of expression issues involving obscenity, libel, and political discourse, for instance, in traditional media such as print, film, radio, television, and the arts. The answer seems to be that none of the familiar legal models or precedents available from previous media quite fits the complex communication contexts evolving in cyberspace. The comparatively novel and diverse possibilities of expression afforded by online CMC have so far eluded consistent classification in traditional legal frameworks. Instead, various entities operating in cyberspace, from single individuals to entire corporations and institutions, have been held liable or not for their online communications depending on which legal models and precedents have prevailed in particular cases.

The enduring problem of how to characterize online environments for judicial purposes, especially relating to U.S. First Amendment protections, is discussed in the 1994 Denning and Lin report, which surveys and provides examples of a variety of legal models available including publisher, distributor, library, common carrier, trusteeship, and information utility, among others (1994, pp. 31–40). The key point, as Denning and Lin observe, is that the extent of liability for the content of online expression depends on the legal characterization applied: for example, in the United States, publishers can be held liable, while carriers have limited liability and distributors have none (p. 37). L. Rose offers a similar range of metaphors used in determining liability in online contexts: publisher, telephone service, magazine distributor, bookstore, public street, and local bar (1995, pp. 8–28). Likewise, Elmer-Dewitt suggests common carrier, television station, and bookstore as possibilities (1996, p. 260). And after reviewing the history of First Amendment concerns in previous media, Wallace and Mangan conclude that cyberspace is best characterized as a constellation of printing presses and bookstores (1997, pp. 193–236).

Unfortunately, despite—or perhaps because of—the number of alternative analogies to be drawn with legal precedents from other media, the courts have so far failed to agree conclusively on how to characterize different parties involved in online CMC. To date, legal verdicts in cases concerning dissent, free speech, and censorship online have proven inconsistent and even contradictory, with judicial interpretations diverging widely, and it is wishful thinking to suppose that matters will be clarified any time soon. Thus, First Amendment follies with respect to cyberspace proliferate, and become exacerbated when, as discussed further ahead, U.S. Constitutional protections regarding freedom of expression meet jurisdictions in the world at large.

DEFINITION SCHIZOPHRENIA: MALEVOLENT CRIMINAL OR MISCHIEVOUS PRANKSTER?

Another set of knotty legal issues stems from a serious definition problem in relation to troublesome behavior in cyberspace. Perceptions of those who provoke disruptions online, as well as decisions about how to deal with them, are uncertain and inconsistent. Should online troublemakers be considered malevolent criminals or mischievous pranksters, or creatures lying somewhere on a continuum between the two extremes? With respect to cyberspace, as Branscomb points out, we are still asking, "what constitutes criminal behavior?" (1996). Questions such as these haunt and bedevil legal authorities and security experts, scholars and journalists, Internet newcomers and sophisticated Internauts around the world. Stoll describes the situation this way: "as communities grow, social and legal structures follow. In our networked community, there is frustration and confusion over what constitutes a crime and what is acceptable behavior" (1988/1991, p. 547). Thus, because the definitional waters are so murky, the regulatory pendulum swings erratically from criminal to prankster and back again. The scales of justice remain unbalanced, with troublesome online behavior being judged seriously illegal here but merely naughty there. This ambiguity and confusion about troublesome online behavior can be described as a form of definition schizophrenia.

Hacking, in particular, seems to straddle the border between felony and tomfoolery, with the dividing line shifting almost as often as the courts render their decisions. Early signs of definition schizophrenia appear in the case of the "Internet Worm" created in 1988 by hacker Robert Tappan Morris (see, e.g., Branscomb, 1995, pp. 90–92; D. E. Denning, 1998, p. 29; Denning & Denning, 1998a, p. ix; L. Rose, 1995, pp. 139, 193; Spafford, 1995). As mentioned above, the outcome of the experimental worm program Morris released while studying computer science at Cornell University was far more dramatic than he anticipated. The Worm invaded and overloaded a significant number of the host computers on the Internet at that time, essentially shutting down the whole network for several days. But, as Branscomb explains, this incident suggests "a dilemma as to whether or not criminal punishment is appropriate under the circumstances" because it remains unclear whether Morris actually committed a crime. No damage to hardware or software occurred and, as Branscomb notes, "most computer crime laws require an intent to inflict harm, which was allegedly lacking in this case" (1995, p. 91). In fact, Branscomb observes that "among some of the young computer literati (often referred to as 'hackers'), [Morris] is looked upon as a folk hero" (p. 91; see also Branscomb, 1996). Nonetheless, as one journalist reports, "on January 23, 1990 a federal jury found Mr. Morris guilty of intentionally disrupting a nationwide computer network, the first jury conviction under the 1986 [Computer Fraud and Abuse] act" (J. Markoff, as cited in R. S. Rosenberg, 1997, p. 235). And folk hero though he may be, according to the online Computer Museum (http://www.tcm.org), Morris was sentenced to three years of probation, 400 hours of community service, and a fine of ten thousand dollars.

Ever since Morris failed to escape paying for his hacking escapade over a decade ago, definition schizophrenia with respect to troublesome online behavior has been on the rise. To illustrate the ongoing dilemma of definition schizophrenia, and the diametrically-opposed resolutions to which such ambiguity can lead, some additional examples are in order. Two major virus cases from 1999 provide an opportunity to compare how their creators were defined and treated: first, the "Melissa" virus launched from the United States by David L. Smith, and then, the "Chernobyl" virus released from Taiwan by Chen Ing-hau.

In the case of Melissa, characterized at the time as "the fastest spreading computer virus in history," Smith's attorney defended his client as lacking intent to harm because the Melissa virus was annoying but not destructive (reminiscent of Morris's Internet Worm). Insisting that "we're dealing with someone more akin to a graffiti artist [than] an international cyberterrorist," Smith's attorney nevertheless did admit that one could not "dismiss the virus as a 'harmless prank'" (as cited in *The New York Times*, April 9, 1999; see also Associated Press, April 7, 1999; Cascio, April 7, 1999; *The New York Times*, April 7, 1999). Indeed, New Jersey state prosecutors did not dismiss Melissa as a harmless prank. Instead, they charged Smith with "five felony counts of computer theft, unlawful computer access, illegal interruption of public communication and conspiracy that could result in prison terms totaling 40 years and fines amounting to nearly a half-million dollars" (*CNN*, April 8, 1999). Ultimately, Smith was sentenced to 20 months in federal prison and a fine of five thousand dollars (U. S. Department of Justice, May 1, 2002).

In contrast, barely a month after the Melissa epidemic, the aptly-named Chernobyl virus surfaced, potent and deadly, decimating hundreds of thousands of computers, primarily in Asia. Although Chernobyl and its variants were "among the most damaging viruses of recent years," creator Chen Ing-hau was treated far more leniently in his native Taiwan than Melissa's creator Smith was in the United States (Reuters, April 30, 1999; see also *CNN*, April 27, 1999; Marriott, June 10, 1999; *MSNBC*, April 30, 1999; Sullivan, May 25, 1999). Chen was not prosecuted at all, nor was he expelled from the college he attended while writing the virus. They merely gave him a demerit, and allowed him to graduate anyway; he then went on to compulsory national military service (Associated Press, April 29, 1999; Guernsey, June 10, 1999). Thus, the troublemaker behind the extremely malign Chernobyl virus is reprimanded in Taiwan as a playful prankster, while the troublemaker responsible for the relatively benign Melissa virus is prosecuted in the United States as a sinister criminal. Such diametrically-opposed outcomes are symptomatic of definition schizophrenia, the contradictory perceptions held of those who provoke trouble in online environments.

THE JURISDICTION CIRCUS: NO RINGMASTER IN CYBERSPACE

The disparity between the resolutions of the Chernobyl caper in Taiwan and the Melissa mayhem in the United States suggests another bewildering set of legal problems in cyberspace, which figuratively but fittingly may be described as the jurisdiction circus. The question that leads to the jurisdiction circus is this: once an offense in cyberspace has been defined as criminal, who will deal with the offender? Or, to put it another way, which legal authority is responsible for controlling troublesome behavior in cyberspace?

The basic jurisdiction dilemma is summarized by P. J. Denning as follows: "modern law enforcement is based on jurisdictions—local authorities who will prosecute local infractions. It is still an open question as to how to deal with the Internet, where there is often no well-defined jurisdiction" (1998a, p. 381). Not surprisingly, legal maven Branscomb identifies "cyberjurisdiction" as a critical dilemma (1996). One survey of legal jurisdiction online, with special attention to domain names, comes from Scheinfeld and Bagley (1996), but a more thorough treatment of personal jurisdiction in cyberspace is offered by Perry et al., who address such matters as where individuals can be sued and whose laws apply, with a view to helping minimize legal risks for Web site operators. After reviewing relevant court cases, Perry et al. conclude that:

> The law of personal jurisdiction based on Internet and Web contacts is, at best, uncertain and unpredictable and, at worst, has the potential of subjecting Web site operators to litigation in the courts of every state in the country . . . and potentially in foreign countries as well. (1998, p. 11)

The crux of the matter in the jurisdiction circus is the transnational nature of cyberspace. As D. R. Johnson and Post explain, "global computer-based communications cut across territorial borders, creating a new realm of human activity and undermining the feasibility—and legitimacy—of applying laws based on geographic boundaries" (1996b). Likewise, Branscomb asserts that "the epidemic of rogue behavior [online] is a global problem which cannot be contained merely by state or even national laws but will likely require a considerable amount of coordination at the international level if the electronic highways are to be safe" (1995, p. 97). International cooperation of this sort is exemplified in Stoll's account of how stalking a European hacker involved teamwork among law-enforcement authorities in California, the U.S. FBI, and the German national law-enforcement agency, the BKA (Bundeskriminalamt) (1989; see also 1988/1991, pp. 534, 543).

But law-enforcement in cyberspace has become an enterprise of overwhelming proportions and daunting intricacy. Consequently, chaos in the jurisdiction circus is compounded by what Gardrat refers to as "practical difficulties of law enforcement" (1998, p. 28). The complexities of international enforcement in cyberspace are stressed by Grabowsky and R. G. Smith (1998, pp. 8, 216–219). As D. R. Johnson points out, "local authorities cannot easily control a global net [and] may not have jurisdiction over all relevant parties" (1996). Branscomb elaborates on this point as follows: "local authorities usually lack the capability of catching offenders who merely transgress local statutes online and are far beyond the geographical jurisdiction within which local authorities can catch and punish them" (1996). And as one report suggests, "even if a suspect is caught, jurisdictional issues arise because of the global nature of such attacks" (Associated Press, May 15, 2000). D. R. Johnson and Post explain how the dwindling relevance of physical location contributes to the difficulties of effective enforcement in online environments:

> The power to control activity in Cyberspace has only the most tenuous connections to physical location. . . . efforts to control the flow of electronic information across physical borders—to map local regulation and physical boundaries onto Cyberspace—are likely to prove futile. . . . The volume of electronic communications crossing territorial boundaries is just too great in relation to the resources available to government authorities to permit meaningful control. (1996b)

Moreover, the unavoidable fact that different places have different standards also creates confusion, ambiguity, and awkwardness in the jurisdiction circus of cyberspace. Nobody better than legal eagle Branscomb to sketch the complex jurisdictional panorama involved in surfing the Internet:

> As users of electronic networks and "netizens" of the new cybercommunities in the Networld, we circle the globe passing through many jurisdictions, potentially contravening local laws, possibly without any apparent knowledge of local custom, and lacking any sense of shame or remorse for our potential wrongdoings. (1996)

As D. R. Johnson and Post perceptively observe, diminished reliance on physical locations and boundaries further muddies the waters surfed by Internauts: "physical borders no longer can function as signposts informing individuals of the obligations assumed by entering into a new, legally significant, place, because individuals are unaware of the existence of those borders as they move through virtual space" (1996b). So, recalling Nystrom's comments (1979) mentioned previously in Chapter Two about where we are telling us who we are and how we ought to behave, it seems that due to uncertainty about where cyberspace is, it remains unclear which legal standards apply in the jurisdiction circus.

In some sense, those who travel through cyberspace are in too many different places at the same time. As a result, it often happens that several conflicting standards appear to apply simultaneously, generating an abundance of legal dilemmas in the jurisdiction circus of cyberspace. Grabowsky and R. G. Smith explain the problem as follows: "telecommunications offences may involve a number of jurisdictions internationally, with the offender, the victim, and the technology necessary to carry out the offence all being present in different countries," which can lead to "the anomalous situation of the same conduct giving rise to criminal liability in one jurisdiction, but not in another" (1998, p. 219). Similarly, Gardrat argues that "the problem at present is not the absence of legal rules, but rather the multiplication of legal rules, their appropriateness, and their application in international contexts"; with such an abundance of conflicting legal regimes, something which is "neither obscene nor defamatory under local law ... may become accessible in other jurisdictions where it is illegal" (1998, p. 27). Additionally, cyberlaw standards around the world are influenced by economic and political factors, among others, a point illustrated a Norwegian judge attending a global conference on cybercrime who remarks that "computer attack, unlike murder or robbery, is still not universally recognized as a crime. Laws to fight it are typically found only in industrialized nations that depend on computers" (as cited in Associated Press, May 15, 2000).

Thus, the jurisdiction circus of cyberspace stages performances worldwide. But even domestically, within the United States for instance, jurisdiction is a tricky business. One Department of Justice official summarized the quandary in this country rather succinctly: "there is no U.S. Attorney for Cyberspace. . . . A U.S. Attorney for a particular district has to bring the case" (as cited in Kaplan, August 20, 1999). An illuminating example of ambiguous domestic jurisdiction producing somewhat bizarre results is an incident often cited in discussions of cyberjurisdiction: the controversial Thomas lawsuit (e.g., P. J. Denning, 1998a; D. R. Johnson & Post, 1996b; Wallace & Mangan, 1997). The Thomases were a married couple who owned and operated a sexually-oriented electronic bulletin board service called "Amateur Action" in the state of California, where they resided. Strange as it might seem, this couple was convicted in the state of Tennessee under federal obscenity statutes for doing something online while physically in California.

Among those who have analyzed the Thomas episode is Godwin, former legal counsel to the Electronic Frontier Foundation (http://eff.org) and admirably qualified to comment on issues like cyberjurisdiction. Godwin notes a chilling effect in the Thomas affair: "a conservative jurisdiction like Memphis [Tennessee] may be in a position to dictate what's allowable on BBSs all over the country" (1996b, p. 269). He further observes that this controversial lawsuit "raises the question of whether it makes sense to define 'community standards' solely in terms of geographic communities." Godwin concludes that the Thomas conviction "sends a frightening message to virtual communities: 'It doesn't matter if you're abiding by your own community's standards—you have to abide by Memphis's as well'" (pp. 272–273). But, as another researcher inquires rather pragmatically, "do we really think that people in Memphis can enforce their pornographic community standards on people in California? ... People in California are never gonna behave in a way that satisfies people in Tennessee" (Sterling, 1998, p. 488). So even domestically, the show goes on in the jurisdiction circus of cyberspace.

In a 1996 article on the Thomas affair, one prophetic investigator speculates about the possible outcome of a similar situation on the international level, posing the following jurisdiction riddle:

> What happens when [material] hops over borders and lands in a different city—or country—whose laws and community standards may differ. . . . The rules of libel in England, for example, are considerably more restrictive than those in the U.S.; what might be considered a fair crack at a public figure in New York City could be actionable in London. (Elmer-Dewitt, 1996, pp. 260–261)

What was mere speculation in 1996 became reality in the year 2000. In a case first attracting public attention in May 2000 and making headlines for quite a while, French authorities tried to compel Yahoo!, an American company operating in the United States, to restrict access in France to Nazi memorabilia available worldwide at Yahoo!'s English-language auction site on the Web. Instead of a national conflict over different moral standards in two states, as in the Thomas episode, this international battle pitted French regulations concerning Nazi-era material against the U.S. Constitutional right to freedom of expression.

With the phrase "jurisdiction dilemma" in the headline of a column about the Yahoo! lawsuit, one journalist echoes questions asked earlier in the domestic context of the Thomas incident, but here on a global scale:

> The [Yahoo!] case points up an enduring legal and cultural puzzle . . . in borderless cyberspace: What happens when the laws and traditions of a country that receives an online message clash with the laws and values of the land where the message originated? (Kaplan, August 11, 2000)

The France-Yahoo!-Nazi litigation kept the company and the courts busy for years. Initially, one of the cofounders of the company, Jerry Yang, stood firm, reportedly saying: "We are not going to change the content of our sites in the United States just because someone in France is asking us to do so" (as cited in Reuters, June 16, 2000; see also Baum, August 14, 2000; Sprenger et al., May 29, 2000). However, eventually, Yahoo! imposed restrictions which satisfied French objections to some extent, but litigation related to the case both in the United States and in France dragged on for several more years (see, e.g., Agence France-Presse, March 17, 2004; *CNN*, March 25, 2005; Weinstein, January 13, 2006). No doubt, cases such as the France-Yahoo!-Nazi affair will continue to appear in the jurisdiction circus of cyberspace.

As if international and domestic confusion did not cause enough legal headaches, another dimension complicates the jurisdiction circus of cyberspace even further: the opposition discussed previously in Chapter Three between external control and internal control of troublesome online behavior. A brief comparison of the three virtual rape incidents mentioned in Chapter Three serves to highlight some of the differences between controlling online troublemakers by external versus internal means. As described earlier in this chapter in the context of First

Amendment follies, the Baker alt.sex.stories newsgroup rape was handled externally by government and university officials offline, with the culprit subject to penalties in the offline world which bore little, if any, connection to his online activities. However, in both LambdaMOO and JennyMUSH, the rapes were handled internally by participants operating within the confines of their virtual communities, who administered digital sanctions that affected solely the perpetrators' online existence, without any appeal to external institutions, authorities, or consequences in the offline world.

Clearly, disruptions occurring within virtual communities can be handled internally, at least to some extent, because most, if not all, cyber gathering places do have internal authorities with power to apply online sanctions: the sysops, wizards, and other such superusers who enforce rules within their electronic domains. The internal actions taken by wizards and other participants to resolve the LambdaMOO and JennyMUSH rape situations demonstrate how virtual communities can band together, led or assisted by system administrators, to handle troublemakers at the local level. D. R. Johnson places the responsibility for enforcement squarely on local shoulders in predicting that internal control will prevail:

> The protection of fairness for individual users in the global Networld will rely less upon the law of territorially-based jurisdictions and more upon the actions of online communities. The efficacy of netlaw will depend more upon sysops who control the on-off buttons and the reactions of their customers, wherever they may reside. (1996)

And so, there are local and global dimensions as well as domestic and international aspects to consider in trying to manage the jurisdiction circus of cyberspace. But there is no centralized organ governing the Internet, nowhere in particular to appeal when online troublemakers cause problems. Nobody can be sure just who is in charge of dealing with troublesome conduct in the online environments of cyberspace. Lacking any central administration, Internet-wide trouble is generally handled by external authorities, whether ISPs, law-enforcement agencies, government institutions, or sporadic combinations thereof. Such authorities, for the most part, act on behalf of nationally-oriented legal frameworks. However, the Internet effectively erases national boundaries. As a result, many players perform a multitude of disparate acts in the jurisdiction circus of cyberspace, and no ringmaster can be found to coordinate the entire show.

The wisest counsel, from the perspective of the present study, on how best to tame the beasts in the jurisdiction circus of cyberspace, and perhaps even to halt the onslaught of First Amendment follies as well as to find a cure for definition schizophrenia, is provided by a pair of eminent scholars in the field of cyberlaw. These two legal experts are D. R. Johnson, practicing attorney and former chairman of the Electronic Frontier Foundation, who co-founded the Cyberspace Law Institute in conjunction with law professor D. G. Post, who serves as the Institute's co-director. Several of Johnson and Post's remarks about jurisdiction in cyberspace have already been cited above, but three of their collaborative articles on this topic deserve to be showcased for their high degree of pertinence to this investigation of misbehavior in online environments.

In "Law and Borders: The Rise of Law in Cyberspace" (1996b), Johnson and Post pinpoint the root of the problem inherent in attempting to apply geographically-based, nationally-oriented legal frameworks to cyberspace. They explain that traditional concepts of law depend upon

> A general correspondence between borders drawn in physical space (between nation states or other political entities) and borders drawn in "law space." For example, if we were to superimpose a "law map" (delineating areas where different rules apply to particular behaviors) onto a political map of the world, the two maps would overlap to a significant degree with clusters of homogeneous applicable law and legal institutions fitting within existing physical borders, distinct from neighboring homogeneous clusters. (1996b)

However, the networked online environments of transnational cyberspace have altered the traditional relationship between physical space and legal place, practically eliminating the relevance of national borders, and consequently disrupting legal senses of place. Reminiscent of arguments discussed previously in Chapter Two that electronic media have undermined the relationship between physical place and social place made by media ecologists such as Meyrowitz in *No Sense of Place* (1985), Johnson and Post offer an analogous argument—no sense of traditional legal place—with respect to online environments:

> Cyberspace radically undermines the relationship between legally significant (online) phenomena and physical location. The rise of the global computer network is destroying the link between geographical location and: (1) the power of local governments to assert control over online behavior; (2) the effects of online behavior on individuals or things; (3) the legitimacy of the efforts of a local sovereign to enforce rules applicable to global phenomena; and (4) the ability of physical location to give notice of which sets of rules apply. The Net thus radically subverts a system of rule-making based on borders between physical spaces, at least with respect to the claim that cyberspace should naturally be governed by territorially defined rules. (1996b)

But if behavior in transnational cyberspace cannot be governed on the basis of geographic physical territory, what other possibilities exist? Johnson and Post address this question in "And How Shall the Net Be Governed? A Meditation on the Relative Virtues of Decentralized, Emergent Law" (1996a). In this article, Johnson and Post review four models of cyberspace governance, criticizing all but one: first, existing regimes extend their territorial jurisdiction; second, existing regimes enter into multi-lateral international agreements regarding online conduct; third, create a new international organization to establish and enforce new schemes; and fourth, develop decentralized local governance. They advocate this fourth option which they call "decentralized emergent law":

> De facto rules may emerge as a result of the complex interplay of individual decisions by domain name and IP [Internet Protocol] address registries (regarding what conditions to impose on possession of an online address), by sysops (regarding what local rules to adopt, what filters to install, what users to allow to sign on, and with which other systems to connect) and by users (regarding which personal filters to install and which systems to patronize). (1996a)

Johnson and Post denounce the lack of effectiveness of the first model which currently dominates worldwide, wherein competing regimes vie to little avail for essentially unattainable supremacy, giving rise to the pandemonium described in the present study as the jurisdiction circus of cyberspace. But Johnson and Post also have pessimistic predictions about the second and third models for governing cyberspace as well, which involve top-down, centralized international organizations and treaties. Instead, favoring decentralized approaches as the only possibilities not doomed to failure, Johnson and Post offer a realistic appraisal of the situation:

> Let's review the alternatives. Can we make territorial laws applicable to online activities that have no relevant or perhaps even determinable geographic location? We doubt it. Can we look to international treaties to set forth workable rules that give good guidance for online commerce? Not in our lifetimes (now measured in accelerated net years). Should we allow the rules of the net to be encoded into software by a technical elite, with no mechanism of accountability to the online population? The question answers itself. Should we create a new international forum for net policy making? Well, maybe not until we demonstrate that less formal mechanisms won't work. Has it been shown that decentralized decision-making will produce unworkable chaos that threatens the vital interests of established governments? Not really. We've hardly tried a collective conversation designed to allow responsible participants to set their own rules and to help all concerned—online and off—seek to understand and respect others' vital interests. Yet that kind of conversation is precisely the kind of activity the net itself is designed—thanks to the engineers—to facilitate. (1996a)

That jurisdiction is so unclear and external legislation and enforcement so unwieldy on the global level suggests greater attention to internal regulation at the local level, within virtual communities, for instance. Such an approach, presented as decentralized online decision-making by Johnson and Post (1996a), is explored further in their subsequent article, "The New 'Civic Virtue' of the Internet" (1997). This article is indispensable for understanding the significance of the present study in the larger context of cybercrime and law-breaking research because Johnson and Post directly point to the local, community level as potentially the most appropriate as well as the most effective level for cyberspace governance. Reiterating arguments from their emergent law article (1996a), Johnson and Post raise doubts about the applicability of territorially-oriented frameworks in cyberspace as follows:

> Who should set the rules that apply to this new global medium? What polity or polities should function as sources of legitimate and welfare-enhancing rules for conduct on the Internet? Who should become the lawmakers of cyberspace?
>
> One obvious answer is that cyberspace should be controlled by those same territorial sovereigns who set the rules governing conduct off line. . . . we argue that this most obvious answer may well be wrong. We question whether a governance system divided into territories demarcated by physical boundaries can achieve key governmental goals in an environment that decouples the effects of conduct from the physical location in which that conduct occurs. (1997)

Johnson and Post go on to elucidate their hopes for the evolution of multiple decentralized systems of local regulation at the online community level, a grass-roots orientation which would involve what they refer to as "civic virtue":

> Rather than relying upon even the best of our democratic traditions to create a single set of top-down laws to impose on the Internet, would-be regulators of cyberspace should instead foster the emergence of diverse and contending rule sets that "pull and tug" against each other (and that help to recruit or discourage potential participants in particular online spaces) in order to allow an optimal overall combination of rules to arise. Rather than relying on the ability of citizens of the global electronic polity to debate thoughtfully in search of a single shared vision of the common good, would-be architects of online governance systems should look for a form of civic virtue that can tolerate continuous conflict and can reside in the very architecture of a decentralized, diverse, complex adaptive system.
>
> The best available solution to conflicts in individual goals and values regarding online conduct may be found by allowing individuals to join distinct, boundaried communities on the Internet, each with its own divergent set of rules, and by allowing those communities to deal with external pressures by devising their own mechanisms for filtering out unwelcome messages and with internal conflict by easing (or requiring) exit. Democratic debate and traditional legislative action may not, after all, be the best way to make the best public policy for the Internet. If we can preserve individual liberty to make educated and empowering choices among alternative online rule sets, our most thoughtful and high-minded collective-action option may be to abandon the process of elections and deliberations regarding some single best law to be imposed impartially on all from the top down. We may instead find a new form of civic virtue by allowing the governance of online actions to emerge "from the bottom up" as a result of the pull and tug between local online "jurisdictions" that do not attempt to act in a dispassionate or disinterested or "public-spirited" manner. (1997)

It seems, then, that controlling troublesome behavior in cyberspace might profitably be pursued by developing internal, rule-based approaches at local levels instead of concentrating primarily on external, law-based approaches operating at global levels. This is the path recommended by Johnson and Post:

> Geographically based governments can and should begin to pay attention to the possibility that the tendency of the Internet to break down geographic borders and eliminate physical clustering of effects requires a whole new perspective on how to measure the virtues of any particular governance mechanism applicable to activities on the Net. . . . The best "collective-action" results for cyberspace will be achieved by treating each separate online location as a distinct, largely self-governing place, with its own rules governing actions that primarily affect its own participants. (Those rules may be made in the first instance by system operators, but they will be ratified, in effect, by individual users' decisions to frequent the online spaces they find empowering.) (1997)

And as the quest to develop approaches for dealing with troublesome online behavior at local levels begins to gather momentum, attracting increasing attention and enthusiasm, a concomitant need arises for greater understanding of how misbehavior and rule-breaking are already being handled internally by existing virtual communities.

Thus, as the preceding discussion of relevant research on cybercrime and law-breaking indicates, with respect to troublesome online behavior, legal experts cannot agree on what constitutes cybercrime, or which laws apply in cyberspace, or who controls the Internet. Because of legal dilemmas described herein as First Amendment follies, definition schizophrenia, and the jurisdiction circus, to date, external efforts to control troublesome behavior in cyberspace have produced muddled and inconsistent outcomes, with drastically inequitable consequences for offenders as well as victims in different physical and cyber places. The folly of attempting to apply U.S. First Amendment protections in transnational cyberspace is becoming more evident with every packet transmitted on the Internet. Due to the ambiguous delineation between malevolent criminal and mischievous prankster, definition schizophrenia runs rampant in the handling of online troublemakers worldwide. Thanks to the judicial anarchy provoked by the Internet's manifold overlapping regimes, the jurisdiction circus in cyberspace has no ringmaster. Furthermore, as Johnson and Post suggest (1997), perhaps no single ringmaster is necessary or even desirable, if the role can adequately be filled instead by a multiplicity of approaches for dealing with troublesome online behavior at local levels.

So, having traversed a bewildering maze of cyberspace illegalities in reviewing issues from literature on cybercrime and law-breaking most relevant to the present study, it is appropriate next to consider research from communication and media theory perspectives that directly addresses misbehavior and rule-breaking in virtual communities, the subject of the following chapter of this report.

Chapter Five
Misbehavior:
Rule-Breaking in Virtual Communities

THE 1994 BRUCKMAN ABSTRACT

In recent years, among the topics that have emerged in virtual community research, issues related to misbehavior and rule-breaking have begun to capture the attention of scholars. However, compared to research on cybercrime and law-breaking on the Internet reviewed previously in Chapter Four, inquiry into misbehavior and rule-breaking in virtual communities is just starting to evolve. Research which directly addresses misbehavior and rule-breaking in virtual communities is still relatively scarce, and as a result, existing literature in this area is somewhat limited. For the most part, this third and most pertinent body of source literature used for the present study consists of articles and reports on issues related to behavior management and social control in online environments; to date, no full-length treatment appears to have been published in this area. Such sources on misbehavior and rule-breaking in virtual communities originate primarily in the realms of communication and media theory, and represent approaches which focus on sociological and psychological dimensions of the lower end of the spectrum of troublesome online behavior. As opposed to cybercrime and law-breaking, discussed in Chapter Four, misbehavior involves the breaking of rules, which are regulations expressed in varying degrees of formality, established and enforced within online environments. Studies of misbehavior and rule-breaking, therefore, emphasize the lower end of the spectrum of troublesome conduct in online environments, situations where rule-making and rule-enforcement are handled internally by participants themselves within their online environments, with appeals to external authorities and institutions offline used only as a last resort.

To introduce the literature on misbehavior and rule-breaking in virtual communities from communication and media theory perspectives, it is appropriate to recall the second of the two key 1994 publications related to trouble in cyber-space mentioned previously in Chapter Three: the brief abstract edited by Bruckman, "Approaches to Managing Deviant Behavior in Online Communi-ties." The 1994 Bruckman abstract presents the agenda and participant position statements for a three-member panel held at the annual meeting of the Special Interest Group on Computer-Human Interaction ("SIGCHI") of the Association for Computing Machinery ("ACM," the "world's oldest and largest educational and scientific computing society," according to its Web site, http://www.acm. org). Unlike the numerous participants in the meetings summarized in the 1994 Denning and Lin report, who were primarily external experts from the realms of computer science and jurisprudence, the three Bruckman panelists have each played prominent internal roles leading well-established virtual communities. Editor of the abstract and herself a panelist, Bruckman founded MediaMOO as a doctoral candidate at the Massachusetts Institute of Technology's Media Lab; she currently teaches and studies virtual communities and education at the Georgia Institute of Technology. The second panelist, Curtis, founder and chief administrator of LambdaMOO, also worked at the Xerox Palo Alto Research Center and has published elsewhere about his virtual community experiences (1997). Figallo, the third panelist, served as managing director of the WELL during its formative years and subsequently as director of community develop-ment for the online magazine *Salon* (http:/salon.com), and has authored a book on hosting Web communities (1998). It is therefore no accident that the 1994 Bruckman abstract displays a strong internal orientation in approaching trouble-some online behavior.

A mere couple of pages, yet extremely insightful, and of the utmost rele-vance for this investigation, the 1994 Bruckman abstract furnishes the earliest published sign of inquiry focusing directly and exclusively on misbehavior within virtual communities. "Short and sweet" most aptly describes the Bruckman piece, which poses fundamental questions that lie at the heart of the present study. The 1994 Bruckman abstract consists of position statements by the three panelists and a moderator, accompanied by a few introductory para-graphs. These introductory paragraphs are so packed with pertinent remarks that they are worth citing in full:

> It is an unfortunate fact of life that where there are multi-user computer sys-tems, there will be antisocial behavior. On bulletin board systems (BBSs), there are those who persist in being obscene, harassing, and libelous. In virtual worlds such as MUDs, there are problems of theft, vandalism, and virtual rape.
>
> Behavior is "deviant" if it is not in accordance with community standards. How are such standards developed? Should standards be established by system administrators and accepted as a condition of participation, or should they be developed by community members? Once a particular person's behavior is deemed unacceptable, what steps should be taken? Should such steps be taken by individuals, such as "filters" or "kill" files on BBSs, and "gagging" or "ignoring" on MUDs? Or should the administrators take action, banning an

individual from the system or censoring their postings? What is the appropriate balance between centralized and decentralized solutions?

Gags and filters are computational solutions to deviant behavior. Are there appropriate social solutions? How effective are approaches like feedback from peers, community forums, and heart-to-heart chats with sympathetic system administrators? Are different approaches effective with communities of different sizes? What is the appropriate balance between social and technological solutions? (1994, p. 183)

Perceptive though it is, zeroing in on major issues and central questions related to misbehavior and rule-breaking in online environments, the 1994 Bruckman abstract on managing deviant behavior in virtual communities does not appear to have triggered a deluge of research in this area. Looking back at the cybercrime and law-breaking literature reviewed in Chapter Four, the 1994 Denning and Lin report encouraged, or at least accompanied, the evolution of an abundance of computer science and jurisprudence approaches to troublesome online behavior, which have proven quite fertile with respect to stimulating diverse lines of inquiry. In contrast, the 1994 Bruckman abstract does not seem to have signaled or provoked a corresponding degree of interest in misbehavior and rule-breaking as research topics in computer-mediated communication ("CMC"), generating comparatively meager results to date in terms of communication and media approaches to troublesome conduct in online environments. For example, the three 1994 panelists themselves have moved on to different issues in virtual community research, apparently not pursuing further inquiry into misbehavior to any significant extent. In 1999, Bruckman organized a workshop on "research issues in the design of online communities" for the annual SIGCHI/ACM meeting, but according to information on Bruckman's own Web site (http://www.cc.gatech.edu/~asb), as well the listings on the ACM's site (http://www.acm.org), this 1999 workshop yielded little, if any, discussion of deviant behavior, theme of Bruckman's SIGCHI/ACM panel five years earlier. Nevertheless, since the 1994 Bruckman panel and abstract, some researchers have begun to investigate various aspects of misbehavior and rule-breaking in virtual communities. The fruits of their labors are reviewed in this chapter, starting with the core concept in the present study: misbehavior.

MISBEHAVIOR AND ITS ALIASES:
NEGLIGENT, NAUGHTY, NASTY, AND BEYOND

In general, the term "misbehavior" refers to conduct which does not conform to norms and which breaks rules, as explained in earlier chapters of this report. To misbehave is to conduct oneself in a manner perceived by others to be aberrant, anti-social, bad, delinquent, deviant, wrong, or as sociologist Goffman puts it, "inappropriate in the situation. . . . felt to be improper" (1963, pp. 3–4). And as noted previously, an overall distinction is drawn in the present study between cybercrime, which involves law-breaking situations and external law-making and law-enforcement; and misbehavior, which involves rule-breaking situations and internal rule-making and rule-enforcement. Thus, misbehavior encompasses the lower end of the spectrum of troublesome conduct in online environments.

Misbehavior goes by many names in the literature related to virtual communities and online CMC. Only a few researchers actually use the word "misbehavior" (e.g., Sproull & Faraj, 1995/1997, p. 49; Suler, 1997a, 1997b; Williams, 2001) or the term "misconduct" (e.g., A. D. Smith, 1999, p. 158). Among the most common synonymous phrases are "anti-social" behavior (e.g., MacKinnon, 1997, p. 207; Mnookin, 1996; Reid, 1999, p. 114; C. B. Smith et al., 1998, p. 111; Suler, 1997a), and "deviant" behavior (e.g., Bruckman, 1994; Suler, 1997a, 1997b; Surratt, 1996; Williams, 2000, 2001). As noted in Chapter One, the word "misbehavior" seems preferable to alternative phrases used by other researchers such as "anti-social" or "deviant" behavior for several reasons. "Misbehavior" avoids certain connotations not applicable in all cases of rule-breaking: for instance, "anti-" may imply purposeful intent and "deviant" may convey a sense of moral perversion; yet a great deal of misconduct is neither intentional nor perverted. The word "misbehavior" seems more general and neutral in that it connotes conduct that does not follow norms, conduct that is awry, off, or somehow out-of-synch, anomalous or dysfunctional perhaps, but not necessarily intentional or perverted. The choice of "misbehavior" as the least judgmental and hence most adequate term also reflects the recommendations of Becker, a sociologist specializing in deviance research, who suggests that "it might be worthwhile to refer to such behavior as rule-breaking behavior" and reserve the term "deviant" for other uses (1963/1973, p. 14). And the phrase "rule-breaking" is similarly favored in this context by deviance sociologists Pfuhl and Henry (1993) as well.

Misbehavior in virtual communities runs the gamut from playful and roguish pranks, tricks, teasing, and mischief that others find annoying, vexing, or irritating, to more serious and malicious offenses, violations, and transgressions that are judged nasty, evil, or injurious. One way to illustrate the variety of misbehavior in which people engage online, as well as the equally diverse perspectives from which researchers approach the topic, is to look at other descriptive words and phrases used in the literature related to virtual communities and online CMC. In the dispassionate range, some investigators explain misbehavior as socially inappropriate, unacceptable, or undesirable conduct (e.g., Baym, 1998, p. 61; Dutton, 1996, p. 279; MacKinnon, 1997, p. 207; Mnookin, 1996; Sproull & Faraj, 1995/1997, p. 42; Suler, 1997a). Then there are rather mild portrayals of misbehavior as breaches of etiquette and manners (e.g., Kollock & M. A. Smith, 1996, p. 116; Stivale, 1996/1997, pp. 138, 140), and "disinhibited behavior" (Joinson, 1998). In a similar vein, some write of "violating the local rules of decorum" (Kollock & M. A. Smith, 1996, p. 117), "violation of group norms" (C. B. Smith et al., 1998, p. 102), "violations of social norms" (Surratt, 1996, p. 363), and "rule violations" (A. D. Smith, 1999, p. 140). Others emphasize the mischievous, obnoxious, and annoying aspects of what Stivale calls "gratuitously irritating behavior" (1996/1997, p. 139; see also Dutton, 1996,

p. 276; Mnookin, 1996; Suler, 1997b). Darker depictions involve "reproachable" or "offensive" conduct (e.g., McLaughlin et al., 1995; C. B. Smith et al., 1998, p. 99; Suler, 1997b) and "disruptive" behavior (Sproull & Faraj, 1995/1997, p. 49). A belligerent component surfaces in such expressions as "downright mean behaviors" (Suler, 1997a), "deliberately aggressive actions" (Stivale, 1996/1997, p. 138), and "aggressive and abusive behaviors" (Reid, 1999, p. 114). Echoes of law-breaking are found in phrases like "virtual crime" and "virtual offense" (e.g., MacKinnon, 1997; A. D. Smith, 1999), and "sub-criminal" behavior (Williams, 2000). And the harshest representations of misbehavior invoke unhealthy images of disease: Danielson uses the phrase "technosocial pathologies" (1996, p. 77), while MacKinnon writes of the "virtual psychopath" who engages in "virtual sociopathy" (1997, p. 207; 1998, p. 165; Williams, 2000). C. B. Smith et al. also employ the expression "virtual sociopathy"; however, these same researchers provide a serviceable, all-around summary definition of misbehavior and rule-breaking as "behavior sufficiently in violation of normative expectations to prompt comment and spark remedial discussion and debate" (1998, p. 98, rephrasing their earlier statement in McLaughlin et al., 1995, p. 95).

This last definition offered by C. B. Smith et al. (1998) suggests an essential point to bear in mind about misbehavior. People's subjective perceptions of and reactions to certain conduct as inappropriate, rather than any inherent or objective qualities of the conduct itself, are the critical factors in determining what does and does not constitute misbehavior on particular occasions in particular environments. Thus, definitions of misbehavior and rule-breaking are relative to situation and context, rather than absolute, as Becker explains in his classic, *Outsiders: Studies in the Sociology of Deviance*:

> The same behavior may be an infraction of the rules at one time and not at another; may be an infraction when committed by one person, but not when committed by another; some rules are broken with impunity, others are not. In short, whether a given act is deviant or not depends in part on the nature of the act (that is, whether or not it violates some rule) and in part on what other people do about it. (1963/1973, p. 14)

Similarly, in *Behavior in Public Places*, Goffman states that "an act can, of course, be proper or improper only according to the judgment of a specific social group, and even within the confines of the smallest and warmest of groups there is likely to be some dissensus and doubt" (1963, p. 5).

It is clear, then, that misbehavior and rule-breaking must be viewed as transactional phenomena, involving socially-constructed and situationally-influenced meanings that people make of conduct and interaction in particular contexts, as discussed previously in Chapter Two. As Becker observes, rule-breaking is "the product of a transaction that takes place between some social group and one who is viewed by that group as a rule-breaker" (1963/1973, p. 10). In another well-known study of social deviance in the traditional offline world, *The Deviance Process*, Pfuhl and Henry agree that "like other forms of social behavior, rule-breaking is volitional and rests on the meanings people create and develop about experiences and events in their effective environment" (1993, p. 83). And because social meaning-making depends so heavily on situational contexts, Pfuhl and Henry conclude that rule-breaking behavior is "an ongoing outcome of the complex process through which people seek to create a sense of social order; most especially it emerges from their rule-making and rule-enforcing activities. . . . an interactional process" (p. 24).

RULES AND NORMS IN VIRTUAL GATHERINGS

Whether online or off, the means of regulating misbehavior are as diverse as the sorts of rule-breaking in which people engage. Nevertheless, in a general sense, regulation of misbehavior involves the rule-making and rule-enforcing activities to which Pfuhl and Henry point (1993, p. 24), which Becker describes as "the situations of rule-breaking and rule-enforcement and the processes by which some people come to break rules and others to enforce them" (1963/1973, p. 2). Arguing that rules can be taken as measure of community or groupness, Becker claims that "all social groups make rules and attempt, at some times and under some circumstances, to enforce them. Social rules define situations and the kinds of behavior appropriate to them, specifying some actions as 'right' and forbidding others as 'wrong'" (p. 1). However, types of rules and ways of enforcing them vary considerably, as Becker explains:

> Rules may be of a great many kinds. They may be formally enacted into law, and in this case the police power of the state may be used in enforcing them. In other cases, they represent informal agreements, newly arrived at or encrusted with the sanction of age and tradition; rules of this kind are enforced by informal sanctions of various kinds. Similarly, whether a rule has the force of law or tradition or is simply the result of consensus, it may be the task of some specialized body, such as the police or the committee on ethics of a professional association, to enforce it; enforcement, on the other hand, may be everyone's job, or at least, the job of everyone in the group to which the rule is meant to apply. (1963/1973, p. 2)

Becker's views, as well as those expressed by Pfuhl and Henry, are congruent with observations made about situations, rules, and rule-breaking in Chapter Two of this report. Furthermore, Becker's discussion also supports the distinction drawn throughout the present study between rules, which refer to internal regulations, expressed in varying degrees of formality, enforced within a community by community members themselves; and laws, which refer to external, highly formalized legislation, enforced by authorities and institutions outside particular communities. And as noted in Chapter Four, people appeal to external laws and penalties as a last resort when internal rules and sanctions fail (see, e.g., Branscomb, 1996; D. E. Denning & Lin, 1994).

Just as crime cannot be contemplated in the absence of law, misbehavior cannot be considered in the absence of rules and norms. As discussed more fully in previous chapters of this report, rules involve regulations, principles, guidelines, customs, and norms governing social behavior; and norms involve standards, models, and patterns of conduct generally regarded as typical of particular social groups. The terms "rules" and "norms" both appear in research that addresses the regulation of misbehavior in virtual communities. Even Rheingold's classic mentions "norms, folklore, ways of acceptable behavior that are widely modeled, taught, and valued that can give the citizens of cyberspace clear ideas of what they can and cannot do with the medium" (1993, p. 64). More recently, Kollock and M. A. Smith emphasize the function of "rules of decorum" in managing virtual communities (1996). Carnevale and Probst refer to "procedures, rules and norms of appropriate content and behavior" (1997, p. 240). Suler considers "rules" and "standards about what is acceptable and unacceptable" (1997a, 1997b). Baym underscores the significance of "behavioral norms" in the emergence of online community (1998, pp. 60–62). Reid views rules as "the collection of rights and responsibilities, expectations and obligations that emerge in social situations" (1999, p. 112). And there are others who discuss "standards of conduct" in virtual communities as well (e.g., MacKinnon, 1997; McLaughlin et al., 1995; C. B. Smith et al., 1998).

Several scholars distinguish between rules and norms in their studies of virtual communities, viewing rules as more formal and authoritative versions of informal, prescriptive norms. According to Surratt, rules are "an established set of norms of interaction which, when violated, result in either formal and [sic] informal sanctions; a means of socializing new members and exerting social control over deviant behavior"; whereas norms are "behavioral codes, or prescriptions, that guide people into actions and self-presentations that conform to social acceptability" (1996, pp. 22, 364). Korenman and Wyatt differentiate rules from norms more carefully and clarify the relationship between them:

> Groups exhibit consistent patterns of behavior that can be described and measured, i.e., roles, norms, etc. In describing group behavior, we ordinarily distinguish between rules for behavior, which are patterns of behavior specified by authority, and norms, which are patterns of behavior developed by the members through interaction. Robert's Rules of Order (1981) is a commonly recognized set of rules for group interaction. . . . In actual practice, many groups modify formal rules to greater or lesser degrees for their own purposes; such modifications constitute norms of interaction. Officially prescribed rules of interaction are usually readily available, but norms are more difficult to identify, describe and analyze. (1996, p. 226)

Korenman and Wyatt go on to point out that the existence of rules is a reasonable measure of "groupness," echoing Becker's claim cited above (1963/1973). Similarly, McLaughlin et al. note that rules for appropriate online behavior can be considered a hallmark of community: "the presence of a set of standards for conduct [may] be construed as prima facie evidence for the existence of on-line communities" (1995, p. 101). According to Baym, "it is to meet the needs of the community . . . that standards of behavior and methods of sanctioning inappropriate behavior develop" (1998, p. 61). This notion that rules are among the social ties that bind online communities together is explained more elaborately in Mnookin's case study of LambdaMOO (1996). Although she refers misleadingly to the ensemble of rules in LambdaMOO as "LambdaLaw," Mnookin emphasizes the cohesive benefits to virtual communities of establishing and formalizing internal standards:

> The existence of LambdaLaw becomes itself proof that LambdaMOO is more than a game, that what happens there is not just recreation but the creation of a virtual community. . . . Law provides dispute-resolution mechanisms and legislative procedures, but it also provides something more: legitimacy. (1996)

Rules and norms in virtual communities are still evolving, as various researchers have observed. For instance, D. J. Phillips notes an initial "lack of established behavioral norms in computer-mediated groups" (1996, p. 40), while MacKinnon writes of "newly developing norms, mores, tradition, or other standards of conduct" (1997, p. 207). In evaluating "the evolving procedures of online governance that attempt to respond to the needs of expanding virtual communities," Stivale detects "ambiguity of what is appropriate or not" (1996/1997, pp. 139, 142), corresponding to similar quandaries with respect to cybercrime and cyberlaw discussed in Chapter Four. Online rules and norms remain unclear, in part, due to lack of experience with virtual environments and constant technological innovation, as Carnevale and Probst point out:

> Electronic communication is a new enough technology that people's expectations, norms, rules of politeness, laws, and policies are not fully worked out. In addition, the fact that the technology itself is changing so rapidly makes it hard to develop standards that can accommodate or anticipate future directions. (1997, p. 240)

Telecommunications researchers Samarajiva and Shields assert that "formal and informal rules governing technologically mediated human interaction have been thrown into flux" (1997, p. 535). Furthermore, the transference of analogies about behavioral rules and norms from traditional offline environments to novel circumstances online turns out to be somewhat awkward. Sproull and Faraj clarify the dilemma as follows:

> In the real world, social contracts take a variety of familiar forms: formal legal codes, professional codes of conduct, association bylaws, community standards. . . . Social contracts in the electronic world are extremely problematic. Because electronic groups are both diverse and ephemeral, attempts to directly apply codes of conduct from the real world often go awry. (1995/1997, p. 48)

Uncertainty due to the relative novelty of online rules and norms is exacerbated by erratic rule-enforcement in virtual communities, according to some scholars. Sproull and Faraj claim that "electronic groups currently have few ways to deal with blatant misbehavior" (1995/1997, p. 49). Stivale remarks on "the absence of any means of effectively enforcing such [online community] standards," noting "a heightened awareness of the difficulties in enforcing sanctions effectively" (1996/1997, pp. 140, 142). And Suler (1997b) observes that especially in larger, more complex communities with cadres of electronic enforcers or superusers, there is a need "to create a standard set of rules for appropriate behavior among users as well as standards for how wizards should enforce them." Nonetheless, as Williams explains, "most online communities have developed a set of rules governing conduct, in tandem with deterrence mechanisms to dissuade any 'inappropriate' action" (2000). One summary of the situation with respect to rules and norms in online environments is provided by Dutton:

> The novelty of the technology has left networked communities relatively normless. Users do not know what etiquette or rules apply to a new medium. E-mail, for example, is not exactly analogous to a letter, a telephone call or a conversation. There is as yet no well established etiquette for electronic communications although there is a developing set of conventions and practices—a so-called "Netiquette"—among experienced users. (1996, p. 271)

NETIQUETTE AND OTHER CODES OF CIVILIZED CYBER CONDUCT

The earliest and most primitive stage in the evolution of rules and norms of online behavior involves the informal system of social control known as "netiquette," an accumulation of "accepted standards of etiquette" for networked environments (Stivale, 1996/1997, p. 139). Netiquette derives from notions of common sense and basic courtesy applied to virtual situations. According to Nguyen and Alexander, "when structures are falling, common courtesy is a strong form of order-seeking behaviour" (1996, p. 103). As Randall puts it, "netiquette is the online version of 'do unto others as you would have them do unto you'" (1997, p. 102). Carnevale and Probst explain that "the Internet has an evolving set of norms about what is appropriate communication. There is increasing interest in 'netiquette' (abbreviation of network etiquette), guidelines and rules for appropriate behavior" (1997, p. 249). Herring also defines netiquette as "network etiquette" (1996b, p. 115), a simple definition echoed by Shade (1996). Mabry defines the term as "norms of network usage" (1998, p. 14), while Wisebrod (1995) offers a picturesque portrayal of netiquette as the "table manners of cyberspace." A very official pronouncement bestowing a certain degree of formality on netiquette, which is generally considered informal in nature, appears in a Canadian lawsuit involving email spam, *1267623 Ontario Inc. v. Nexx Online Inc.* (1999). In the court's ruling, Justice Wilson defines netiquette as the "growing body of acceptable, though as yet largely unwritten, etiquette with respect to conduct by users of the internet" (for summaries of this case and its legal implications, see Evans, July 9, 1999 and Kaplan, July 16, 1999). And a down-to-earth explanation of how netiquette works that incorporates a teenager's perspective on the subject is provided by Tapscott in *Growing Up Digital: The Rise of the Net Generation*:

> The most obvious codes of a given culture are its systems of etiquette. These codes are not so much about which fork to eat your salad with as they are codes about how people show respect for one another. On the Internet, a system of tacit codes popularly known as *Netiquette* has evolved. There is a considerable debate about how deeply these rules of Netiquette have penetrated the Internet community since, as many have noted, the medium is impossible to control. However, on the Net, as in society, cultural codes are maintained not through control, but through contract. Members of a culture agree to uphold certain behaviors to maintain their rights. . . . In Netiquette, as in etiquette, respect for others translates into respect for other's rights. "This is your site. By logging on to your site I expect to follow the rules you have set. Just like I don't expect to walk into someone's house or a business cursing or causing a disturbance," says 14-year-old Eric Mandela of Rahway, New Jersey. "I feel that your Internet server is like your house or business, or any other place where kids hang out, and it should be run by your rules. You should be allowed to censor anything you want, and if people don't want to follow these rules, they can go somewhere else. If someone is causing a disturbance, you should have the right to ban them. Also, they should have the right to put anything legal they want on their site." (1998, pp. 66–67)

A popular treatment of the topic is provided in Shea's book, *Netiquette* (1994), often mentioned in the related literature (e.g., Branscomb, 1996; C. B. Smith et al., 1998). Reminiscent of the "Ten Commandments of Computer Ethics" (Computer Ethics Institute, 1997) cited previously in Chapter Four, Shea provides the following ten "Core Rules of Netiquette":

Rule 1: Remember the human
Rule 2: Adhere to the same standards of behavior online that you follow in real life
Rule 3: Know where you are in cyberspace
Rule 4: Respect other people's time and bandwidth
Rule 5: Make yourself look good online
Rule 6: Share expert knowledge
Rule 7: Help keep flame wars under control
Rule 8: Respect other people's privacy
Rule 9: Don't abuse your power
Rule 10: Be forgiving of other people's mistakes
(http://www.albion.com/netiquette/corerules.html)

The way Shea's book (also available on the Web) is described in her publisher's electronic catalog effectively expresses the value of such an etiquette manual in providing guidance on avoiding inappropriate behavior online:

People who wouldn't dream of burping at the end of dinner post offensive messages to international forums. Middle managers inadvertently send romantic email messages to the company-wide email alias. People at computer terminals forget that there are real live people on the other end of the wire. Topics are lost in noise, feelings are hurt, reputations are damaged, time and bandwidth are wasted.

This book brings etiquette to the bustling frontiers of cyberspace. In a series of entertaining essays, the author establishes the do's and the don'ts of communicating online, from the Golden Rule to the art of the flame, from the elements of electronic style to virtual romance. Accessible to both network wizard and clueless newbie, this is the first book to offer the guidance that all users need to be perfectly polite online.
(http://www.albion.com/catNetiquette.html)

There happens to be scholarly precedent for attending to popular etiquette manuals as evidence on patterns of social interaction. For instance, in his study of behavior in public places, Goffman justifies quite explicitly the research value of such material:

I want to explain my use of quotations from etiquette manuals. When Mrs. Emily Post makes a pronouncement as to how persons of cultivation act, and how other persons therefore ought to act, sociologists often become offended. Their good reason for snubbing Mrs. Post is that she provides little evidence that the circle about which she speaks has any numerical or social significance, that its members do in fact conduct themselves as she says they do, or even that these persons—or any others—consider that one ought to so conduct oneself.

These doubts impute much more creativity to etiquette writers than they possess. Although these writers do not empirically test their claims as to what is regarded as proper, it seems to me they are still describing some of the norms that *influence* the conduct of our middle classes, even though on many occasions other factors will predominate. Moreover, these books are one of the few sources of suggestions about the structure of public conduct in America. It is my feeling that the main drawback to using these books as data for social science is not the unvalidated nature of the statements they contain—for statements can always be checked by research—but rather that these books tend to provide a mere catalogue of proprieties instead of an analysis of the system of norms underlying those proprieties. (1963, p. 5)

More recently, in explaining "how the city dweller 'learns the ropes' of urban living," sociologist Lofland provides an interesting survey of etiquette books in the United States from 1881 to 1962, stressing the important role such manuals play in many areas of public behavior. One example cited by Lofland includes chapters devoted to "'correct' public behavior" such as "Etiquette of the Street," "Etiquette of Public Places," "Etiquette of Travelling," and "General Rules of Conduct" (1973, pp. 116–117). Lofland also notes that "many nineteenth- and early twentieth-century American etiquette books were, in fact, very much concerned with bodily movement and control in public" (1998, p. 47, n. 4). And in examining the social impact of media, Meyrowitz remarks that "printing fostered the preparation of 'training manuals' for princes and priests (such as those written by Machiavelli and Gracian) and led to the publication of many etiquette manuals aimed at people of different ages and sex" (1985, p. 314), and that in the sixteenth century "etiquette books for children, along with special guides for their parents, were printed" (p. 259). It seems, then, that in face-to-face interaction offline as well as in computer-mediated interaction online, etiquette manuals serve as important ingredients in providing guidance on appropriate social behavior.

The literature on etiquette in cyberspace transcends mere definitions of the term "netiquette," of course. Some researchers consider netiquette in particular virtual environments. For example, netiquette in Usenet newsgroups is discussed by MacKinnon (1995) as well as Shade (1996), who also reports on netiquette in IRC; Curtis (1997) lists the main points of "manners" in LambdaMOO; and Rutter and G. Smith discuss how netiquette provides "a basic code and fundamental basis of the friendliness" in RumCom.local, an independent newsgroup (1999a). Surratt covers netiquette in IRC, Usenet newsgroups, and a BBS system known as FidoNet (1996). As MacKinnon notes (1995, p. 115), plenty of primers and guides about netiquette exist as well (e.g., Horton, 1994; Rinaldi, 1994; Von Rospach, 1999). C. B. Smith et al. offer similar observations about the prevalence of guides to "netiquette and other standards of communicative practices" (1998, p. 97). One famous example is the often cited tongue-in-cheek piece entitled "Dear Emily Postnews" (Templeton, 1994). Additional examples come from the numbered series of authoritative documents known throughout the Internet as "RFCs" (Network Working Group Requests for Comments), including *RFC 1855: Netiquette Guidelines* (Hambridge, 1995), as well as *RFC 2635: Don't Spew, a Set of Guidelines for Mass Unsolicited Mailings and Postings (Spam)* (Hambridge & Lunde, 1999). In addition, netiquette is often mentioned in other virtual community and CMC literature (e.g., Baym, 1995; Danielson, 1996; D. E. Denning & Lin, 1994; Dery, 1996; Kiesler et al., 1984/1991; Maltz, 1996; Moore, 1995; D. J. Phillips, 1996; M. S. Rosenberg, 1992; M. A. Smith, 1992). And netiquette surfaces occasionally in the popular press as well. For example, one journalist suggests a "rekindled interest in etiquette" resulting from interaction in cyberspace (Kelly, 1997); another presents ten commandments of email (Spring, March 31, 1999); and yet another claims that there are dozens of email etiquette primers (Hafner, December 10, 1998).

Several scholars regard netiquette guides and similar documents as primary vehicles for disseminating rules of conduct in various online environments (e.g., Machado, 1996; Maltz, 1996). Kollock and M. A. Smith describe the role of documentation such as primers in socializing participants in Usenet newsgroup post environments:

> Rules and institutions exist on a global and local level throughout Usenet. At the global level, there are some concerns that are common to all newsgroups, and a set of documents exist which chart out rules that should govern participation.... These documents discuss rules of etiquette, suggestions for using the

Usenet efficiently, cautions against wasting bandwidth or being off-topic, and many other issues. (1996, p. 121)

And Werry provides examples of how participants in chat environments develop and spread their own traditions of netiquette guidelines:

> As with many other forms of computer-mediated communication, IRC has a general code of conduct that one is required to observe. All of the various manuals that exist for IRC have fully detailed sections on "netiquette," as does the IRC on-line help facility. Such texts might be said to perform a function akin to Castiglione's *Book of the Courtier*, providing as they do a handbook of cyberspace conduct. (1996, p. 50)

MacKinnon offers a related illustration of how netiquette functions in Usenet newsgroups:

> Usenet's parallel method or analog for conveying mores, norms, and traditions is known as "netiquette." As the term implies, it is literally "network etiquette," and it helps to reinforce the standards of behavior that users might miss from the lack of verbal cues. Several attempts have been made to summarize the norms of netiquette. The most widely cited is Gene Spafford's series of documents, which he compiled and edited from the suggestions of Usenet users. Either heeded or ignored by many, the estimates of the validity of Spafford's guidelines vary, but they are often invoked to resolve a dispute or to "advise" one another. . . . enforcement of netiquette begins with the individual users. . . . Netiquette, then, is the Usenet analog for the external world's system of mores, norms, and tradition. While not a precise duplication of the external world's social structure, netiquette provides Usenet users with guidelines or standards of behavior. (1995, p. 115)

MacKinnon refers here to the same Spafford mentioned previously in Chapter Four of this study in connection with research on computer viruses. What MacKinnon reports about Spafford's contributions to Usenet netiquette is confirmed on Spafford's Web site (http://www.cerias.purdue.edu/homes/spaf), which states that "Spaf published the first set of newusers documents for Usenet ca. 1981 (and continued to maintain and post them for the next 12 years)."

Closely related to netiquette is the genre of online guidelines known as Frequently Answered Questions ("FAQs") (see, e.g., FAQ about viruses, L. Jones, 1995; about IRC, H. Rose, 1996). C. B. Smith et al. emphasize the function of FAQs in disseminating netiquette throughout virtual communities such as Usenet newsgroups:

> Such conventions are usually propagated regularly for the benefit of new readers in informative postings known as FAQs, a well-known and ubiquitous acronym for "frequently asked questions." . . . FAQs are usually generated by volunteers, newsgroup readers who tire of seeing the same old questions and as a result begin to post Socratic dialogues of recurring questions and answers. So

widespread is the FAQ phenomenon that readers of more esoteric newsgroups have created tongue-in-cheek FAQs which are more on the order of inside jokes than they are informative.... For many newsgroups, however, FAQs have become indispensable forms of information distribution and a means of archiving the history and evolution of a particular newsgroup. Maintenance, distribution, and updating of FAQs are important functions which are not undertaken lightly. (1998, p. 97, references omitted; see also McLaughlin et al., 1995, p. 106)

FAQs play important roles in various online environments. For example, Surratt discusses FAQs in IRC and Usenet newsgroups, as well as the FidoNet BBS system (1996), and others researchers also mention FAQs in connection with behavior management and social control (e.g., Maltz, 1996; McLaughlin et al., 1995; Wisebrod, 1995). Broad distribution of user-oriented documents such as FAQs and RFCs is aided nowadays by easily accessible online archives, particularly on Web sites (e.g., http://www.faqs.org), but Branscomb describes the genesis of FAQs on the Internet and how they first started circulating:

The computer literati—the console cowboys and girls of the electronic frontier—preferred an anarchical but benign electronic environment in which everyone would behave more or less civilly because it was the right and proper way to use the new capabilities efficiently. However, the experienced users who came to inhabit these new cyberspaces sought to regularize civilized behavior in [this] new Networld by establishing new forms of "netiquette." These were posted in FAQs (frequently asked questions) by the various discussion groups that popped up spontaneously on Usenet—more than 10,000 by 1996—and countless more in self-generated groups called Listservs. (1996)

And according to Kollock and M. A. Smith, "the production of FAQs illustrates the ways in which local rules are produced and modified endogenously, by the members themselves" (1996, p. 122).

Higher up on the scale of formality than netiquette guides, RFCs, and FAQs are agreements known as Acceptable Use Policies ("AUPs") and Terms of Service ("TOSs"). These more formal documents prohibiting certain kinds of objectionable behavior are described by D. E. Denning and Lin as "contractual agreements" (1994, p. 222). AUPs and TOSs typically serve to establish contractual relationships between users and commercial Internet Service Providers ("ISPs"), but similar documents are employed in other network contexts as well, as Denning and Lin explain:

With most commercial network service providers, a condition of use to which all users must agree is that users will abide by a certain set of rules about acceptable behavior; violators can be punished by the provider's discontinuing their access to the system. Contractual relationships between users and providers can be tailored according to the needs of the parties involved.... Bulletin board operators often operate in similar fashion: they write their own rules and set them forth the first time a new user logs in.... Many universities have codes of acceptable network behavior as well. . . . When adopted, such codes are a part of the rules and regulations governing the academic community, and all relevant academic mechanisms for enforcing rules and regulations are available to university policymakers for dealing with miscreant electronic behavior. (1994, pp. 26–27)

The rise in AUPs and TOSs in educational contexts has been commented on in the popular press (e.g., Rodberg, 1999a, 1999b; for examples of academic network policy statements, see Data Communications Task Force, 1995; DelFavero, 1997). The relevance of policy documents such as AUPs and TOSs is also mentioned in Dutton's research on "network rules of order" in two post environments (1996). Dutton describes one system requiring "a written agreement to abide by a long, detailed series of rules"; and another system employing "formal policy regarding the use of the BBS . . . spelled out in a handbook that was periodically distributed to students and scrolled by users when they logged onto the system" (1996, p. 281). Dutton also provides a summary table comparing the formal written policies of these two online communities (p. 282). General guidelines for developing online service agreements like AUPs and TOSs are provided in an appendix to L. Rose's *Netlaw* (1995, pp. 262–266), and one published illustration is a 1992 AUP of the Internet's NSFNET backbone service cited by Randall (1996, pp. 248–249). Up-to-date examples of AUPs and TOSs are readily available by logging on to almost any network system anywhere.

Having reviewed descriptions of misbehavior as well as observations about the function of rules, norms, and netiquette in regulating online conduct, the stage is set for examining more closely the third body of source literature used in the present study. This core literature which most directly addresses misbehavior and rule-breaking in virtual communities approaches the topic from communication and media theory perspectives and concentrates on issues related to behavior management and social control.

BEHAVIOR MANAGEMENT AND SOCIAL CONTROL IN ONLINE ENVIRONMENTS

Of the various research areas discussed in the present study, the most pertinent body of source literature encompasses investigations which directly address misbehavior and rule-breaking in virtual communities. Drawing primarily on communication and media theory perspectives, such sources represent approaches which focus on sociological and psychological dimensions of the lower end of the spectrum of troublesome conduct in online environments. The core collection of significant literature on misbehavior and rule-breaking in virtual communities is comprised of articles and reports from communication and media journals and CMC anthologies, as well as several pieces published online, a couple of chapters of a doctoral dissertation in sociology, and a few sections of a mass-market book on employees of Internet-related companies. To date, no overview, general survey, or book-length treatment devoted to the subject of misbehavior in online environments appears to have been published; the present study may be the first endeavor of this nature. The thirty or so items making up the core collection of significant sources related to misbehavior and the regulation of online conduct all concentrate on some aspect of behavior management and social control within virtual communities, examining either specific aspects of online misbehavior, or misbehavior in specific online environments. Taken as a group, these core sources cover a broad range of activities which, in the present investigation, have been grouped into three sets: rule-breaking, rule-making, and rule-enforcement. Discussed further ahead in Chapter Six of this report, these three sets of intertwined activities constitute what researchers in this area refer to in general as behavior management and social control.

The core research on behavior management and social control in online environments offers valuable information and ideas concerning misbehavior and rule-breaking, as well as rule-making and rule-enforcement. Furthermore, this body of core literature also reveals major relevant themes beyond the infamous triad of flaming, spamming, and virtual rape discussed in Chapter Three. For example, in this core literature, distinct areas and issues can be discerned, among them: how people establish, revise, disseminate, apply, and implement rules of online conduct; the roles of offenders and enforcers, and their possible motivations and personality profiles; and the technical mechanisms and sociological measures for sanctioning those who misbehave. The discussion ahead reviews and assesses the contributions and limitations of this set of core literature on misbehavior and the regulation of online conduct in virtual communities.

Among the earliest to focus on behavior management and social control in online environments are McLaughlin, Osborne, and C. B. Smith, three researchers whose provocative 1995 article from a CMC anthology, "Standards of Conduct on Usenet," serves as a stepping stone for subsequent research (e.g., Baym, 1998; D. J. Phillips, 1996). In their 1995 case study of Usenet newsgroups, McLaughlin et al. examine existing standards of conduct and how participants violate them (i.e., rule-making and rule-breaking). Providing a taxonomy of "reproachable conduct," and also an embryonic bibliography of relevant literature, this article represents perhaps the first published attempt to systematize the study of misbehavior in virtual communities, although limited to a single type of post environment, namely, Usenet newsgroups. These same three co-authors, with their names reordered as C. B. Smith, McLaughlin, and Osborne, continue their case study of newsgroups in a later CMC anthology article, "From Terminal Ineptitude to Virtual Sociopathy: How Conduct is Regulated on Usenet" (1998). Rewording both their earlier definition of "reproachable conduct" as behavior eliciting "remedial discussion and debate," as well as their taxonomy of reproachable conduct (i.e., rule-breaking), C. B. Smith et al. concentrate in this article on ensuing "corrective" or "remedial" episodes, considering "reproaches" to newsgroup "offenders" as well as offenders' reactions to being reprimanded (i.e., rule-enforcement). Although broader and more up-to-date than their earlier piece, this 1998 article contains a heavy dose of statistical analysis of the posting patterns of "reproachers" and "offenders," such quantitative statistics not nearly as illuminating as the authors' qualitative taxonomies; and again, discussion is restricted to one type of post environment. Nevertheless, these three researchers clearly advance the study of misbehavior with their two perspicacious pieces (i.e., McLaughlin, Osborne, & C. B. Smith, 1995; C. B. Smith, McLaughlin, & Osborne, 1998).

Another first-rate article from a CMC anthology, "Managing the Virtual Commons: Cooperation and Conflict in Computer Communities" (1996) by Kollock and M. A. Smith, similarly addresses behavior management and social control through a case study of Usenet newsgroups. Their examination of the "informal social control mechanisms" involved in managing behavior in this set of post environments is informed by a review of design principles found in traditional offline communities that successfully manage collective resources: principles related to group size and boundaries, rules and institutions, and monitoring and sanctioning. Kollock and M. A. Smith identify roughly four types of newsgroup violations (i.e., rule-breaking), and discuss monitoring and sanctioning techniques as well (i.e., rule-enforcement), but their strength lies in focusing on the evolution and dissemination of rules (i.e., rule-making) by means of documents and compilations such as FAQs, manuals, and primers intended to socialize newcomers both to particular newsgroup communities and to the Usenet community in general. Though dealing exclusively with newsgroups, Kollock and M. A. Smith's research is rich enough to apply to other types of online environments as well.

One more topnotch article on behavior management and social control in Usenet newsgroups, also from a CMC anthology, is Baym's "The Emergence of On-Line Community" (1998). This lucid and meticulous discussion draws on the case study of rec.arts.tv.soaps ("r.a.t.s.") about which Baym has published elsewhere: in her doctoral dissertation (1994); in CMC anthologies (e.g., 1993/1997b, 1995), and in *Tune In, Log On: Soaps, Fandom, and On-Line Community* (1999). In this 1998 article, arguing that "a sense of community emerges from stable social meanings," Baym suggests that one of the ways such shared social meanings arise in online CMC is through the creation of "norms that serve to organize interaction and to maintain desirable social climates. . . . rules that shape what [participants] can do" (p. 62). According to Baym, along with new forms of expression, public identities, and relationships in online environments, behavioral norms (i.e., rule-making) constitute one of four "facets of the creation of community" (p. 51). Baym considers each of these facets in relation to five sets of variables influencing CMC in general: "factors of external context, temporal structure, system infrastructure, group purposes, and participant characteristics" (p. 51). In discussing the role of behavioral norms online, Baym also mentions several kinds of misbehavior (i.e., rule-breaking) typical of newsgroups such as flaming (p. 59), as well as "the sociopolitically loaded practice of 'trolling' . . . asking obviously stupid questions" (p. 53). Additionally, Baym comments on differences in moderation (i.e., rule-enforcement) between closed, commercial environments such as America Online ("AOL") where postings can be "yanked before they ever appear" versus the open, public environment of unmoderated Usenet newsgroups, where "people turn, in effect, to shaming people into compliance by drawing attention to their violations" (p. 61). Although Baym's discussion emphasizes asynchronous posting, she is among the few CMC scholars to stress the role of temporal factors online (see also Sternberg, 1998; Strate, 1996b). Rich in relevant CMC theory and post environment data, Baym's work is an instance of depth triumphing over breadth, in that she confines her analysis to a single Usenet newsgroup, r.a.t.s., when it might profitably be applied to other newsgroups as well as to other types of online environments.

Providing a welcome break from Usenet newsgroups, a journal article by Dutton, "Network Rules of Order: Regulating Speech in Public Electronic Fora" (1996), presents an extremely strong case study comparing behavior management and social control in two California BBSs: "PEN," the Santa Monica Public Electronic Network, and "USCBBS" at the University of Southern California, both post environments. Dutton addresses an important and neglected area—what participants themselves think—building a taxonomy of user concerns regarding misbehavior (i.e., rule-breaking) based on responses from participants of both BBSs to open-ended surveys about online rights and responsibilities. Echoing the theme of 1994 Denning and Lin report on rights and responsibilities in networked communities, to which Dutton explicitly refers (having himself participated in the meetings summarized in the report), Dutton contrasts the formal policies of each BBS embodied in written user agreements (i.e., rule-making). He also considers issues such as sanctions and system operator involvement (i.e., rule-enforcement). Although Dutton's research is confined to post environments in BBSs, he offers helpful insights about various aspects of misbehavior while extending the field of inquiry beyond Usenet newsgroups to other post environments.

Several studies involving online behavior management and social control widen the scope of investigation from post environments to include chat environments as well. An expansive albeit superficial article that privileges generality over specificity is "Atheism, Sex, and Databases: The Net as a Social Technology" (1995/1997) by Sproull and Faraj, reprinted in a CMC anthology from a collection on public Internet access. Sproull and Faraj survey a range of virtual communities including Usenet newsgroups, listservs, MUDs and MOOs, the WELL and other BBSs, commercial ISPs such as AOL and CompuServe, and the Web. Sproull and Faraj's main purpose is to emphasize the social rather than informational nature of electronic gatherings in general, so they do not address particular issues related to breaking, making, or enforcing rules of online conduct. However, they do express similar sentiments as Denning and Lin (1994) and Dutton (1996) about the difficulties of balancing online rights and responsibilities. Other than actually using the word "misbehavior" and ruminating about diverse occurrences of this phenomenon, Sproull and Faraj's contribution furnishes some food for thought but little concrete data.

A far more substantial account of how order is maintained in chat environments is Reid's "Hierarchy and Power: Social Control in Cyberspace" (1999), a case study comparing four MUDs of two different types (adventure-oriented and socially-oriented). Reid is among the most experienced and proficient chat ethnographers around, having written about IRC (1991, 1996a) as well as LambdaMOO (1995) and JennyMUSH (1996b, 1998). In this 1999 article from a CMC anthology, Reid tackles "mechanisms" and "overt forms" of social control (i.e., rule-enforcement), specifically, hierarchies of power based on various participant levels in MUDs. Reid provides a revealing taxonomy comparing different system privileges of superusers known as "gods" and "wizards" as well as basic users and guests; and she admirably covers four distinct MUD communities. However, the value of her research on social hierarchies in virtual communities could be enhanced if extended to other aspects of misbehavior in MUDs beyond rule-enforcement (such as rule-breaking and rule-making), or if the user hierarchies she identifies in MUDs were contrasted with similar hierarchies in chat environments like IRC, post environments like newsgroups and listservs, or meta-environments like AOL, CompuServe, and BBSs.

A legal approach to behavior management and social control in virtual communities is taken by several scholars, including authors of two articles in the special issue devoted to emerging cyberlaw of the *Journal of Computer-Mediated Communication* edited by Branscomb, mentioned in previous chapters of this report. In one article of the special journal issue, "Virtual(ly) Law: The Emergence of Law in LambdaMOO" (1996), Mnookin contributes a solid case study focusing on the evolution of the LambdaMOO "legal system" (i.e., rule-making), which employs internal rules to resolve online disputes within that community. Mnookin's account of the Bungle virtual rape in LambdaMOO transcends similar discussions (reviewed in Chapter Three herein) because she moves beyond the incident itself to delve into the actions of community leaders and members subsequent to and as a result of the rape. Mnookin explains in detail how Curtis, founder and "archwizard" of LambdaMOO (and, as noted above, also a member of the 1994 Bruckman panel on managing deviant behavior), handed over control of this virtual community to its participants by instituting "a petition system, a process through which the players in LambdaMOO could enact legislation for themselves," including procedures for arbitration and dispute resolution, as well as stipulations for sanctions and penalties. Mnookin's article is strengthened by extensive references to historic internal LambdaMOO documents, such as Curtis's (1992) memorandum to the community introducing the new LambdaLaw system. Although Mnookin studies just a single chat environment and concentrates on rule-making, with little on rule-enforcement other than a few comments about sanctions and the role of wizards, she offers highly generalizable insights worthy of extension to other online environments. Mnookin sees her research in "legal anthropology" as a "chance to examine a legal order separate from our own that has received no previous scholarly attention. . . . [providing] the opportunity to see how participants are creating both social and legal order within a virtual sphere." And

Mnookin suggests that looking at law within LambdaMOO (i.e., rules) "might turn out to reveal something about law outside of LambdaMOO as well."

The second article that deals with behavior management and social control in the CMC journal issue edited by Branscomb is Maltz's "Customary Law & Power in Internet Communities" (1996), a rather unfocused survey of rule-making in online environments. Addressing informal as opposed to formal rules, with netiquette as a leading example, Maltz deals with documents like FAQs and primers produced by and for users as means of consolidating and disseminating rules (i.e., rule-making), but takes minimal note of rule-enforcement issues like sanctions. Maltz covers similar territory as Mnookin in describing the development of LambdaLaw after the Bungle affair, but overall, Maltz's approach seems comparatively superficial and tepid. On the other hand, by including material on Usenet newsgroups as well as LambdaMOO, Maltz strives to broaden the topic of rule-making in virtual communities. Maltz is also to be commended for providing ample footnotes and references relevant to rule-making in both post and chat environments.

Another article about behavior management and social control from a legal perspective is "Controlling the Uncontrollable: Regulating the Internet" (1995) by Wisebrod, published in a media and law journal. Wisebrod offers a survey of regulation within Usenet newsgroups that also takes into account legal concerns throughout the Internet in general. Covering similar territory as Maltz (1996), but much more adequately and with a different focus, Wisebrod discusses in detail two pivotal cases relating to sanctions for misbehavior in newsgroups (i.e., rule-enforcement). First, Wisebrod reviews the Canadian government ban on publication of material concerning the 1993 criminal prosecutions of Karla Homolka and her husband Paul Teale, a ban which was successfully imposed on traditional media in Canada, but ultimately subverted by the transnational nature of newsgroups devoted to publicizing information about the Homolka case. The second case Wisebrod describes is the well-known spate of commercial spamming in newsgroups described in Chapter Three, the 1994 episode in which the "green card lawyers," Canter and Siegel, "spammed nearly 6,000 Usenet newsgroups with an advertisement for their service of assisting non-Americans wishing to enter the work-permit raffle." Despite perceptive analyses of these two Usenet newsgroup incidents, as well as a thorough set of germane references, Wisebrod's piece does not break new ground in the study of online misbehavior.

The last article from something akin to a legal orientation in the core collection on behavior management and social control is Danielson's "Pseudonyms, Mailbots, and Virtual Letterheads: The Evolution of Computer-Mediated Ethics" (1996), published in a CMC anthology. Danielson provides a survey of evolving standards of virtual ethics (i.e., rule-making), which roams through a variety of online environments, including BBSs, IRC, listservs, and newsgroups. Asserting that "computer-mediated communities such as Usenet lack many organized defenses against abuse," Danielson tries to develop ethical filtering systems based on software robots (i.e., rule-enforcement) in hopes of implementing a code of "Artificial Morality." As he explains, "to filter is to commend some and to sanction other behaviors, to discriminate and thus to begin to stake ethical claims" (p. 76). Danielson's article is the perhaps the most offbeat item in the core collection of misbehavior literature. However, given that most post environment researchers opt to study newsgroups, a point in Danielson's favor is that he considers listservs, a genre of post environment discussed less frequently in the related literature.

Another view that researchers bring to bear on the study of behavior management and social control in online environments draws on approaches to conflict mediation and dispute resolution in offline contexts. An excellent article in this tradition is A. D. Smith's "Problems of Conflict Management in Virtual Communities" (1999), from a CMC anthology. Not a career media theorist, but rather a professional mediator applying her skills to benefit the virtual community she investigates, A. D. Smith offers a powerful case study of "problems, strategies, and techniques of maintaining social order in cyber communities," in which she assesses the "application of well-established real-life tools of conflict management to virtual disputes" based on her first-hand experience in a MUD called MicroMUSE (1999, p. 134). She offers taxonomies both of online disputes (i.e., rule-breaking) and of intervention strategies (i.e., rule-enforcement), with special attention to sanctions and the roles of wizards (including wizard listservs, a feature encountered in many virtual communities). Additionally, A. D. Smith also mentions the evolution of internal codes of conduct (i.e., rule-making). Capped by a bibliography particularly replete with general literature on conflict mediation and dispute resolution, A. D. Smith's study of MicroMUSE complements Mnookin's (1996) report on LambdaLaw, both pieces investigating the evolution of internal regulation in chat environments, but in different MUDs and from different perspectives.

Along similar lines, addressing behavior management and social control from something of a conflict management angle is "Defending the Boundaries: Identifying and Countering Threats in a Usenet Newsgroup" (1996) by D. J. Phillips. In this journal article, Phillips offers a scrupulous case study of soc.gandl, a newsgroup that "confronted a perceived 'invasion' of 'barbarians,' who 'killed' one of their members," causing the group to examine strategies available for dealing with such crises, with a view to protecting the community from future disruptions (1996, p. 39). Phillips focuses on threats and defenses (i.e., rule-breaking and rule-enforcement), devoting particular attention to the role of peer sanctions, moderation, and network administrators in keeping newsgroups in line. Enriched by references to similar issues in other virtual communities, such as the r.a.t.s. newsgroup studied by Baym (1993/1997b, 1994, 1995, 1998, 1999) and Dibbell's accounts of the LambdaMOO Bungle rape (1993, 1996, 1998), as well as some mention of BBSs and commercial networks like AOL, Phillips produces an eminently satisfactory treatment of behavior management and social control in Usenet post environments offering insights equally applicable to other online environments.

A survey treatment of behavior management and social control that tackles conflict resolution in MOO chat environments is "Dissolution and Fragmentation: Problems in On-Line Communities" (1998), an article by Kolko and Reid from a CMC anthology. Kolko and Reid present a rather pessimistic view of the potential for collaboration and cooperation in regulating online conduct (i.e., rule-making and rule-enforcement), suggesting that virtual communities "encourage multiplicity but not flexibility" (p. 219). Focusing on situations where communities fail to accomplish desired regulatory objectives, Kolko and Reid contrast, for example, a harassment case in an unnamed, research-oriented MOO where "the roots of the decision to change the structure of the community were tangled and complicated by the vastly different ideas and expectations of the parties involved" (p. 214), with the Bungle rape in LambdaMOO described by others (e.g., Dibbell, 1993, 1996, 1998; Mnookin, 1996; Stivale, 1996/1997). According to Kolko and Reid, online environments encourage "the relentless fragmentation of the self in ways that hinder community formation" (p. 220). And because "the displaced and dispersed nature of virtual space reinforces the psychological fragmentation of the on-line self" (p. 226), Kolko and Reid claim that dissolution occurs with respect to selves, spaces, and places online. While offering valuable data about problems related to rule-making online, the rather limited scholarly horizons displayed in this article diminish its appeal (a criticism also applicable to Reid's 1999 study of hierarchies and power in MUDs mentioned above), in that Kolko and Reid do not venture much beyond the parameters of CMC research set by Turkle's *Life on the Screen* (1995). Although they draw a bit on postmodernist theories of space and geography, there is a conspicuous lack of references to sociological work on identity and self (e.g., Mead, 1934; Goffman, 1959). Overall, Kolko and Reid's article demonstrates a distinctive but relatively narrow perspective on behavior management and social control in a single type of chat environment.

Another survey article in the area of conflict resolution, also from a CMC anthology, is "Conflict on the Internet" (1997) by Carnevale and Probst. Their efforts "to detail the forms and impact of electronic communication on the manner in which social conflicts are manifest and resolved" (p. 233) result in a rather sketchy treatment. However, Carnevale and Probst offer a useful definition of social conflict as "the perception of divergent interests, which means that the parties believe that they have incompatible preferences among a set of available options," emphasizing that "divergent interests can be found in all social arenas, from relations between children on the playground to international relations" (p. 234). Focusing on taxonomies of conflict resolution procedures as well as negotiation strategies (i.e., rule-making and rule-enforcement), Carnevale and Probst identify "three broad classes of procedures for resolving conflicts . . . (a) working together to find a solution; (b) taking the conflict to a third-party decision maker, and (c) taking independent action" (p. 234). Well-organized but rather shallow, the contributions of this article to the study of behavior management and social control in online environments lie primarily in the respectable list of references Carnevale and Probst provide, as well as the fact that they discuss newsgroups, BBSs, and the Web, thus covering a variety of virtual communities.

Among the topics figuring prominently in the core literature on behavior management and social control are issues related to rule-breaking and rule-enforcement in online environments. Several researchers offer studies that address specific types of misbehavior, while others probe the activities of virtual bad guys and good guys from a number of distinct directions. A linguistic perspective on a particular variety of misbehavior in online environments is presented in "Spam: Heteroglossia and Harassment in Cyberspace" (1996/1997) by Stivale, a professor of French. In this article originally published in a literary journal, Stivale outlines a basic taxonomy of spam (i.e., rule-breaking), categorizing this phenomenon into three types: playful, ambiguous, and pernicious. As noted in Chapter Three of this report, Stivale also includes under the rubric of spam the type of online sexual harassment generally referred to as virtual rape. In addition, Stivale discusses the effectiveness of both external laws and internal rules (i.e., rule-making), with interesting references to the Canter and Siegel green card newsgroup spam covered by others (e.g., Moore, 1995; Wisebrod, 1995) as well as the Baker newsgroup and Bungle MOO rapes described in previous chapters herein. Though somewhat limited in scope, the value of Stivale's study derives from his concentration on one genre of misbehavior in post as well as chat environments.

A similar study of behavior management and control that focuses on a particular type of rule-breaking, but from a social psychology perspective, is Joinson's "Causes and Implications of Disinhibited Behavior on the Internet" (1998). In this survey article from a CMC anthology, Joinson links flaming and what he describes as "excessive self-disclosure" in developing "a general model of disinhibition on the Internet that stresses the joint role of both context and self-awareness" (p. 43). As Joinson explains, "flaming may be a subset of disinhibited communicative behavior on the Internet, but it is not the only disinhibited behavior on the Internet" (p. 47). According to Joinson, "disinhibition on the Internet is not defined as flaming or hostile communication, but rather is seen as any behavior that is characterized by an *apparent* reduction in concerns for self-presentation and the judgment of others" (p. 44). After reviewing various psychological theories and models to account for disinhibited behavior (i.e., rule-breaking) in both face-to-face and CMC environments, Joinson concludes that "just because people are privately self-aware does not mean that their behavior is regulated only by internal standards and goals. Rather their behavior is a product of self-regulation and context-dependent norms" (p. 57). One such context-dependent norm he identifies is a general attitude of informality among relative strangers online: "the social norm of Net behavior allows people the freedom to contact those they do not know in an informal manner" (p. 56). Joinson also refers to the role of netiquette guides and FAQs (i.e., rule-making) in orienting online conduct, pointing out that the Usenet newsgroup alt.flame issues its own special FAQ, which suggests that "flaming has certain rules and regulations—not something one would expect for an allegedly uncontrollable, hostile activity" (pp. 44–46). Especially noteworthy is Joinson's inclusion of material about disinhibited behavior on the Web (pp. 47–48), although he mostly refers to "surfing" or "browsing" behavior, which typically involves passive viewing rather than active social intercourse. An added boon of Joinson's work is that, hailing from the United Kingdom, he introduces references and examples not often cited in North American bibliographies. All in all, Joinson provides a sound treatment covering one genre of misbehavior in several post environments.

Bringing a psychotherapeutic perspective to the topics of rule-breaking and rule-enforcement, Suler offers a matched pair of lively and perceptive articles from his electronic book, *The Psychology of Cyberspace* (1996–1999), much of which is devoted to his own participant-observer experiences on the Palace, a genre of chat environment. In one piece, "The Bad Boys of Cyberspace: Deviant Behavior in Online Multimedia Communities and Strategies for Managing It" (1997b), Suler discusses rule-breakers ranging from mischief-makers and pranksters that he labels "SNERTs" (Snot-Nosed Eros-Ridden Teenagers) to more severe abusers he deems "the truly obnoxious trouble-makers." Outlining virtual offense types (i.e., rule-breaking) with an emphasis on offender personalities and effective "intervention" strategies for "managing deviant behavior" and "attempting to control offensive behavior" (i.e., rule-enforcement), Suler describes several levels of punishment, varying in severity from mild reproach to utter banishment, as well as three dimensions for categorizing enforcement strategies: preventative versus remedial, interpersonal versus technical, and user versus superuser. Suler's second article of relevance to the present study, "Knowledge, Power, Wisdom ... and Your Very Own Asterisk: Wizards at the 'Palace'" (1997a), concerns the superusers called "wizards" (i.e., rule-enforcers). Suler's article on wizards covers similar territory as its bad boys companion piece, but zeroes in on system administrators who have the responsibility, power, and dubious privilege of dealing most directly with the electronic antics of bad boys. The insights Suler provides about the personalities, motivations, and activities of rule-breakers and rule-enforcers in these two pieces are thought-provoking and his research commendable for its depth. However, Suler's tight focus on just one type of chat environment (i.e., the Palace), as well as his exclusively psychological viewpoint, detract from the overall substance of these studies. An additional deficiency is that Suler fails to provide many references other than to his own material, taking for granted familiarity with general psychological principles and building no bridges to related areas of inquiry. Thus, Suler's work is long on data and short on connections to disciplines outside his own area of expertise, but his observations about bad-boy SNERTs and superuser wizards are admirable in detail as well as in applicability to rule-breakers and rule-enforcers in other online environments.

An approach similar to Suler's in ethnographic flavor comes from two journalists, Lessard and Baldwin, who often write about Internet affairs for computer magazines. In their book *Netslaves: True Tales of Working the Web* (2000; see also http://www.netslaves.com), Lessard and Baldwin critique human relations practices in "new media" companies through a series of case studies of personality types they identify among Internet industry employees. Though their title misleadingly implies an emphasis on the Web, Lessard and Baldwin actually concentrate on large, commercial meta-environments, ISPs whose names are barely disguised and easily deciphered: "Cyber-America" as America Online; "CompuTime" as CompuServe; and "Synergy" as Prodigy. Writing in a breezy and colorful style, with plenty of tongue-in-cheek commentary clearly intended to amuse, Lessard and Baldwin's account of people found behind the scenes in the Internet industry takes inspiration from Terkel's classic, *Working* (1974), and demonstrates a similar "roving reporter" method. Based on their explorations as "amateur anthropologists" (p. 5), Lessard and Baldwin develop a "hierarchical pecking order" (p. 6) of "netslaves" working in the "New Media Caste System" (p. 15), ranging from lowly technicians they call "garbagemen" to Web-designing "cab drivers," "cowboy and card shark" programmers, project-managing "fry cooks," and so forth, up to top-level "robber barons" such as Bill Gates of Microsoft (p. 202). Among the various characterizations offered by Lessard and Baldwin, of primary interest for the present study of misbehavior are their depictions of two kinds of rule-enforcers working in virtual communities hosted in commercial meta-environments: "cyber-cops" and "social workers." As an example of the first category, they describe a character they call "Officer Kilmartin":

> Kilmartin was a Cop—a Cyber-Cop who patrolled the mean streets of Synergy from dusk to dawn in search of perverts, freaks, stalkers, and other undesirables threatening Synergy's carefully managed "family" image. It was tedious, tiring work, yet he kept doing it. He found the seamy underside of online behavior strangely intriguing. He had grown accustomed—in a sense, addicted—to a daily dose of deviance. (2000, pp. 43–44)

To illustrate the second category, Lessard and Baldwin recount the trials and tribulations of Cindy, the "Celebrity Chat Queen for Cyber-America" (pp. 64–76); but they also portray fairly accurately the sorts of activities in which moderators, hosts, and other types of socially-oriented rule-enforcers engage:

> From colorful tents pitched inside chat rooms, bulletin boards, and special-interest Web sites, these tireless souls did everything from solving marital problems and providing sustenance to weary surfers to serving as hosts and liaisons for celebrities and other notables visiting the electronic community. What's more, the members of this caste all seemed to be experts in their particular field of interest. . . . Social Workers are by definition understanding types, but instantaneously transform into modem-wielding Furies whenever they feel their territory is being threatened. . . . the urge to protect their communities. . . . it's their job to keep the conversations lively and on-topic and to imbue their communities' inhabitants with a sense of safety, of having a place to go to escape the stresses of their everyday life. (2000, p. 61)

In addition, Lessard and Baldwin also present cases of upstanding employees who turn into rule-breaking renegades, particularly to take revenge upon employers they feel have wronged them (pp. 139–140), as well as several examples of rule-breaking such as cybergang uprisings (pp. 48–49) and email bombs (p. 130). Albeit anecdotal in tone and not particularly profound, selected portions of Lessard and Baldwin's book contribute vivid data about rule-breaking and rule enforcement in large-scale, commercial meta-environments, infrequently addressed in the core literature on behavior management and social control.

Some of the most rigorous work on rule-breaking and rule-enforcement in online environments comes from MacKinnon, a former police officer later employed as a political scientist at the Advanced Communication Technologies Laboratory of the University of Texas. Drawing on his combined background in law-enforcement and political science, MacKinnon addresses what he describes as political anthropology and governance in virtual environments in "The Cybergovernance Trilogy," a series of articles about online crime and punishment published in CMC anthologies. The first of MacKinnon's articles, "Searching for the Leviathan in Usenet" (1995), covers censorship and moderation in Usenet newsgroups (i.e., rule-enforcement), while the third piece, "The Social Construction of Rape in Virtual Reality" (1998), examines the Bungle LambdaMOO episode (i.e., rule-breaking and rule-enforcement), providing a fine complement to Mnookin's (1996) focus on rule-making aspects of the Bungle affair. For the present study, however, the most illuminating segment of MacKinnon's trilogy is the second article, "Punishing the Persona: Correctional Strategies for the Virtual Offender" (1997), in which MacKinnon builds on the virtues of the other two pieces about Usenet and LambdaMOO, here taking on "virtual governance, crime, and punishment" in both post and chat environments. His taxonomies of virtual crimes (pp. 209–212) and hierarchical punishment guidelines, including "correctional strategies" and "virtual penalties" (pp. 223–231), constitute prime examples of serious scholarly attention to these areas (i.e., rule-breaking and rule-enforcement). This 1997 article is especially robust on the history of punishment, though MacKinnon digresses a bit about corporal sanctions (pp. 214–217). He even discusses hackers, constructing a "rogues' gallery" in which he compares Mitnick's Internet-wide hacking penetrations (mentioned in Chapter Four herein) with the Bungle MOO and Baker newsgroup rapes, considering Mitnick to have been a virtual rapist as well (pp. 208–214). MacKinnon's view both downgrades the level of Mitnick's offenses and upgrades the severity of the virtual rapes, hearkening back to the definition schizophrenia discussed in Chapter Four that runs rampant in the realm of cybercrime and law-breaking. But overall, MacKinnon's 1997 analysis furnishes an outstanding example of research on behavior management and social control in both post and chat environments; and if that were not sufficient, MacKinnon also contributes a laudable set of references, including many of the core studies of misbehavior and rule-breaking reviewed herein.

More recent scholarship on behavior management and social control in online environments which focuses on rule-breaking and rule-enforcement comes from Williams, a social scientist in the United Kingdom who studies criminal justice. Building on the work of MacKinnon (1995, 1997, 1998), as well related CMC research, Williams offers two survey articles from a unique perspective that blends criminology with the linguistic theory of "speech acts" proposed by Austin in *How to Do Things with Words* (1962). In Austin's framework, illocutionary speech acts are performed in producing utterances of warning, promise, or request, as Williams illustrates: "at the same time as what is being said, something is also being done; the policeman stating 'I am charging you with assault' is not saying something which has a delayed consequence, the consequence is immediate" (2001, p. 155). Williams clarifies the relevance of such illocutionary verbal performances to the study of online misbehavior by explaining how interpersonal CMC privileges text over most other modes of communication, therefore inviting harassment and abuse like virtual rape by means of text-based offensive discourse:

> The very nature of interaction within computer-mediated communication has forged a convention that allocates more "functions" to text than usually granted in the actual world. Within virtual environments, text functions as dialogue, action, description and emotion which combined makes context. Such a burden on text arguably leaves it susceptible to misuse, being employed as an effective vehicle for derision. (2000)

In "Virtually Criminal: Discourse, Deviance, and Anxiety Within Virtual Communities" (2000), a journal article, Williams discusses derisory discourse (i.e., rule-breaking) in the Baker newsgroup and Bungle MOO rapes, as well as a chat environment known as CyberWorlds, stressing that enforcement has a double purpose of both sanctioning offenders and alleviating harm to victims and anxiety in witnesses and other community members. Williams's second article, "The Language of Cybercrime" (2001), appearing in an Internet crime anthology, covers several well-known defamation lawsuits involving ISP liability issues, as well as the Bungle incident and the JennyMUSH rape reported by Reid (1999) discussed in Chapter Three herein. In his second article, Williams focuses on suitable forms of redress (i.e., rule-enforcement) for the harm inflicted by verbal assaults (i.e., rule-breaking), which he describes as "words that wound." He suggests that "harms online may vary in severity, and that any form of redress should reflect such difference" (2001, p. 164). However, Williams claims that "recognizing the level of harm induced by such acts seems the first milestone to overcome" (2001, p. 163) because virtual injuries are often dismissed as inconsequential. He criticizes the lack of importance attributed to online misbehavior by asserting a fundamental unity between life in physical and digital environments:

The "real" and "virtual" are not separate experiences and as such the nature of online communication enables a perpetrator to inflict recognizable levels of harm upon a victim via textual slurs and abuse. . . . It is important to understand that events within online settings are not wholly separate from those in the offline world. Such a strict dichotomy between the "real" and the "virtual" must be nullified if the consequences of abusive acts online are to be fully acknowledged. . . . the consequences of online abuse and harassment can manifest in the "real" world even if the act was performed in a "virtual" setting. (2001, pp. 152–154)

And to underscore how online problems intermingle with and impact on life offline, Williams invokes the LambdaMOO rape example:

When Legba was sexually assaulted by Mr. Bungle, it was the online persona that was victimised and "physically" assaulted through text. However, the psychological effects and harms were experienced by the creator of Legba's persona (Dibble, 1993). It seems clear that any injurious illocution online strikes at the identity of the computer user in the offline world. (2001, p. 162)

In general, Williams's work appears aimed at convincing criminologists to take more seriously "sub-criminal behaviour that can fragment online community cohesion" (2000), i.e., the lower end of the spectrum of trouble in cyberspace, as he explains:

Credit card fraud, computer hacking, and the dissemination of child pornography over computer networks are but a few of the "high tech" crimes reported on and sensationalised by the media. Yet what is to be made of these other forms of deviance that are performed on a daily basis within virtual environments whose legal status remains dubious? The acts of harassment and even rape have arguably been re-engineered from their "physical" manifestations into derisory and harmful textual performances that are present within online community interaction. Those who misuse computer-mediated communication to disrupt online social interaction are beginning to be labelled as deviants and criminals, who have as their source of derision their online victims. Unlike other "high tech" crimes, both the practice and the consequences of these acts of deviance take place within the virtual environment, making these deviant performances unique in both aetiology and motivation. (2000)

In his own field of criminology, according to Williams, "the academic community has yet to acknowledge forms of online sociopathic behaviour as either 'valid' forms of criminality or inquiry" (2000). Moreover, Williams criticizes CMC research for being "often characterised by a lack of insight into more criminological matters of deviance, regulation and forms of online justice" (2000). With this pair of articles that combine perspectives from two highly germane disciplines, criminology and linguistics, in addressing one genre of misbehavior—derisory discourse—in both post and chat environments, Williams makes a solid contribution to the study of misbehavior online.

From down under, two Australians, Rintel and Pittam, provide a trio of pieces that also approach behavior management and social control in online environments from linguistic perspectives, with sociological and anthropological influences as well. First, on his own, Rintel's provocative paper published on his Web site, "Nothing Worth Saying?: Communicatory Freedom on Internet Relay Chat" (1995), presents a linguistic case study of comp.unix.admin, a Usenet newsgroup populated by systems administrators. Framed in the context of free speech debates, Rintel offers a content analysis of issues raised in one newsgroup "thread" or series of posts from 1991, revolving around the pros and cons of IRC from a security point of view, examining "how the thread functions metalingually to reveal what these administrators believe are the important concepts of communicatory freedom and control of Internet communications systems generally" (1995). What is striking about this study of a post community discussing chat communities is that Rintel provides data from system administrators about dealing with troublesome online behavior (i.e., rule-enforcement) such as software piracy and password hacking on IRC (i.e., rule-breaking). Furthermore, pointing to the inherent problems underlying the jurisdiction circus discussed in Chapter Four herein, Rintel rightly asserts that systems administrators can play key roles in regulating behavior in cyberspace:

> The Internet is generally unregulated. Due to the circumstances of its inception, growing from the largely academic ARPANET, no single government, corporation, or institution of any kind owns the majority of connections to the Internet, and therefore no single body has the authority to regulate or police it. . . . While it is true to say that no one body can control the Internet by right of internationally recognised law, there is one group that could effectively wield control over most of the policy about communication on the Internet— the system administrators of the various computers that make up the networks. (1995)

Rintel follows up his work on IRC in two collaborative pieces with Pittam. In "Communicative and Non-Communicative Silence on Internet Relay Chat: Management and Function" (1997a), a convention paper, Rintel and Pittam present a case study of how silence is managed on IRC in comparison with face-to-face interaction, based on content analysis of logs from two IRC channels, #penpals and #australia, grounded in Goffman's (1959) work on presentation of self. Rintel and Pittam mention various sorts of misbehavior found on IRC (i.e., rule-breaking) such as flooding, "the rapid transmission of several lines of text" which "forces all conversations to scroll by quicker than normal, taking up space on the screen" (1997a). They astutely observe that "newbies" (novice users) often commit flooding due to anxiety about what they perceive as overly protracted silence from other participants. Rintel and Pittam also consider techniques for dealing with misbehavior on IRC (i.e., rule-enforcement) such as the role of silence in ignoring offenders, and technical methods employed by privileged superusers, such as "opers" using the "kill" command to remove troublemakers from entire IRC networks, as well as their forced removal from IRC channels by "chanops" using the "kick" command. In "Strangers in a Strange Land: Interaction Management on Internet Relay Chat" (1997b), Rintel and Pittam provide a similar content analysis of the same set of IRC logs. In this journal article, they compare interaction management strategies used in opening and closing encounters on IRC and in face-to-face situations, informed not only by Goffman's (1959) work, but by elements from Hall's (1959, 1966) anthropological research as well. As in their other study, Rintel and Pittam mention several genres of IRC misbehavior (i.e., rule-breaking), giving more examples of newbies flooding IRC channels, as well as another common newbie sin: typing in all upper-case letters, a format normally reserved online for special textual emphasis. Additionally, Rintel and Pittam note the use of offensive nicknames as well as disputes over nickname ownership and provocative public statements. Again, they review techniques of forcibly removing offenders from IRC channels and servers by means of kicks, bans, and kills (i.e., rule-enforcement). Of particular interest in this second article is how Rintel and Pittam highlight levels of online experience among "relatively new [versus] more experienced users" as well as "whether interactants appear to be strangers or not" as influential factors in organizing social interaction online:

> On IRC, perhaps more so than with other media, experience and depth of acquaintance may form related continua that together have a dynamic impact on the management strategies adopted. While a user's experience is likely to grow over time, the user's place on the acquaintance dimension will vary depending on the other interactants. When meeting a stranger, each user has a constant place on the experience dimension and an initially low place on the acquaintance dimension. One can imagine a user being an experienced stranger and experienced acquaintance, or a novice stranger and a novice acquaintance, within the same interaction. In each case, the amount and type of interaction management strategies may be different, which may have a corresponding effect on the type of relationship that is established. (1997b)

Though limited mostly to providing useful data on rule-breaking and rule-enforcement in IRC chat environments, Rintel and Pittam's pieces nevertheless demonstrate a fruitful blend of linguistic content analysis with Goffman's sociological approach.

Two sociologists from the United Kingdom, Rutter and G. Smith, contribute a duet of articles, both case studies of RumCom.local, a newsgroup on an independent ISP-based system. In "Ritual Aspects of CMC Sociability" (1999a), a conference paper, Rutter and G. Smith develop a hybrid sociological approach: "a useful framework for understanding the role of information in sociable exchanges is provided by the tradition of studies of sociability established by Simmel and by Goffman's sociology of the interaction order." They apply this sociological framework in analyzing the netiquette operating in RumCom.local (i.e., rule-making), stressing that "the enactment of netiquette is a complex phenomenon deeply linked to the development of a sense of community."

Elaborating on the socially significant relationship between netiquette and community, Rutter and G. Smith argue that:

> The issues addressed by netiquette ... should not be dismissed as merely superficial or as secondary to the substantive, informational nature of CMC. Netiquette is far from "mere" and it extends beyond the stipulative lists of AUPs. ... [netiquette] includes not only ... established and accepted guidelines for computer-mediated communication ... but also those more subtle and local rules of interaction. These rules of netiquette codes have to be interpreted by users and implemented appropriately and these practical issues involve judgmental work that is open to disagreement and dispute by newsgroup coparticipants. This negotiation contributes not only to the sense of community found within the group but also the development of virtual boundaries around it, which mark it as separate for other internet users and newsgroups. (1999a)

Rutter and G. Smith provide another case study of RumCom.local, this time centering on identity management in cyberspace, in "Presenting the Off-Line Self in an Everyday, Online Environment" (1999b), published on the Web. The major conclusion they reach in this second piece is that users often present non-fictional online selves which greatly resemble their offline identities, evidence that participants "blur distinctions between on- and offline selves" (1999b). While Rutter and G. Smith's pair of studies is restricted to one post environment, they do tackle a newsgroup system other than Usenet for a change, and their research also contributes by applying Goffman's ideas about interaction in combination with Simmel's (1949) notions of sociability to the analysis of rule-making activities online.

A similar but richer sociological approach to post environments comes from Danish cultural sociologist Gotved. In "Newsgroup Interaction as Urban Life" (2000), Gotved offers a case study of rec.arts.books.tolkien, a Usenet newsgroup devoted to fantasy author J. R. R. Tolkien. Building on Baym's rec.arts.tv.soaps research (1993/1997b, 1995, 1998), in this conference paper, based on her doctoral dissertation written in Danish, Gotved focuses on norms of interaction (i.e., rule-making) and strategies for upholding such norms (i.e., rule-enforcement). Noting that "establishing as well as enforcing such norms is a continuing challenge" (2000), Gotved identifies a set of norms in this particular newsgroup that parallel general netiquette guidelines, as well specific guidelines which she refers to as "parochial" norms, in accordance with urban sociologist Lofland's distinctions (1998) discussed previously in Chapter Two herein. As an example of "public netiquette" Gotved offers the general Usenet principle, "Do not use newsgroups as sources for homework"; for "parochial netiquette," she cites this particular group's norm, "Show respect to Tolkien." And based on the distinction between public and parochial norms, Gotved observes that "the strategies to make the norms respected among the participants differ accordingly, drawing a continuum from polite teasing to flaming." Gotved also emphasizes the gradual evolution of community norms: "perhaps the single most important issue in establishing such commonly accepted guidelines and strategies is time, closely followed by a certain amount of often returning participants." Reminiscent of the argument made in Chapter Two herein about rules becoming more readily apparent when broken than when maintained, Gotved remarks that "normative guidelines are always most striking when they are broken and the process of reestablishing the boundaries (and thereby the working consensus) starts up." And in addition to rule-making issues, Gotved also considers typical genres of newsgroup violations (i.e., rule-breaking) such as "trolling" found also in Baym's r.a.t.s. studies: "it is not the core participants in rec.arts.books.tolkien who troll, but newbies or non-serious regulars, who try to coax the serious Tolkien fan into long and detailed explanations of a given topic." But most remarkable in Gotved's paper is her sociological perspective rooted not only in the work of Goffman (1959) on presentation of self, but also on the urban studies of Lofland (1973, 1998) as well as Simmel's views on metropolitan strangers (1950). Gotved's assertion that "there is a likeness between the modern metropolis and cyberspace," both recalls and complements media ecologist Strate's piece on containers, computers, and cities (1996a). But Gotved emphasizes Simmel's notion of the stranger in her explanation of the urban nature of online environments:

> Cyberspace is in fact often described in the same manner as the early metropolis, where the sociologist Simmel around 1900 painted a fearing picture of the changed life forms. The ever-changing social environment, with strangers all over and a lot of fast-moving traffic caused nervous breakdowns in the human relationship with the surroundings. . . . The term "urbanism" does not refer to the life in any actual city, but to the broader culture in the modernity, where life forms are characterized by mobility, diversity, and networks of relations. Even the regions distant from actual urban space are merged with the urbanism, through different media and personal networks as well as communication and information technology.
>
> In urbanism (online as well as offline) life is characterized primarily by the heavy presence of strangers in the open public space. The individual is an anonymous character in the heterogeneous crowd and it is neither a possibility nor a wish to know all the people around. Of course there are nuances to this picture; nuances made from localities, habits, and transport corridors. There are neighborhoods and newsgroups where one is recognized, stores where one is a regular customer, people of whom one has a remote knowledge. But the main condition in urban space is anonymity in surroundings filled with strangers on the move. (2000)

Finally, expressing similar sentiments as Williams (2001), Gotved stresses the continuum between life online and off:

> The distinction between tangible life and cyber-spatial life is perforated, and the networks of relations span both at the same time. Despite the different kinds of appearances and lines of action in physical and virtual areas, it is basically the same: interactions, organisations, and communities in urbanism. Human activity on the net reflects, involves, and responds on life as a whole; different

kinds of community of interest arise and fall in constant overlaps between actual experiences and digital mediating. . . . The net and the city overlap, they influence each other and are interwoven in complex patterns. . . . Everyday social interactions on an interpersonal level are visible on the net as well as in the city; the net is not a parallel world but a commonplace part of town. (2000)

Fuller appreciation of Gotved's research efforts must await publication in English of further material from her Danish dissertation. At present, the greatest contribution Gotved makes in this abbreviated English version is to reinforce the relevance of Goffman's research and to call attention to the pertinence of Lofland and Simmel's inquiries in urban sociology to the study of behavior management and social control in online environments.

Paradoxically, the most appealing of all the core studies that deal with behavior management and social control online is also the most obscure: a Goffmanesque doctoral dissertation by Surratt, *The Sociology of Everyday Life in Computer-Mediated Communities* (1996). Not a single reference to Surratt's research was encountered in other literature, though it appears in key-word searches of dissertation abstracts available electronically. Surratt presents a fascinating, multi-layered triple case study in which she compares various aspects of community life in both post and chat environments on FidoNet (a BBS), IRC, and Usenet newsgroups. Furthermore, she assembles data from several communities within each of these environments: three FidoNet nodes, two IRC channels, and three Usenet newsgroups. Addressing "norms of behavior, forms of deviance and methods of social control" (p. 54), Surratt covers the full panoply of activities related to misbehavior (i.e., rule-breaking, rule-making, and rule-enforcement). In contrast to Lessard and Baldwin's mass-market volume on "netslaves" (2000), Surratt's dissertation is the solitary book-length treatment of an academic nature in the core collection of misbehavior literature, although only two chapters are directly relevant. In chapter seven on "deviance and social control," Surratt examines "the forms of deviance that are constructed in CMC communities and the means of social control that participants have established in order to deal with that deviance" (p. 363). Chapter eight, on "social differences and inequality," travels through similar terrain as Reid's (1999) study of user hierarchies in MUDs; however, Surratt deals with no less than three such hierarchies in discussing superusers on IRC channels and servers ("chanops" and "IRCops," respectively), as well as "sysops" in FidoNet and Usenet. Besides these two pertinent chapters, the remainder of Surratt's dissertation includes comprehensive surveys of relevant sociological and virtual community research (including much of the core literature reviewed herein), enhanced by abundant data samples taken from posts, transcripts, and logs of the various communities she studied, further augmented by a meticulous bibliography especially plentiful in sociological material (e.g., Goffman, 1959, 1963; Mead, 1934; Oldenburg, 1989/1997). Moreover, Surratt points to the work of deviance sociologists Becker (1963/1973), as well as Pfuhl and Henry (1993), a pertinent line of inquiry not mentioned elsewhere in the related literature. Overall, Surratt provides some of the finest research to date on misbehavior in virtual communities; her dissertation supplied key guidance during early phases of the present investigation. If the authors of the core literature on behavior management and social control in online environments were a team, Surratt would certainly deserve the Most Valuable Player award for best all-around performance on the varsity squad of misbehavior studies. Although largely unknown, with everything to recommend it except possibly age, once uncovered, Surratt's 1996 dissertation glitters as the hidden treasure of the core collection on behavior management and social control in online environments.

A postscript to this discussion of core literature on behavior management and social control in online environments which provides a fair indication of the status quo in this line of inquiry comes from none other than Bruckman, editor of the pivotal 1994 abstract described at the outset of this chapter, "Approaches to Managing Deviant Behavior in Virtual Communities." Although Bruckman may not have pursued this topic any further at SIGCHI/ACM meetings, on January 20, 1999, in MediaMOO, the chat environment she helped create, Bruckman chaired a live symposium on the very same theme. An abstract and edited transcript of this brief but significant online event are incorporated in "Managing Deviant Behavior in Online Communities" (Bruckman, 1999). The guest panelists for Bruckman's 1999 symposium included: Glos, producer at ThirdAge Media, an online community Web site for "45+" users; Koster, developer of LegendMUD and member of the Ultima Online gaming community design team; and Moore, former director of Fujitsu's avatar-based WorldsAway community, now an independent consultant in the field of online communities. In addition, other notable virtual community leaders also showed up in the audience, such as Horn, founder of the Echo BBS and author of *Cyberville*, the 1998 book about her "online town," as well as Anderson, a seasoned LambdaMOO administrator. (Because I had corresponded with Bruckman to express interest in her 1994 abstract and related projects, and in light of my being a CMC researcher with experience as an enforcer in virtual communities on IRC, Bruckman invited me to attend the MediaMOO symposium, and my remarks appear in the transcript under the name "Janster.") The 1999 Bruckman transcript thus contains comments from savvy community leaders and other veteran managers about rule-breaking, rule-making, and rule-enforcement in a variety of online environments.

But what is most important to emphasize here, at the end of this review of literature on misbehavior and rule-breaking in virtual communities, a discussion opening with Bruckman's 1994 panel and closing with Bruckman's 1999 symposium, is that even after a span of five years, researchers continue to raise the same issues. It is instructive to compare the concerns highlighted in the two Bruckman pieces. Restating ideas from the 1994 abstract cited at the beginning of the present chapter, the summary passage Bruckman uses to introduce the 1999 symposium transcript is likewise worth quoting:

An increasing percentage of the general population have had direct experience with those pesky individuals who spoil the party. Anti-social behavior in online communities ranges from the merely annoying to the downright scary. But who determines what is too annoying to tolerate? And what can community members [and] leaders do about it? Too many community managers are reinventing the wheel; as a community, we need to learn from one another's experiences. In this symposium, we have the opportunity to learn from [representatives] of two large commercial entertainment communities about what works, what doesn't, and what it all means. (1999)

Although starting this review of literature related to misbehavior and rule-breaking in virtual communities with Bruckman's 1994 panel abstract and finishing with Bruckman's 1999 symposium transcript may lend a certain symmetry to the discussion, the latter piece, unfortunately, offers no closure. Instead, Bruckman's 1999 MediaMOO symposium transcript demonstrates beyond a doubt that critical questions about the regulation of online conduct in virtual communities still remain unanswered.

THE STATUS QUO:
THEORIES AND ANALYSES IN SEARCH OF A PARADIGM

Since Bruckman's 1999 MediaMOO symposium, the status quo with respect to research on misbehavior and rule-breaking in virtual communities has not changed significantly. Scholars continue to call for further investigation in this area. The situation is summed up in Williams's plea that online misbehavior be taken more seriously:

We find new forms of sociopathic behaviour, which present themselves in abundance, being disregarded due to their "virtual status," while similar crimes in the real world are subject to intensive investigation. . . . increasingly populated online environments are having to incorporate justice models, regulatory frameworks and security patrols in order to curtail any disruptive or potentially harmful behavior. These structures, in tandem with the aetiology of online deviance and anxiety, deserve thorough investigation. . . . If the virtual environment is to become a "second home" for a large proportion of the population, as is the case for many already, then structures that protect their fundamental rights in the actual world must be duplicated in the virtual. By unravelling the tie between the motivations of virtual deviance and regulatory practices it is hoped that enhanced methods of governance that incorporate elements of justice and fundamental human/avatar rights can be delineated, in so doing reducing levels of online anxiety and maintaining community integrity. (2000)

Yet, as suggested in the preceding review of core literature on behavior management and social control in online environments, an abundance of relevant material has begun to accumulate, offering valuable information and ideas on which to base further inquiry. At the end of Chapter Two of the present report, a telling assessment of the state of related research was cited from the work of MacKinnon: "the literature on virtual communities and cyberspace is increasing at a phenomenal rate and thereby boasts a plethora of competing theories and analyses in search of a paradigm" (1998, p. 148). The preceding review of core research about misbehavior online offers ample evidence that even today, MacKinnon's assessment of the status quo remains accurate.

Alas, there is a significant lack of integration among different research perspectives on behavior management and social control in online environments, and this fragmentation hinders progress in developing coherent approaches to the study of misbehavior in virtual communities. For instance, rarely mentioned in the core collection of relevant literature is the pair of ground-breaking 1994 publications that represent the two approaches to trouble in cyberspace introduced in Chapter Three. The 1994 Denning and Lin report discussed in Chapter Four is mentioned by Branscomb (1996) and Dutton (1996); but then, Branscomb was a member of the steering committee behind the Denning and Lin report, and Dutton participated in the meetings summarized therein. As for the 1994 Bruckman abstract contemplated at the outset of the present chapter, Surratt (1996) seems to be the sole researcher to refer to this seminal publication on misbehavior in virtual communities; but then, no references to Surratt's authoritative dissertation can be found in the core literature either.

These theories and analyses of in search of a paradigm can be seen as loose threads, separate but related lines of inquiry which beg to be woven together into a more substantial and cohesive intellectual fabric. Such various strands of research on misbehavior in virtual communities are displayed by reviewing the major perspectives offered in the core collection on behavior management and social control in online environments covered in this chapter. First, there are *general CMC* perspectives on misbehavior offered by Baym (1998), Bruckman (1994, 1999), Dutton (1996), Kollock and M. A. Smith (1996), McLaughlin et al. (1995), Reid (1999), C. B. Smith et al. (1998), and Sproull and Faraj (1995/1997). Then there are *legally-oriented* perspectives on misbehavior, such as those taken by Branscomb (1996), Danielson (1996), Denning and Lin (1994), Maltz (1996), Mnookin (1996), and Wisebrod (1995). And related to law and governance, there are also perspectives on misbehavior presented from *political science* by MacKinnon (1995, 1997, 1998), and *criminology* by Williams (2000, 2001). Perspectives involving *conflict resolution and mediation* are applied to misbehavior as well, such as Carnevale and Probst (1997), Kolko and Reid (1998), D. J. Phillips (1996), and A. D. Smith (1999). Even *journalism* is represented by Lessard and Baldwin's perspective (2000). Misbehavior is approached from *linguistic* perspectives by Rintel and Pittam (1997a, 1997b; Rintel, 1995), Stivale (1996/1997), and Williams (2000, 2001). Joinson's *social psychology* perspective (1998) is complemented by Suler's *psychotherapy* perspective (1997a, 1997b). And last but certainly not least, especially fertile perspectives from *sociology* are brought to bear on the study of misbehavior by Gotved (2000), Rutter and G. Smith (1999a, 1999b), and Surratt (1996). These various loose strands of research on behavior management and social control in online environments, woven together, highlight patterns and differences in misbehavior and the regulation of conduct in virtual communities which, in turn, help clarify the parameters of research into computer-mediated interpersonal communication in general.

It seems that researchers who broaden their scholarly vision by looking beyond the confines of mainstream CMC research make productive connections with other disciplines. Such interdisciplinary connections bring novel perspectives and additional lines of inquiry into play, thereby enriching the study of communication overall. Several contributors to the core collection on behavior management and social control in online environments furnish instructive examples of scholarship that crosses academic boundaries to great advantage. For instance, Surratt's study (1996), grounded in the sociological perspectives of Mead (1934) and Goffman (1959, 1963), not only points to the pivotal 1994 Bruckman abstract, but also to deviance sociologists Becker (1963/1973) and Pfuhl and Henry (1993), and even to urban sociologist Oldenburg (1989/1997). Similarly grounded in Goffman's work, Gotved's research (2000) not only builds on the work of Baym (1993/1997b, 1995, 1998), but also indicates the relevance of perspectives from urban sociologists Lofland (1973, 1998) and Simmel (1950). By directing attention to fresh approaches which enhance understanding of misbehavior and the regulation of online conduct, scholars such as Surratt and Gotved, among others, broaden the study of online CMC in general. Moreover, without going into too much detail, scrutiny of the bibliographies of older research cited in recent studies of online misbehavior reveals a related universe of interdisciplinary scholarly discourse. For instance, urban sociologist Lofland (1973, 1998) refers to Becker, Goffman, Hall, Mead, Mumford, Oldenburg, Simmel, and even to media ecologist Meyrowitz. Likewise, Oldenburg (1989/1997) mentions Hall, Lofland, and Simmel. Deviance sociologist Becker (1963/1973) cites Goffman, Mead, and Simmel; and Becker, in turn, is cited by Pfuhl and Henry (1993), who refer to Goffman and Simmel as well. Thus, some of the most provocative work on misbehavior in cyber places, as well as on behavior in public places offline, comes from scholars who integrate their work with research perspectives from beyond their own disciplines.

Given the status quo, in which related theories and analyses await consolidation, the study of misbehavior and rule-breaking in virtual communities is ripe for the application of a paradigm which can tie together the sorts of independent strands of pertinent research reviewed above. The field of media ecology provides such an overarching interdisciplinary framework and, as discussed in previous chapters of this report, no media ecologist to date has considered online misbehavior in any depth. Despite a certain lack of internal integration among intellectual traditions within the field, described in Chapter Two, one of the hallmarks of media ecology is to encourage cross-fertilization among different disciplines. The field of media ecology is based on intellectual traditions which excel at making connections among apparently unrelated perspectives, the work of McLuhan (1964) furnishing a cardinal example. In fact, media ecologists expect as a matter of course to look beyond any single perspective, and as result, scholars in the field are comfortable in interdisciplinary contexts. This is the specialty of the media ecology paradigm: to integrate diverse perspectives and combine approaches from different disciplines in studying various aspects of human interaction in communication environments of all kinds. Media ecologists bring multiple perspectives to bear on communication issues because of an underlying assumption that every environment entails complex systems of interconnected relationships. Because of this view, in situations involving new communication technologies, media ecologists anticipate changes on many fronts, and therefore seek a wide range of perspectives on which to draw in addressing their research targets. Media ecology thus offers a general paradigm capable of weaving together disparate research approaches into more coherent intellectual substance. In particular, the present investigation applies a media ecology framework in distilling and synthesizing relevant research on misbehavior and the regulation of online conduct in virtual communities. Demonstrating a media ecology approach to interpersonal communication in computer-mediated environments, then, the chapter which follows summarizes the findings of this research project on misbehavior in cyber places.

Chapter Six
The Regulation of
Online Conduct in Cyber Places

BREAKING, MAKING, AND ENFORCING RULES ONLINE

This investigation of misbehavior in cyber places is grounded in approaches to interpersonal computer-mediated communication ("CMC") in online environments drawn from the field of media ecology. The context of this study and its theoretical framework were explained in earlier chapters by reviewing media ecology research on space, place, situations, rules, rule-breaking, and mediated interpersonal communication, and by surveying mainstream scholarship concerning online CMC as well as virtual communities. The research method used was philosophical inquiry, and the corpus of data examined consisted of three bodies of literature related to troublesome behavior in a variety of online environments. Principal and supplementary sources provided documentary evidence for analysis. Principal sources included published analyses and accounts of troublesome online behavior, from both scholarly and popular literature, available in print as well as electronically. Supplementary sources involved material pertaining to the regulation of conduct produced by and for users of online environments. Asynchronous post environments and synchronous chat environments, as well as meta-environments offering both modes of communication, were considered: the Internet overall; electronic mailing lists ("listservs"); Usenet newsgroups; Internet Relay Chat ("IRC"); Multi-User Dungeons or Domains ("MUDs") and MUDs-Object-Oriented ("MOOs"); the Palace; independent bulletin board systems ("BBSs"); networks like America Online ("AOL") and CompuServe; and the World Wide Web.

The investigation yielded both general and specific findings. Discussion of these results begins by summarizing general findings which have already been mentioned throughout this report. Then, specific findings are presented which address the primary research problem of this philosophical study: to analyze and assess, on the basis of the literature, how people regulate misbehavior in virtual communities on the Internet.

Throughout the preceding chapters which examine the source literature used to provide data for this investigation of online misbehavior, four general findings are evident. These general findings serve as the foundations for the design of this study and the overall structure of this report.

The first general finding involves the organization of relevant source material into three areas: trouble brewing in cyberspace (Chapter Three), cybercrime and law-breaking on the Internet (Chapter Four), and misbehavior and rule-breaking in virtual communities (Chapter Five).

Related to this first general finding is the second general finding: the identification of major relevant issues discussed in each of these bodies of source material, displayed in the selection and arrangement of topics in the three corresponding chapters.

In the source material on trouble brewing in cyberspace (Chapter Three), the emergence of an infamous triad of online behavior (i.e., flaming, spamming, and virtual rape) was identified as a factor contributing to the evolution of a frontier mentality that persists even today. Evidence was presented of an ensuing climate in which many people perceive the Internet as besieged; and two kinds of research approaches to troublesome online behavior were distinguished. A pair of key publications was singled out as representing these two types of research approaches to trouble in cyberspace: on the one hand, externally-oriented approaches focusing on cybercrime and law-breaking throughout the Internet (represented by the 1994 Denning and Lin report); and on the other hand, internally-oriented approaches, focusing on misbehavior and rule-breaking within virtual communities (represented by the 1994 Bruckman abstract).

The source material on cybercrime and law-breaking on the Internet (Chapter Four) was gathered primarily from the realms of computer science and jurisprudence, and found to emphasize the higher end of the spectrum of troublesome conduct in online environments, situations where law-making and law-enforcement are handled by external authorities and institutions offline. In the context of the Internet, laws were defined as external, highly formalized legislation, established and enforced outside online environments. Research approaches to cybercrime and law-breaking throughout the Internet were characterized as taking technical perspectives stressing technological and legal dimensions of troublesome online behavior. Significant issues identified in research on cybercrime and law-breaking on the Internet include: online security, attacks, and viruses; hackers and other denizens of the cyberspace underground; First Amendment follies involving dissent, free speech, and censorship online; definition schizophrenia causing confusion in distinguishing between malevolent criminals and mischievous pranksters; and the jurisdiction circus in transnational cyberspace with no ringmaster in sight.

The source material on misbehavior and rule-breaking in virtual communities (Chapter Five) was gathered primarily from the realms of communication and media theory, and found to emphasize the lower end of the spectrum of troublesome conduct in online environments, situations where rule-making and rule-enforcement are handled internally by participants themselves within their online environments, with appeals to external authorities and institutions offline used only as a last resort. In the context of virtual communities, rules were defined as internal regulations, expressed in varying degrees of formality, developed and enforced within online environments. Research approaches to misbehavior and rule-breaking in virtual communities were characterized as taking humanistic perspectives stressing sociological and psychological dimensions of troublesome online behavior. Significant issues in research on misbehavior and rule-breaking in virtual communities involve behavior management and social control in online environments, leading to specific findings of this investigation discussed further ahead.

The third general finding of this study consists of the identification of a core collection of pertinent research on behavior management and social control in online environments, discussed in Chapter Five. To have unearthed, assembled, and reviewed for the first time a specialized collection including over thirty core sources which directly address aspects of online misbehavior is an accomplishment which in and of itself constitutes a substantial result of this investigation.

The last general finding, revealed by analyzing the core collection on behavior management and social control in online environments, involves the organization of the study of misbehavior into three distinct but related areas, corresponding to three sets of intertwined activities: rule-breaking, rule-making, and rule-enforcement. The organization of misbehavior as a research topic into these three related sets of activities raises several questions.

Why organize activities revolving around misbehavior into the three areas of rule-breaking, rule-making, and rule-enforcement? The answer is that misbehavior clearly involves the breaking of rules; while the regulation of misbehavior—i.e., what people do about misbehavior—involves the making of rules and their enforcement. Support for this tripartite division exists in the related literature. For example, deviance sociologists Pfuhl and Henry divide the subject along similar lines: a set of rule-breaking activities on the one hand, and on the other, two sets of activities, rule-making and rule-enforcement, which together, encompass the ways people deal with misbehavior. According to Pfuhl and Henry, "deviance, then, is an ongoing outcome of the complex process through which people seek to create a sense of social order; most especially it emerges from their rule-making and rule-enforcing activities" (1993, p. 24). Cybercrime experts D. E. Denning and Lin likewise differentiate between rule-making and rule-enforcement: "although making rules for electronic networks is challenging, enforcing the rules may be even more problematic" (1994, p. 23). And the three paragraphs of the pivotal Bruckman abstract about managing online misbehavior (1994, p. 183), cited at the outset of Chapter Five herein, reflect this tripartite distinction as well. Bruckman's first paragraph describes misbehavior, i.e., rule-breaking:

It is an unfortunate fact of life that where there are multi-user computer systems, there will be antisocial behavior. On bulletin board systems (BBSs), there are those who persist in being obscene, harassing, and libelous. In virtual worlds such as MUDs, there are problems of theft, vandalism, and virtual rape.

The second paragraph addresses issues related to rule-making, and moves on to raise matters of rule-enforcement as well:

Behavior is "deviant" if it is not in accordance with community standards. How are such standards developed? Should standards be established by system administrators and accepted as a condition of participation, or should they be developed by community members? Once a particular person's behavior is deemed unacceptable, what steps should be taken? Should such steps be taken by individuals, such as "filters" or "kill" files on BBSs, and "gagging" or "ignoring" on MUDs? Or should the administrators take action, banning an individual from the system or censoring their postings? What is the appropriate balance between centralized and decentralized solutions?

And the third paragraph elaborates on rule-enforcement issues:

Gags and filters are computational solutions to deviant behavior. Are there appropriate social solutions? How effective are approaches like feedback from peers, community forums, and heart-to-heart chats with sympathetic system administrators? Are different approaches effective with communities of different sizes? What is the appropriate balance between social and technological solutions?

Another question which arises about the three sets of activities related to misbehavior—i.e., rule-breaking, rule-making, and rule-enforcement—is why address them in this order, the answer to which is not so obvious. Common sense suggests that rule-making precedes rule-breaking and rule-enforcement: after all, if misbehavior involves breaking rules and incurring disciplinary consequences, there must be rules to break and enforce. Nevertheless, though perhaps a counter-intuitive notion, rule-making activities often follow rule-breaking and rule-enforcement, as reactions to and ways of dealing with behavior which transgresses previously unstated, informal rules and norms. Implicit support for taking rule-breaking as the initial point of departure can be found in the three-paragraph sequence from the 1994 Bruckman abstract cited above. Explicit support for this order is provided by sociologists Pfuhl and Henry. In discussing the chapter structure of their volume on deviance, Pfuhl and Henry offer the following reason for starting with rule-breaking: "Breaking Rules could have followed our subsequent discussion of making rules, since, in many cases rule making is the prior activity. However, behaviors that become deviant may also exist before they invoke the action to ban them" (1993, p. xiii). So rule-making activities do not necessarily precede rule-breaking activities. Nor do they necessarily precede rule-enforcement activities either. Even before explicit rules have been made, misbehavior may occur that provokes impromptu, on-the-spot reactions to stop the objectionable conduct and deal with the offender. Instances of spontaneous enforcement may then stimulate subsequent rule-making activities which justify and institutionalize such ad-hoc enforcement after the fact. More significant than questions of sequence or order, though, are the distinctions and relationships among these three sets of activities: on the one hand, misbehavior, i.e., rule-breaking; and on the other hand, ways and means of regulating online conduct and dealing with misbehavior, i.e., rule-making and rule-enforcement.

These, then, are the general findings of this report on misbehavior and the regulation of conduct in virtual communities. The general findings furnish the background and context for contemplating the specific findings of the study, presented below according to the three sets of intertwined activities distinguished herein: rule-breaking, rule-making, and rule-enforcement.

In analyzing the specific findings of this investigation of online misbehavior, several situational variables were taken into account, in accordance with the media ecology framework used for this study, described in Chapter Two, based on approaches to interpersonal communication which focus on social behavior in group situations in mediated as well as face-to-face environments (e.g., Goffman, Meyrowitz, and Nystrom). Related theoretical literature suggested initially that situational variables involving space, place, and rules are extremely relevant in assessing how people deal with misbehavior in virtual communities. But further analysis of the data provided in the source material revealed three additional situational variables to be critically important in understanding patterns and differences in rule-breaking, rule-making, and rule-enforcement online. These additional situational variables in online environments relate to roles, degrees of co-presence, and levels of access.

The first situational variable revealed by the analysis to be significant involves *roles* enacted in online environments. Associated with the three sets of corresponding activities, three primary roles related to misbehavior in virtual communities were identified: rule-breaker, rule-maker, and rule-enforcer. The analysis also uncovered several secondary roles in online environments that are infrequently discussed in the related literature, such as victim, witness, bystander, and absent-but-concerned community member. In a sense, these secondary roles make up a fourth class of participant that might generally be characterized as "rule-follower": ordinary rule-abiding citizens who may or may not take part in the primary activities. Although the notion of a fourth set of roles is not developed in this study, such secondary roles related to misbehavior online no doubt merit further inquiry in their own right. In addition, the relationships among online roles and those who enact them differ in terms of hierarchies of authority, status, privilege, and prestige within particular virtual communities.

The second situational variable found to be significant involves *degrees of co-presence* in online environments. Though this study assumed from the outset a certain degree of spatial co-presence in that virtual community participants frequent given cyber places, the results of this investigation indicate that varying degrees of temporal co-presence are also factors affecting patterns of rule-breaking, rule-making, and rule-enforcement online . In particular, temporal differences between asynchronous post environments (in which communication is delayed) versus synchronous chat environments (in which communication is almost immediate) appear to influence activities related to misbehavior and the regulation of online conduct in important ways.

The last situational variable discovered to be significant in analyzing online misbehavior involves *levels of access* to particular online environments. In accordance with the theoretical discussion of space and place in Chapter Two, the extent to which virtual communities are public or private turns out to be pertinent in analyzing misbehavior online. Specifically, whether a community is open to the public (e.g., a Usenet newsgroup) or restricted to members (e.g., an AOL message board) makes a difference in activities related to misbehavior. Furthermore, as with offline space and place, there are semi-public, parochial virtual communities in the mid-range such as private AOL chat rooms, to which some but not all AOL members have access while non-members do not. Likewise, there are communities where levels of access are flexible and not necessarily fixed: for example, IRC channels may be instantly converted from public to private with a single command. On the other hand, membership in some private virtual communities is extremely limited, often with requirements such as participants demonstrating special interests or expertise, or corroborating their identities in the offline world (e.g., academically-oriented communities such as MediaMOO, as well as many scholarly and institutional listservs). Differences in levels of access between relatively open virtual communities and those which are closed or gated in some fashion were found to be key ingredients in determining patterns related to misbehavior and the regulation of online conduct.

The significance of these three situational variables for understanding misbehavior in cyber places—roles, degrees of co-presence, and levels of access—is further explained below in connection with specific findings of this investigation, according to the three types of activities involved in the regulation of online conduct in virtual communities: rule-breaking, rule-making, and rule-enforcement. This summary of specific findings of the study is intended to outline and highlight major issues related to misbehavior in online environments rather than to explore them in depth, a task left for future researchers.

BREAKING THE RULES: VARIETIES OF VIRTUAL MISBEHAVIOR

The first specific finding related to rule-breaking online confirms a pair of basic assumptions underlying this investigation: first, misbehavior in virtual communities on the Internet is widespread; and second, the regulation of online conduct is a prominent concern for those who participate in virtual communities. As discussed previously, there is a broad spectrum of troublesome online behavior ranging from playful and mischievous pranks to serious and malicious transgressions, giving rise to the distinction drawn herein between misbehavior at the lower end of the spectrum and cybercrime at the higher end.

The second finding, particularly evident in the core literature on behavior management and social control reviewed in Chapter Five, is that within the realm of online misbehavior, there is likewise a spectrum of rule-breaking with various gradations that differ according to degrees of severity. Misbehavior in virtual communities runs the gamut from playful and roguish pranks, tricks, teasing, and mischief that others find annoying, vexing, or irritating, to more serious and malicious offenses, violations, and transgressions that are judged nasty, evil, or injurious. So, for instance, flooding or spamming individual participants is generally viewed as less problematic than equivalent impositions on entire virtual communities. In addition, assessments of the severity of particular instances of rule-breaking often depend on whether or not the behavior in question is perceived as intentional. Misbehavior seen as committed on purpose tends to provoke harsher reactions than misbehavior perceived as resulting from accident, ignorance, or negligence,. For example, some online mischief, such as distributing virus programs in chat rooms or in listserv posts, is viewed as more threatening than mundane mishaps like erroneously sending a private message to a whole cyber group, a common and often embarrassing occurrence familiar to most Internauts. While hasty enforcement actions may be taken to counter transgressions that have urgent consequences, even severe offenses tend to be forgiven if participants feel no harm was meant. Similarly, rule-breaking activities online viewed as lighthearted in spirit, such as pranks and tricks, appear to be tolerated more readily than misbehavior judged hostile or harmful.

Related to assessments of severity and intent, a critical finding of this study is that, in online environments as in the offline world, misbehavior and rule-breaking must be considered transactional phenomena, involving socially-constructed and situationally-influenced meanings that people make of conduct and interaction. In other words, participants' subjective perceptions of and reactions to certain online conduct as inappropriate are the foremost factors in determining what constitutes misbehavior in any given virtual community on any given occasion, rather than objective or inherent qualities of the conduct itself.

Another finding concerning rule-breaking activities online is that the types of misbehavior encountered in virtual communities mimic and reproduce at local levels themes evident in global Internet-wide abusive behavior. Paralleling electronic abuse throughout the Internet described in literature on cybercrime and law-breaking (reviewed in Chapter Four), significant themes related to rule-breaking in virtual communities include: attacks, censorship, deception, defamation, dissent, eavesdropping, fraud, harassment, hijacking, liability, monitoring, obscenity, piracy, pornography, privacy, sabotage, surveillance, terrorism, theft, trespassing, vandalism, and violence. Within virtual communities in all types of online environments, acting alone as well as in gangs, people engage in misbehavior that affects both individuals and larger groups. People commit offenses against other participants such as hostile or aggressive discourse (e.g., flaming, spamming, and virtual rape) and attacks carried out by technical means (e.g., flooding and denial of service). Misbehavior in virtual communities can involve property (e.g., stealing nicknames and channels on IRC), digital architecture and objects (e.g., vandalism and theft in MUDs and MOOs), Web sites (e.g., mutilation of page displays), and domain names (e.g., hijacking and squatting), to name just a few types of online targets.

As for the situational variable of co-presence in relation to rule-breaking, this investigation found that, overall, synchronous chat environments, as well as meta-environments which include synchronous chat options (e.g., AOL and CompuServe), appear to be subject to more misbehavior, both quantitatively and qualitatively. People seem to engage in misbehavior more frequently in synchronous than in asynchronous environments, and the types of misbehavior in synchronous chat environments appear more diverse as well. The delay involved in asynchronous post environments, which do not involve temporal co-presence, may help dissipate some of the heated feelings which incite misbehavior in some cases. In contrast, synchronous chat situations require immediate response and action, thereby encouraging people to act on their feelings without pausing to reflect on the consequences. Moreover, in synchronous chat environments, because people are temporally co-present, more opportunities are available for misbehavior than in asynchronous situations. For example, in synchronous chat environments like IRC, MUDs, MOOs, or the Palace, troublemakers commit technological assaults on other participants by sending excessive amounts of data which overload victims' systems and disconnect them (e.g., deliberate flooding). An equivalent offense in asynchronous post environments such as listservs or newsgroup is an "email bomb," whereby an offender floods a group with waves upon waves of posts in rapid succession. Such email bomb incidents in asynchronous environments, however, are reported far less frequently in the literature than analogous flooding in synchronous environments. In addition, rule-breaking in synchronous environments such as IRC and AOL chat rooms appears to have spurred a popular class of "war" software, including not only customized programs which permit attacks involving stronger bombardment of more victims, but also special viruses transmitted synchronously in chat environments designed to disrupt participants' online lives in various ways. Yet analogous weapons of destruction for use in asynchronous post environments rarely surface. Given the greater incidence and variety of misbehavior found in synchronous environments than displayed in asynchronous environments, this analysis suggests that due to the temporal co-presence required in synchronous environments, participants may be more inclined to misbehave, and may have more opportunities to do so. Consequently, in comparison with asynchronous post environments, it appears that temporally co-present participants in synchronous chat environments run higher risks of being involved with misbehavior.

Finally, regarding the situational variable of access to open versus closed virtual communities, there were two specific findings related to rule-breaking. One finding is that virtual communities which are open to the general public appear to be subject to greater degrees of misbehavior than private or semi-public communities which are closed or gated in some fashion. For instance, there is far more flaming and derisory discourse observed in Usenet newsgroups than on invitation-only professional listservs. No doubt this has to do with higher levels of identification and accountability often demanded for membership in gated or restricted systems. A related finding, hardly surprising, is that the number of people having access to a given cyber place also makes a difference. The larger the community, the more rule-breaking occurs; and this applies to both open and closed virtual communities. For example, on major international public IRC networks such as DALnet and Undernet, flooding attacks have escalated recently as channels and networks have grown exponentially. According to discussions on IRC-related listservs, newsgroups, and Web sites, over the past five years or so, as IRC channels went from 20 to 200 participants and IRC networks went from 500 users to over 50,000 logged on at the same time, flooding of individual participants evolved into what have come to be known generically as "denial-of-service" attacks, colloquially referred to among IRC aficionados as "nuking" and "smurfing," whereby entire IRC networks composed of dozens of servers are bombarded by gangs of packet-wielding vandals. Similarly, as closed meta-environments like AOL have increased their membership tremendously, misbehavior involving commercially-oriented spam has become more prevalent. Although AOL houses virtual communities in a meta-environment gated by membership fees, the fact that AOL so widely distributes free sample software kits, combined with an onslaught of credit card fraud worldwide, in effect, causes AOL's environment to be far less effectively gated than its membership requirements might suggest.

RULE-BREAKERS:
NETIQUETTE NEWBIES, PACKET PRANKSTERS,
AND MODEM MISCREANTS

In the introduction of this report, a passage from Postman (1988) was cited in which he compares two cultures from long ago, praising the civic-minded Athenians of ancient Greece and condemning the barbaric Visigoths of medieval Europe. Those who misbehave and break rules online can be described as the Visigoths of cyberspace. However, as suggested in the title of this section, various manifestations of the role of rule-breaker in virtual communities were uncovered in this investigation. Online rule-breakers span a range similar to the variety of misbehavior described above, in terms of perceptions of severity and intent, and the same relativity exists in terms of people's perceptions of rule-breaking roles and those who enact them. As in face-to-face environments offline, the primary factors involved in determining who is or is not considered a rule-breaker in a given online situation are the meanings people make in their social transactions. For example, among gangs of online rule-breakers, the role is greatly admired; and prominent offenders sometimes develop legendary fame in their virtual communities, much as hackers gain heroic reputations in some quarters, as discussed in Chapter Four.

This study found rule-breaker roles in online environments to be similar to equivalent roles in the offline world. Newbies or novice users often break rules because of ignorance of technical and social conventions; average and even experienced users sometimes commit infractions inadvertently; pranksters violate behavioral standards in order to amuse and have fun; and the most serious miscreants perpetrate malicious offenses intended to inflict harm or cause damage. Chronic offenders, whether uninformed, negligent, or deliberate, appear to tax the patience of norm-abiding community members more easily than occasional rule-breakers. Newbies and accidental rule-breakers tend to be forgiven more easily than those perceived as having sinister intentions. Among deliberate rule-breakers in virtual communities, general character types, personality profiles, and motivations were discerned that parallel those of law-breakers discussed with respect to cybercrime in Chapter Four. In addition, reflecting overall patterns of Internet use, rule-breakers in virtual communities were found primarily to be males, generally in their teens or early twenties. Females and older users who misbehave online typically appear to be model participants provoked to an extreme, and their misbehavior is often attributable to disruptions of previously harmonious participation in their virtual communities. In fact, such female and older offenders frequently are former rule-enforcers who have turned renegade. But perhaps the most important feature found to be common to all characterizations associated with rule-breakers, online or off, is that they are perceived by the rest of the community as not belonging. Abiding by the rules, whether in virtual or traditional communities, is one of the foremost measures of group identification; those who misbehave are often described as outlaws or outsiders. It seems that by enacting (or being perceived as enacting) the role of rule-breaker in virtual communities and online environments, participants also mark themselves as strangers.

MAKING THE RULES:
BEHAVIORAL STANDARDS FOR ONLINE GATHERINGS

Rule-making in virtual communities encompasses activities whereby people establish, revise, disseminate, apply, and implement rules of online conduct. As noted above, online rules, like those offline, do not necessarily precede misbehavior or disciplinary measures. Often, people only conclude that a certain class of behavior is inappropriate when particular conditions arise or after the behavior first occurs and provokes disapproval. Such evolving perceptions lead to decisions that rules need to be established; hence the emergence of recognizable rule-making activities subsequent to rather than in advance of rule-breaking or rule-enforcement. For example, IRC software was originally limited to plain text, but over the years features were added that permit sending colored text as well as sounds. These new features were subsequently judged in some IRC communities to be excessive waste of bandwidth and therefore prohibited. But such rules forbidding the use of color or sound on particular IRC channels had no reason to be established or enforced until the behavior prompting them was noticed and deemed objectionable.

The first specific finding of this study concerning rule-making is that rules of online conduct demonstrate different levels of explicitness and formality, reflecting anthropologist Hall's three levels of culture: informal, formal, and technical (1959, pp. 60–96). The least formal are norms, often unstated rules related to general behavioral patterns; the origins of netiquette lie in this informal, unstated realm. As discussed in Chapter Five, netiquette principles become explicit when codified into documents such as Frequently Asked Questions ("FAQs"), lending them increasing formality and authority. At more formal levels are rules of online conduct contained in Acceptable Use Policies ("AUPs") and Terms of Service ("TOSs"), agreements which begin to resemble legal contracts in degree of authority. And there is also a meta-level of technical rules applicable to online rule-making and rule-enforcement activities themselves: special sets of instructions that stipulate appropriate behavior for rule-makers and rule-enforcers performing their online roles. In online environments, such technical meta-rules involve procedures for making and disseminating general rules, and appropriate means of enforcing sanctions against rule-breakers. For instance, one of the most common meta-rules applicable to rule-enforcers in many virtual communities is that first offenders should be given a warning before being more severely punished. Overall, behavioral standards in virtual communities were found to span a range from informal norms, through more formal and technical rules which approach external laws in terms of formality and authority.

A second finding related to rule-making is that behavioral standards for online gatherings involve local as well as global rules of conduct. That is, local rules apply to particular virtual communities, whereas global rules apply to most communities in the same type of online environment. Thus, local rules tend to be more specific to a given context in cyberspace. For example, in Usenet newsgroups, the general global rule is to avoid flaming; yet in alt.flame, a newsgroup devoted to the art of flaming, the specific local rule is that flaming is required. Hence, in the context of alt.flame, flaming is appropriate conduct while the lack of flaming is considered misbehavior.

The situational variable of co-presence was found to have some significance for rule-making activities online. In synchronous chat environments, where people are temporally co-present, opportunities for give-and-take negotiation in working out rules are facilitated by the possibility of immediate response. However, the fact that asynchronous post environments inherently involve written records facilitates rule-making processes to some extent, although most current chat software permits "logging" that produces equivalent written transcripts of synchronous online sessions.

With respect to rule-making and the situational variable of access, analysis revealed that behavioral standards in closed virtual communities tend to be more specific, depending on the same sorts of limitations required for membership in such communities. However, size is also a factor. Small closed communities like private listservs or restricted chat rooms tend to rely on informal norms and netiquette, while large closed meta-environments like AOL and CompuServe, which host a multiplicity of virtual communities, favor more formalized AUPs and TOSs. A significant finding of this study is that in open, public virtual communities, most activities involving rule-making require collaborative processes not always easy to achieve online. The supposition that participants in virtual communities based on common interests enjoy a homogeneity of views in a climate of social harmony is negated by substantial evidence that conflict and negotiation are abundant in activities related to rule-making online. In fact, rule-making activities seem to be among the most important factors binding virtual communities together and giving their participants a sense of group identity. In contrast, in closed meta-environments like AOL, rules tend to be provided more impersonally by top-level authorities far removed from daily online affairs. Consequently, in such meta-environments there is less evidence of community participation in rule-making processes. Furthermore, as in any kind of social organization, the larger the group, the more difficult collaborative cooperation becomes. The larger the virtual community, and the more technically complex the online environment in which it is embedded, the more likely that formal rule-making activities will emerge, and that responsibility for rule-making will be undertaken by participants enacting specialized online roles.

RULE-MAKERS:
NETIZENS AGAINST DIGITAL MISCONDUCT

If online rule-breakers represent the Visigoths of cyberspace, then rule-makers are among its Athenians. One of the specific findings of this study is that the roles of rule-maker and rule-enforcer online are closely related, with considerable overlap between the two. In fact, in some virtual communities, no distinction is made between rule-maker and rule-enforcer, the same individual or set of individuals enacting both roles. However, the responsibilities of these two online roles were found to differ significantly. Whereas rule-enforcers deal with concrete instances of misbehavior, rule-makers deal with misbehavior in the abstract. Thus, the role of rule-maker has a more preventative nature, addressing categories of rule-breaking and rule-breaker rather than particular instances of misbehavior by given individuals, a pattern which is typical offline as well as online. Additionally, the larger the virtual community and the more complex the online environment which hosts it, the more likely it is that rule-makers are distinguished from rule-enforcers.

A second specific finding related to the role of rule-maker in virtual communities is that volunteers often fill this function. Volunteer participants with a high sense of responsibility and dedication to their virtual communities and online environments, sometimes called "netizens," perform duties associated with rule-maker roles for numerous reasons except financial gain. For example, there are volunteer rule-makers such as Spafford, mentioned in Chapter Five, who spent over a decade maintaining and updating FAQs in Usenet; evidence of the pride he takes in this achievement is available on his personal Web site. But because online volunteers have other commitments offline, particularly to earn a living, the time they can afford to devote to their rule-maker duties is restricted in various ways. It sometimes becomes problematic when volunteer rule-makers put their offline activities first and neglect their online roles. Paid rule-makers, on the other hand, have more clearly defined duties and schedules, and the regular enactment of their roles is therefore more predictable and reliable. However, the personal commitment of employee rule-makers who are paid to fill their online roles is not necessarily of the same caliber as that of volunteer rule-makers.

Additional findings related to rule-makers in virtual communities involve patterns of gender and age which differ from those identified for online rule-breakers. Whereas young males appear to have a penchant for breaking rules in cyberspace, they rarely aspire to become online rule-makers. Similarly, although females and older participants tend not to become rule-breakers online, both demographic groups are commonly encountered among the ranks of rule-makers in virtual communities. These demographic patterns appear to be related to issues of status and prestige. In virtual communities, rule-makers often are perceived as having high status: their opinions and experience are valued and they are given authority to interpret and resolve cases of rule-breaking. However, online rule-makers who are not involved in enforcement tend to remain in the background of ordinary community affairs with a less visible presence, and therefore may be perceived as lower in status than rule-enforcers, whose activities are far more apparent on a day-to-day basis. Such differences in prominence, prestige, and status mirror analogous roles in face-to-face environments and traditional situations: in everyday life offline, law-makers tend to be less visible than law-enforcers, whose activities are more readily and routinely apparent to the general population.

ENFORCING THE RULES:
STRATEGIES AND TECHNIQUES
FOR HANDLING ONLINE TROUBLEMAKERS

The first specific finding of this study related to rule-enforcement is that there are various strategies and techniques for dealing with misbehavior in virtual communities, corresponding to the numerous sorts of rule-breaking in which participants engage. Nevertheless, this investigation revealed two principal dimensions used to distinguish among types of rule-enforcement strategies and techniques in online environments. One significant dimension involves the distinction between internal and external control, already covered above. But another important distinction is often made between technical and social measures of applying sanctions and penalties in virtual communities, and each category has pros and cons. Technical mechanisms are seen as relatively efficacious and impartial, but imperfect (e.g., software filters attempting to block pornography or spam). However, excessive reliance on exclusively technological enforcement mechanisms is sometimes perceived as lacking beneficial long-term educational and preventive value. Technical enforcement methods online appear most effective in the short term, and in cases where immediate action is necessary. As opposed to technological means, rule-enforcement involving social measures in online environments demands a great deal of people power. Reliance on human resources rather than software to carry out enforcement is viewed as more socially beneficial, especially in building and maintaining a sense of community. But people-intensive enforcement strategies and techniques in online environments require volunteers or employees with varying levels of scope and power, or at a minimum, supportive cooperation from other participants (e.g., to impose sanctions such as public shaming or shunning). A related finding is that in online environments, as in the offline world, rule-enforcement serves several purposes: stopping offensive behavior, alleviating harm to victims, reducing anxiety in bystanders, and preserving the integrity of the group as a whole. Overall, a similar range of severity is evident in sanctions and penalties matching the range of severity and intent found in varieties of rule-breaking. The general enforcement principle operating in most virtual communities appears to be that the punishment should fit the crime; hence lighter penalties are given to newbies and first offenders, in tones that are more informative, remedial, or reproachful than punitive.

The situational variable of co-presence was found to be quite significant for issues related to rule-enforcement online. In synchronous chat environments requiring temporal co-presence, rule-enforcement tends to be extremely demanding and time-consuming. For example, monitoring behavior in busy chat rooms and channels can be exhausting and draining even for veterans. Also, because synchronous rule-breaking often has immediate effects, rule-enforcement must be timely to be effective. Effective enforcement in synchronous environments often requires a keen level of attention, especially in larger virtual communities, and this in turn leads to specialized division of labor within the ranks of online rule-enforcers. For instance, in chat environments on IRC and AOL, some enforcers specialize in detecting misbehavior while others act to discipline those who misbehave. In addition, a wider array of technological measures appears to develop in synchronous chat environments to compensate for the heightened human attention required by temporal co-presence. For example, special software "scripts" have been developed for IRC channel and server operators to automate enforcement procedures like kicking, banning, and killing, as well as detection and removal of participants engaging in undesirable behavior like flooding, obscene language, virus distribution, or "clones" (excessive multiple connections by a single user).

The situational variable of access was found to be significant in rule-enforcement activities online. Enforcement in open, public virtual communities is more difficult due to participants' lack of accountability. In closed or gated virtual communities, enforcement is easier because offenders can more readily be identified and shut out of the online environment. However, as is the case with AOL, a closed meta-environment of gigantic proportions, size has important implications for rule-enforcement online. Despite limiting access to members only, the fact that AOL distributes a never-ending stream of free trial software encourages offenders who were closed out of the community to return with fresh, unsullied accounts, and initiate further cycles of misbehavior. Although it seems to be technically feasible for AOL to track and cancel offending accounts, it is time-consuming (even with the aid of customized tracking software), and the sheer number of offending accounts makes it nearly impossible to conduct effective rule-enforcement in this type of meta-environment. As a result, vast amounts of commercially-oriented spam originate from such AOL accounts, and similar situations involving lack of accountability and spam occur with free email accounts from providers like Yahoo! and Hotmail. In short, this investigation suggests that the larger and more complex the online environment, the more difficult to achieve effective enforcement, and the more resources and energy required to do so.

RULE-ENFORCERS:
MODERATORS, SYSOPS, WIZARDS, AND GODS ON CYBER PATROL

Like online rule-makers, rule-enforcers are also Athenians in cyberspace, participants with overall responsibility for and technical authority over their virtual communities. But unlike rule-makers, who primarily contemplate misbehavior in the abstract, rule-enforcers are the ones in the online trenches dealing first-hand with actual cases of misbehavior. The first specific finding in this area is that, especially in virtual communities which distinguish between rule-makers and rule-enforcers, participants who enact the latter set of roles deal with concrete instances of misbehavior, fulfilling more of a remedial function as opposed to the duties of online rule-makers which are more oriented towards prevention. A related finding is that because rule-enforcers generally confront rule-breakers directly in actual rather than hypothetical circumstances, in online as well as offline environments, the risk of reprisal from those they have disciplined tends to be greater for rule-enforcers than for rule-makers, whose activities are rarely apparent at the time rule-breaking is committed or punished.

Another specific finding related to rule-enforcer roles in virtual communities is that they range from more socially-oriented moderators, hosts, and guides, to more technically-oriented sysops, wizards, and gods. Rule-enforcer roles online appear to fall into three groups. First, there are those involved in community integration, along the lines of social workers. Second, rule-enforcers implementing technical sanctions function mostly as police. And finally, the least glamorous type of online enforcement role, especially attractive to so-called "geeks" and "nerds," involves environmental or system maintenance, something akin to janitors or custodians. As with rule-makers, the difference between volunteers and paid employees in virtual communities was also found to be significant in relation to rule-enforcer roles online, and for similar reasons. Especially evident in chat environments is the phenomenon of enforcer "burn-out," a consequence of synchronous interaction being more immediate and therefore more time-consuming, demanding, and literally exhausting, particularly over long-term periods. More frequently than rule-enforcers in asynchronous post environments, rule-enforcers in synchronous chat environments tend to take leaves of absence or retire altogether from their appointed roles after extended tours of online duty.

Demographic findings of this investigation reveal that, like the ranks of rule-makers in virtual communities and for the same sorts of reasons, cadres of online rule-enforcers tend to be populated by females and older participants, although youngsters sometimes fill rule-enforcer roles as well. The value of experience and maturity in performing rule-enforcer roles online is quite apparent: women and other caregivers with practice raising children (notorious offline troublemakers) seem to demonstrate considerable adeptness at dealing with rule-breakers in virtual communities and surprising willingness to spend time and energy doing so. Furthermore, some women (as well participants of all genders who are shy and withdrawn in face-to-face situations) may not wield similar authority or demonstrate equivalent technical expertise in their offline environments; for such individuals (including youngsters), roles as online rule-enforcers may be empowering. Age also turns out to be significant in determining who may or may not attain rule-enforcer status in virtual communities, because so many online offenses involve activities and materials deemed harmful to minors (e.g., pornography). Yet ascertaining unequivocally the age of someone wishing to become an online enforcer is not always easy to accomplish. As a result of age-related issues like these, AOL dismissed all online rule-enforcers under eighteen several years ago (the bulk of whom were volunteers).

Another finding is that unlike the case with rule-maker roles, many participants in virtual communities aspire to become rule-enforcers, due to this set of roles being at the top of the hierarchy in terms of authority, power, status, and prestige online. Enforcer roles are often envied and coveted, and among the most frequent questions asked by new participants in almost any virtual community is how to become a rule-enforcer in that group, reflected by the fact that most virtual community FAQs include answers to such inquiries. The most common advice seems to be: become a regular participant in the virtual community and wait to be asked to join the ranks of its rule-enforcers; begging for such status is considered the worst possible road to achieving it. Because of their high status and special privileges, online rule-enforcers are sometimes exempt from standards applied to regular participants, and when enforcers do misbehave, their offenses may not be treated as strictly. However, online rule-enforcers are often subject to special responsibilities as well, having to adhere to extra rules about how to carry out their enforcement activities. For example, on both IRC and AOL, enforcers must follow up in writing certain types of disciplinary actions, such as terminating the connection or account of an offending user. Additionally, it seems that enforcers in virtual communities need "back regions" (see, e.g., Goffman, 1959; Meyrowitz, 1985) to "rehearse" their performances. Such back region gatherings for online enforcers (e.g., exclusive listservs, Web sites, and internally-restricted chat lines), in turn, give rise to sub-communities of rule-enforcers (often joined by rule-makers) within the larger group. And naturally, sub-communities of online enforcers develop their own internal rule-breakers, rule-makers, and rule-enforcers.

Finally, it was found that rule-enforcer roles in virtual communities tend to be defined objectively rather than through subjective perception. Situational variables equivalent to those of dress and demeanor in face-to-face environments were apparent in many online environments. For example, rule-enforcers like IRC chanops and IRCops, as well as wizards and gods on MUDs, MOOs, and the Palace, typically have special symbols (e.g., asterisks) available to mark their online names as having privileged status. Similarly, on AOL, screen names containing certain lexical items like "Guide" and "Ranger" are reserved for the exclusive use of rule-enforcers. In tandem with requirements to sport such markers that serve as professional badges or uniforms, rule-enforcers in virtual communities are often subject to sets of technical meta-rules concerning their own standards of behavior while thus identified as being on-duty performing their enforcer roles. This sort of professional identification displayed in online environments parallels authentication measures in the offline world, and serves similar purposes of reassuring people they are dealing with legitimate authorities.

Having summarized above the general and specific findings of this investigation of misbehavior and the regulation of online conduct in virtual communities on the Internet, it must be emphasized that the goal of this study was not to examine in detail the results reported herein, each of which deserves further inquiry. Rather, the purpose of this project was to gather and integrate relevant research, to distill and combine information and ideas from such research, and to suggest clearer paths for future investigators to pursue in greater depth by providing a more coherent sense of the main issues and primary parameters in the study of misbehavior in cyber places.

Chapter Seven
Conclusion:
A New Sense of Place

FROM PHYSICAL TO BEHAVIORAL BOUNDARIES

The purpose of this investigation was to analyze and assess how people regulate misbehavior in virtual communities on the Internet. In addressing the conclusions drawn from this study, it is essential to note that the discussion which follows applies to cultural contexts typical of industrialized regions in the West such as the United States, where high technology is well developed and Internet use fairly commonplace. Although access to the Internet is now routinely available in major urban centers worldwide, and many online environments and virtual communities host international populations, circumstances vary around the globe, and conclusions drawn from this investigation are not necessarily generalizable to regions with different degrees of Internet penetration.

In *No Sense of Place* (1985), Meyrowitz argues that electronic media have significantly diminished people's sense of physical and social place. Given the time period of Meyrowitz's research, the impact of interpersonal computer-mediated communication ("CMC") in online environments had not yet become apparent, and Meyrowitz's analysis therefore focuses on social consequences of television and other forms of electronic media. As noted in previous chapters, some scholars hold views similar to Meyrowitz's about electronic media weakening people's sense of place. For example, Gumpert laments time and again about the loss of public places for socializing as people turn instead to electronically-mediated communication (e.g., Gumpert, 1987, pp. 167–189; Gumpert & Drucker, 1996, p. 36; 1997, pp. 5–6; Gumpert & Fish, 1990a, pp. 3–4). Healy observes that in the age of electronic communication "we long for place as well as space" (1997, p. 66). And extending Meyrowitz's argument to online CMC, Strate et al. assert that cyberspace intensifies "no sense of place" (1996b, p. 14).

However, there is a critical difference between electronic media like television and the online environments afforded by CMC which must not be underestimated. In relation to media such as television primarily employed for mass communication, average users are merely passive receivers, consuming content produced by others, and not actively generating anything on their own (except perhaps fodder for audience demographics studies). The messages of mass media, for the most part, travel only in one direction (see, e.g., Avery & McCain, 1982/1986; Cathcart & Gumpert, 1983/1986). In contrast, users of online CMC who frequent virtual communities can participate actively in interpersonal communication, which alters circumstances radically. In online environments, messages may flow in both directions, with participants able to send as well as receive, allowing them to produce their own content in exchange for consuming content generated by others (see, e.g., Cutler, 1996, p. 325; Strate, 1999, p. 405). Even relatively passive CMC requires more active participation than do mass media. If such creatures as "mouse potatoes" exist online analogous to the offline "couch potatoes" associated with television viewing, they would be the largely inactive participants often referred to online as "lurkers." Nevertheless, even lurkers get pulled into social interaction online when their lack of participation (i.e., lurking) is considered misbehavior and other users treat them as rule-breakers.

According to Meyrowitz, television and other electronic media like telephone and radio have dispersed conceptions of place and made people feel placeless, both physically and socially. This absence of a sense of place may result not only from a deficiency in physical spaces for social interaction, but also from a lack of participation in social activity, an excess of passivity induced by the relentless consumption of one-way mass media so prevalent in cultural contexts where high technology flourishes. The findings of the present study suggest that, for better or for worse, interpersonal communication in online environments reassembles people in new sorts of cyber gathering places where opportunities for active participation in social interaction abound. Countering the diminished sense of place resulting from low levels of participation inherent in mass media, such cyber gathering places complement and substitute for traditional offline places, filling the social void left by the lack of place that Meyrowitz identifies, which accompanies passive consumption of mass media such as television.

To have no sense of place is an unnatural, unbalanced, and undesirable condition for human beings. People require places to socialize, the sorts of environments Oldenburg describes as "third places" where they can gather for social interaction beyond what occurs at home or at work (1989/1997). Perhaps the main conclusion reached in this study is that the gradual loss of traditional offline gathering places coupled with the rising availability of online environments have encouraged people to explore social interaction in new cyber places, and people have amply exploited the availability of these novel spaces to claim as their own. Thus, as opposed to the dispersing impact of electronic media described by Meyrowitz and others, it appears that virtual communities in online environments present opportunities for interpersonal communication through which people's sense of social place may come to be restored, or through which they may begin to develop a sense of social place if they were previously unacquainted with such feelings. It seems that having discovered online environments to serve as third places for socializing, people are using online CMC to quench their thirst for active participation in social groups, a need increasingly difficult to satisfy exclusively in face-to-face environments offline.

A revealing illustration of how participants may come to feel a strong sense of place online is provided by Dery:

> Those who spend an inordinate amount of time connected by modem via telephone lines to virtual spaces often report a peculiar sensation of "thereness"; prowling from one conference to another, eavesdropping on discussions in progress, bears an uncanny resemblance to wandering the hallways of some labyrinthine mansion, poking one's head into room after room. "One of the most striking features of the WELL," observed a user named Ioca, "is that it actually creates a feeling of "place." I'm staring at a computer screen. But the feeling really is that I'm "in" something; I'm some "where." (1993, p. 565)

Rintel cites a similar comment from a sysop who "describes IRC metaphorically as a 'place,' like a '. . . street corner where local hoodlums hang out'" (1995). D. R. Johnson and Post also refer to cyber places in similar fashion, and in addition, they astutely observe that part of how people orient themselves with respect to place involves being able to recognize boundaries upon crossing them:

> There is a "placeness" to Cyberspace. . . . You know when you are "there." No one accidentally strays across the border into Cyberspace. . . . a primary function and characteristic of a border or boundary is its ability to be perceived by the one who crosses it. (1996b)

But having no physical limits or borders other than on or off, what is it about cyber places that forms the perceptible boundaries that Johnson and Post claim are so necessary and that users seem to notice? Certainly not physical structures built of bricks, as Kolko and Reid emphasize, noting "the absence of impermeable walls within a virtual community" (1998, p. 224) and the "permeability of virtual structures" (p. 226). The key idea comes from Rutter and G. Smith, who claim that "the development of virtual boundaries" can be attributed to rule-making activities (1999a). One conclusion drawn from this study of online misbehavior, therefore, is that in cyber gathering places, boundaries tend to be marked by behavioral patterns rather than by physical properties. By setting and following behavioral boundaries, participants develop and experience a sense of belonging and group identity. They gain meanings to make in their lives by regaining social situations in which to interact, even if not physically co-present. And because behavioral boundary-setting promotes interaction among groups of participants, the attention paid to the regulation of online conduct in virtual communities contributes to the evolution of a new sense of social place.

GROWING INTEREST IN LOCAL REGULATORY APPROACHES

As noted throughout this study, troublesome online behavior is attracting increasing attention in many spheres, and interest is growing in the development of alternative models and approaches for regulating online conduct (see, e.g., Schnurr, 2000). In August 2000, *New Scientist* magazine published an interview with Cailliau, a Belgian computer engineer considered a cyberspace pioneer for having worked with Berners-Lee in developing the World Wide Web. Several of Cailliau's observations in this interview concern the need for online behavioral standards, and he raises various issues, some of them controversial, such as requiring people to have a license to surf the Internet much as they need a license to drive on physical highways. What is most impressive about Cailliau's attitude is that he calls not only for a global framework, but also for *intervention at the local level* to provide education and guidance for people in general about appropriate and inappropriate behavior online. Cailliau says:

> The Net is a space in which you encounter others, so there has to be some regulation of behaviour. . . . This is something to implement in international conventions and for citizens to reflect and decide on. Unfortunately we have a global network, a global economy and global companies, but we have not got a global legal system. . . . What I want is behaviour regulation. We should all know what our rights and duties are. (August 26, 2000)

On the occasion of Cailliau's interview, the anonymous author of a French news wire release suggests that "regulation of the Internet is one of the hottest issues in cyberspace, made more acute by rising incidence of computer vandalism, pornography and fraud and other cross-border crimes that have exposed gaping holes in national laws" (Agence France-Presse, August 27, 2000, as cited by Vinton G. Cerf in post to the Internet Societal Task Force electronic mailing list, August 28, 2000).

Indeed, it seems that despite law-making and law-enforcement efforts in cyberspace, the time has come to transcend nationally-oriented regulatory frameworks and consider locally-oriented alternatives. Legal dilemmas in cyberspace such as First Amendment follies, definition schizophrenia, and the jurisdiction circus will continue to perplex scholars, professionals, and laypersons alike until *local* strategies are developed for regulating troublesome behavior on the Internet. To assume that a single global legal framework for cyberspace can be developed to cover a sufficient range of cultural contexts, which vary tremendously around the world, is simply naive. Wisebrod (1995) cites a newspaper article according to which "Professor Anne Branscomb, a Harvard researcher on information issues, has predicted that the Internet will subdivide into a matrix of small communities, each with a unique Netiquette." Branscomb herself explains as follows this prediction that a mix of approaches will prevail:

> Certainly there will be many inputs into the emerging law on the electronic frontier—a new Netlaw for the future. It will not be completely *sui generis* (as though springing from the head of Minerva) but a blend of existing local laws, customary law as practiced by netizens, and new methods of dealing with strange new occurrences and opportunities that arise only in computer-mediated cybercommunities. (1996)

Dutton is another who suggests that multiple sets of local, internal rules might be more effective and appropriate in online environments than external laws:

> Just as there are different rules when one enters a video arcade as opposed to a church, there could be many different networks with different norms governing their operation. . . . All public meetings have rules of order, which govern turn taking as well as other protocols for speakers. Rules of order are designed to facilitate rather than to constrain group communication and decision making. . . . the regulation of speech in public electronic fora is critical to their effective use as a vehicle for enhancing democratic communication. It would therefore be ironic if laws and precedents designed to protect democratic communication were used to prevent the development and enforcement of appropriate network rules of order. . . . policy is likely to require compromise among competing positions, the development of stronger and more widely held norms among the user community. . . . Public electronic fora seem to require innovative approaches to the development of rules and regulations. (1996, pp. 286–287)

Thus, despite pessimism in some quarters about the potential for local regulation of conduct within virtual communities (e.g., Kolko & Reid, 1998), there are signs that others are starting to pay closer attention to local regulatory approaches and possibilities (e.g., Rintel, 1995; D. R. Johnson & Post, 1996a, 1996b, 1997). A conclusion drawn from this study, then, is that evidence is mounting of ever-increasing interest in discarding national and global legal frameworks for governing cyberspace in favor of local regulatory approaches such as those encountered in virtual communities for dealing with misbehavior in cyber places.

To put it plainly, as the Internet has grown, the rise of troublesome online behavior has challenged and strained existing regulatory frameworks. Such frameworks, for the most part, attempt to regulate behavior in cyberspace on the basis of nationally-oriented legal systems. However, nationally-oriented legal systems are inherently inadequate for regulating online behavior, given the global scope of the Internet and the transnational nature of cyberspace.

To describe cyberspace as transnational helps remind us that national boundaries have little significance online. People often think of the Internet as being international, that is, connecting different nations. But the Internet does more than just connect nations. The Internet cuts across nations, thus tending to make national boundaries irrelevant. So when nationally-oriented regulatory frameworks are applied to solve Internet troubles in transnational cyberspace, all sorts of legal dilemmas occur.

Furthermore, the transnational nature of cyberspace demands that cultural relativity be taken into account. In many instances, the multicultural contexts of transnational cyberspace render nationally-oriented legal provisions, such as the U.S. First Amendment, irrelevant or moot in connection with standards of political and religious freedom, obscenity, or libel, among others. For example, imagine the uproar over French versus U.S. reactions to Nazi memorabilia online (discussed in Chapter Four), compounded by German and Israeli perspectives added to the mix. Or compare the levels of tolerance in China for political discourse online with freedom of expression protections often defended in the West. Or take the norms for online obscenity and pornography in regions where Islamic values of modesty dominate, in contrast with more liberal orientations prevalent in places such as Scandinavia and parts of Latin America. Because beliefs and attitudes about appropriate conduct do vary tremendously around the world, measures for dealing with troublesome online behavior ought to respect diverse points of view and make allowances for different and sometimes incompatible cultural sensitivities. Attempts to derive the lowest common denominator among disparate legal regimes have failed and will continue to fail, as there are simply too many divergent cultural points of view to factor into the calculations. It is unrealistic to expect a single legal framework for dealing with troublesome online behavior to adequately cover a sufficient range of the innumerable cultural contexts and traditions represented in transnational cyberspace.

The time has come to consider alternative approaches for dealing with the legal dilemmas caused by troublesome online behavior in transnational cyberspace. We must abandon nationally-oriented legal frameworks, but we must not be misled by futile efforts to develop global, universal, centralized, top-down, or "one-size-fits-all" legal perspectives. Instead, we should encourage a multiplicity of decentralized locally-oriented solutions for regulating online behavior. Rather than persist in seeking national or global answers which likely will never be found, it may well be more productive in the long run to stimulate and embrace a variety of decentralized local approaches which respect and accommodate diverse standards and multiple strategies for regulating conduct in the online environments of transnational cyberspace.

MISBEHAVIOR OFFLINE:
ATHENIANS AND VISIGOTHS IN EVERYDAY LIFE

Life in online and offline environments forms a continuum, as Internauts have long understood, and as CMC researchers are beginning to argue and others to accept. The illusory opposition between virtual worlds and the so-called "real world" is increasingly being abandoned or ignored, as people come to realize that in general, what happens online is part and parcel of what happens offline, although there is no denying the numerous differences between the two kinds of environments.

As described in previous chapters, the passage by Postman (1988) cited in the introduction of this report, in which he praises the civic-minded Athenians of ancient Greece and condemns the barbaric Visigoths of medieval Europe, is quite applicable to the study of misbehavior. So it is not surprising to discover that issues raised in this investigation of misbehavior in cyber places find parallels in face-to-face situations in everyday life offline where people break rules as well. Similarities between misbehavior in online and offline environments are particularly evident in public and semi-public contexts where people interact with strangers, the sorts of transitional spaces discussed by Nystrom (1978) and Strate (1999). As Strate points out, "anything goes" in transitional cyberspace (p. 406). More and more nowadays, in offline areas of everyday life, we are seeing instances of behavior guided by this principle that "anything goes." There appears to be a general decay in civility in the same high-technology contexts where Internet use abounds, particularly contemporary Western culture exemplified by that of the United States.

Social interaction in public and semi-public transitional space, of which cyberspace is one kind, means above all having to deal with strangers. The argument that cyber gatherings involve communities of participants who share interests and do not have to work out any differences is dispelled by the notion that a large proportion of social interaction in cyber places involves relative strangers. As discussed in earlier chapters, the role of stranger is raised in studies of misbehavior offline as well as online. Gumpert explains the significance of strangers or outsiders in helping to consolidate feelings of shared community: "the collective identity which crystallizes community . . . is dependent upon the awareness that some people or groups are excluded from 'our community.' The 'outsiders' which threaten the community help to define it" (1987, p. 171).

Online environments are not the only contexts in which people transacting among strangers seem to be veering out of control. Symptoms of social malaise and lack of attention to appropriate and considerate behavior are surfacing in offline environments as well. For instance, there are numerous accounts of conflicts over which sorts of face-to-face behavior are appropriate where and when. One newspaper article reviews misbehavior involving a popular high-technology gadget: "Taking the Offensive Against Cell Phones" (Guernsey, January 11, 2001). In a paper on "Understanding Road Rage," a media ecologist contemplates the antics of automobile drivers who misbehave on non-virtual highways (Schuchardt, 2000). A flight attendant complains bitterly about airplane passenger misbehavior in a magazine piece entitled "Flying in the Age of Air Rage" (Hester, 1999). And journalists write about misbehavior in the workplace: "Overworked, Overwrought: "Desk Rage" at Work" (Nissen, November 15, 2000); and "Etiquette Crisis at Work: Employees Say They've Had Enough of Incivility, Bad Manners" (Jacoby, November 29, 1999). Another newspaper article explains how sports events provide occasions for misbehavior too: "New

Rules for Soccer Parents: 1) No Yelling. 2) No Hitting Ref." According to this report on "sideline rage," there is "a rising tide of misbehavior at high school and youth sports, especially among adult spectators" leading to "a wellspring of new rules, workshops and state legislation aimed at curbing misconduct" (Wong, May 6, 2001). And even a humble, ordinary object wielded without consideration for others can stimulate misbehavior in water-logged public environments: "Umbrellas in Their Midst, New Yorkers Ponder 'Rain Rage'" (Saulny, January 30, 2001). The situation is effectively summarized on the Web site of the U.K. National Workplace Bullying Advice Line: "road rage, air rage, office rage, desk rage, work rage, bike rage, trolley rage . . . rage is the word of the moment" (http://www.successunlimited.co.uk/rage.htm). Such examples of misbehavior in offline contexts illustrate an increasing awareness that etiquette guidelines and behavioral road maps are necessary, an invigorated notion that differences between appropriate and inappropriate behavior make a difference in civil society. And as one journalist suggests, a "rekindled interest in etiquette" may result from social experiences in cyberspace (Kelly, 1997).

Today, we socialize in new kinds of public places, such as virtual communities on the Internet, where face-to-face physical presence is not required. In these sorts of online environments, for example, situational improprieties range from cyberspace flame wars that overheat the tempers of a few, to email virus epidemics which overwhelm the mailboxes of many. We also continue to frequent traditional public places offline, but these environments are transformed by the introduction of new media technologies, such as cell phones in restaurants, theaters, and classrooms. In traditional environments to which new media have been introduced, situational improprieties range, for instance, from conflicts regarding hand-held cell phones versus highway safety, to debates over camera-enabled cell phones versus personal privacy (see, e.g., Sternberg, 2003, 2009).

In circumstances where strangers interact in public, in life offline as online, similar problems arise in determining how to deal with misbehavior. It seems somehow frivolous to contemplate formal guidelines for appropriate umbrella etiquette; but regulating misbehavior involving cell phones, transportation, and jobs may not seem so silly. Situations in the offline world where people misbehave suggest that, just as in the online world, local regulation, often of the socially-integrative sort, may offer more hope than enacting intricate, unenforceable, and sometimes ludicrous legislation. It may be more productive in the long run to work towards instilling a better sense of ordinary manners, politeness, and basic consideration and respect for others in all sorts of environments in everyday life, whether on or offline. In this regard, D. R. Johnson and Post's arguments in favor of mixed rules of "civic virtue" (1997) suggest appealing possibilities.

Recall Lofland's observations that "places are *especially meaningful spaces*, rich in associations and steeped in sentiment" (1998, p. 64), and that "the critical component of 'place' is sentiment" (p. 75, n. 18). When people develop attachments to the cyber places they frequent, a sense of social place emerges, a meaningful investment of sentiment which encourages participation and respon-sibility rather than misbehavior and disruption. According to Strate, "those who gain a sense of group membership become part of a virtual community and often develop a sense of responsibility towards the social cyberspace in which it is situated, much as residents of a neighborhood may take responsibility for the area's cleanliness and safety" (1999, p. 404). Just as they come to care about their cyber selves and identities, topics much discussed in CMC research, people also invest sentiment in the *cyber places* where they gather for social interaction. It is this very investment of sentiment that prevents people from simply logging out of online environments and turning off their computers when confronted with misbehavior, that makes them care enough to participate in regulating online conduct in their virtual communities.

Deviance sociologist Becker raises one of the most important points of all about misbehavior in any environment. Becker recommends asking why people do *not* misbehave rather than the more obvious question of why they do:

> In analyzing cases of intended nonconformity, people usually ask about moti-vation: why does the person want to do the deviant thing he does? The question assumes that the basic difference between deviants and those who conform lies in the character of their motivation. Many theories have been propounded to explain why some people have deviant motivations and others do not. . . .
>
> But the assumption on which these approaches are based may be entirely false. There is no reason to assume that only those who finally commit a devi-ant act actually have the impulse to do so. It is much more likely that most peo-ple experience deviant impulses frequently. At least in fantasy, people are much more deviant than they appear. Instead of asking why deviants want to do things that are disapproved of, we might better ask why conventional people do not follow through on the deviant impulses they have. (1963/1973, pp. 26–27)

According to Becker, inverting the question is more revealing: the answer turns out to be that commitments people make to group norms and values stemming from the social allegiances they develop are what dissuade them from misbehaving:

> Something of an answer to this question may be found in the process of com-mitment through which the "normal" person becomes progressively involved in conventional institutions and behavior. In speaking of commitment, I refer to the process through which several kinds of interests become bound up with car-rying out certain lines of behavior to which they seem formally extraneous. What happens is that the individual, as a consequence of actions he has taken in the past or the operation of various institutional routines, finds he must adhere to certain lines of behavior, because many other activities than the one he is immediately engaged in will be adversely affected if he does not. . . .
>
> In fact, the normal development of people in our society (and probably in any society) can be seen as a series of progressively increasing commitments to conventional norms and institutions. The "normal" person, when he discovers a deviant impulse in himself, is able to check that impulse by thinking of the

manifold consequences acting on it would produce for him. He has staked too much on continuing to be normal to allow himself to be swayed by unconventional impulses. (1963/1973, pp. 27–28)

What Becker describes is the social imperative to conform to situational norms of appropriate behavior identified by Goffman as the overarching rule of "fitting in" (1963, p. 11), powerful enough to compel people to behave themselves even under extreme conditions, as demonstrated by Milgram's experiments on obedience to authority (1974). The social obligation to "be good" in the presence of others is key to understanding misbehavior in practically every environment where people interact.

In virtual communities, it sometimes happens that online rule-breakers turn into rule-abiding netizens or even online rule-enforcers. Becker's explanation of the social imperative to conform suggests a reason for such a switch. Offenders may come to develop bonds in virtual communities they formerly tormented, and these social affinities overcome their rule-breaking impulses, which become weaker and in some cases, subside altogether. It seems that if people inclined to misbehave build ties instead that produce a social stake, a meaningful investment in belonging to a group or community, in not being a stranger or outsider, they may resist and suppress their desire to break the rules in light of the greater well-being of the community and their standing in it. Those who care about fitting in are more wary of misbehaving. And the reverse happens too, as illustrated by the occasional online rule-enforcer who turns renegade. Such conversions from rule-enforcer to rule-breaker, according to Becker's explanation, may be due to damaged ties that previously bound newly-misbehaving participants to the virtual communities they used to serve, causing them to feel betrayed or to seek revenge. Those who care little about fitting in are more likely to misbehave.

To have a meaningful investment in a cyber gathering place is to feel like an Athenian, and this is also what makes people disinclined to behave like virtual Visigoths. By offering settings for people to experience group interaction and community building, cyber gathering places provide those shared social spaces invested with special sentiment or attachment, those "'homes away from home' where unrelated people relate" (Oldenburg, 1989/1997, p. ix). The final conclusion reached in this investigation is that by re-engaging ourselves in Athenian activities online, we can perhaps restore some sense of social place and civic responsibility that seems to be breaking down in modern life. As we learn to dwell more comfortably in the virtual gathering places of cyberspace, we may learn to be more at ease transacting with strangers in our offline environments, and may not be so inclined to enter into the sorts of social conflicts described above with reference to public activities involving cell phones, automobiles, airplanes, offices, sports events, and even umbrellas.

Perhaps the need for civic virtue seems more compelling in cyberspace than in face-to-face situations offline, because in online environments, it is behavior itself and behavior alone which sets boundaries, as there are no physical boundaries other than on or off. Those who belong to cyber gathering places and participate in them as Athenians seem less likely to threaten or disrupt their communities as Visigoths might. According to Joinson, "it is possible that Net users come to see themselves differently following their on-line behavior. Whether changes then manifest themselves in different behavior in real life is unknown, though certainly worthy of research" (1998, p. 53). Although personally I can vouch only for my own behavior and experiences in virtual communities, the conclusions drawn from this study suggest that gathering for social interaction in cyber places and participating actively in the regulation of online conduct may help promote a new sense of social place and civic concern.

To conclude this investigation of misbehavior in cyber places, it is fitting to recall the passage cited at the outset of this report, in which Postman compares the traditions and values of those two cultures from long ago: the community-building Athenians of ancient Greece and the community-destroying Visigoths of medieval Europe:

> To be an Athenian is to take an interest in public affairs and the improvement of public behavior. . . . A modern Visigoth is interested only in his own affairs and has no sense of the meaning of community. . . . Eventually, like the rest of us, you must be on one side or the other. You must be an Athenian or a Visigoth. (1988, pp. 188–189)

I hope that by attempting to shed light on the activities of online Athenians and Visigoths as they gather in cyber places, this study of misbehavior may also contribute to enriching our understanding of the ways Athenians and Visigoths in all environments behave and communicate in everyday life, both online and off.

References

1267623 Ontario Inc. v. Nexx Online Inc. [Ruling]. O.J. No. 2246, Court File No. C20546/99 (Ontario Superior Court of Justice, June 14, 1999). Retrieved July 24, 1999, from http://www.digitaldesk.com/stuff/netiquette.htm

Aftab, P. (2000). *The parent's guide to protecting your children in cyberspace*. New York: McGraw-Hill.

Agee, W. K., Ault, P. H., & Emery, E. (1985). *Introduction to mass communications* (8th ed.). New York: Harper & Row.

Agence France-Presse. (2000, August 27). *Web pioneer supports surfing licenses, global laws on cyberspace* [Article cited by Vinton G. Cerf in post to the Internet Societal Task Force electronic mailing list, August 28, 2000].

Agence France-Presse. (2004, March 17). *France to try ex-Yahoo! boss in Nazi auction case*. Retrieved April 4, 2004, from http://www.expatica.com/source/site_article.asp?subchannel_id=58&story_id=5722

Agre, P. E. (1998). Designing genres for new media: Social, economic, and political contexts. In S. G. Jones (Ed.), *CyberSociety 2.0: Revisiting computer-mediated communication and community* (pp. 69–99). Thousand Oaks, CA: Sage.

Albrecht, R. (2004). *Mediating the muse: A communications approach to music, media, and cultural change*. Cresskill, NJ: Hampton Press.

American Cancer Society. (n.d.). *Fraudulent chain letter* [Bulletin]. Retrieved March 5, 1999, from http://www.cancer.org/chain.html

Anderson, B. (1996). Providing explicit support for social constraints: In search of the social computer. *Proceedings of SIGCHI, CHI 96*. Retrieved July 30, 1999, from http://www.acm.org/sigchi/chi96/proceedings/doctoral/Anderson/ba_txt.htm

Anderson, T., & Kanuka, H. (1997). On-line forums: New platforms for professional development and group collaboration. *Journal of Computer-Mediated Communication, 3*(3). Retrieved February 8, 1999, from http://jcmc.huji.ac.il/vol3/issue3/anderson.html

Aronson, S. H. (1986). The sociology of the telephone. In G. Gumpert & R. Cathcart (Eds.), *Inter/media: Interpersonal communication in a media world* (3rd ed.) (pp. 300–310). New York: Oxford University Press. (Original work published 1971)

Associated Press. (1999, March 15). Reno announces alliance to curb cybercrime. *The New York Times*. Retrieved March 16, 1999, from http://www.nytimes.com/library/tech/99/03/biztech/articles/16reno.html

Associated Press. (1999, March 30). Investigators search for author of "Melissa" virus. *CNN*. Retrieved March 30, 1999, from http://cnn.com/TECH/computing/9903/30/computer.virus.ap

Associated Press. (1999, April 7). Lawyer for alleged "Melissa" virus creator questions charges. *CNN*. Retrieved April 8, 1999, from http://cnn.com/TECH/computing/9904/07/computer.virus.ap

Associated Press. (1999, April 29). Taiwan college identifies virus. *The New York Times*. Retrieved May 1, 1999, from http://www.nytimes.com/library/tech/99/04/biztech/articles/29virus.html

Associated Press. (2000, May 15). World leaders join forces to fight Internet attacks. *CNN*. Retrieved May 16, 2000, from http://cnn.com/2000/TECH/computing/05/15/internet.crimes.ap/index.htm

Austin, J. L. (1962). *How to do things with words*. New York: Oxford University Press.

Avery, R. K., & McCain, T. A. (1986). Interpersonal and mediated encounters: A reorientation to the mass communication process. In G. Gumpert & R. Cathcart (Eds.), *Inter/media: Interpersonal communication in a media world* (3rd ed.) (pp. 121–131). New York: Oxford University Press. (Original work published 1982)

Aycock, A., & Buchignani, N. (1995). The e-mail murders: Reflections on "dead" letters. In S. G. Jones (Ed.), *CyberSociety: Computer-mediated communication and community* (pp. 184–231). Thousand Oaks, CA: Sage.

Barnes, S. B. (1995). The development of graphical user interfaces from 1970 to 1993, and some of its social consequences in offices, schools, and the graphic arts (Doctoral dissertation, New York University, 1995). *Dissertation Abstracts International, 56*(11), 4184 (UMI No. AAT 9609383).

Barnes, S. B. (1996a). Cyberspace: Creating paradoxes for the ecology of self. In L. Strate, R. Jacobson, & S. B. Gibson (Eds.), *Communication and cyberspace: Social interaction in an electronic environment* (pp. 193–216). Cresskill, NJ: Hampton Press.

Barnes, S. B. (1996b). Internet relationships: The bright and dark sides of cyber-friendship. *Telektronikk, 96*(1), 26–39.

Barnes, S. B. (2000). Bridging the differences between social theory and technological invention in human-computer interface design. *New Media & Society, 2*(3), 353–372.

Barnes, S. B. (2001). *Online connections: Internet interpersonal relationships*. Cresskill, NJ: Hampton Press.

Barnes, S. B. (2003). *Computer-mediated communication: Human to human communication across the Internet*. Boston: Allyn & Bacon.

Barnes, S. B., & Strate, L. (1996). The educational implications of the computer: A media ecology critique. *The New Jersey Journal of Communication, 4*(2), 180–208.

Bartle, R. (1996, April). *Hearts, clubs, diamonds, spades: Players who suit MUDs*. Retrieved May 1, 1999, from http://journal.tinymush.org/v1n1/bartle.html

Baum, R. (2000, August 14). Yahoo! Nazi case raises questions. Reuters. Retrieved September 20, 2000, from http://www.totaltele.com/view.asp?ArticleID=29878&pub=tt&categoryid=626

Baym, N. K. (1994). Communication, interpretation, and relationship: A study of a computer-mediated fan community (Doctoral dissertation, University of Illinois at Urbana-Champaign, 1994). *Dissertation Abstracts International, 55*(12), 3682 (UMI No. AAT 9512297).

Baym, N. K. (1995). The emergence of community in computer-mediated communication. In S. G. Jones (Ed.), *CyberSociety: Computer-mediated communication and community* (pp. 138–163). Thousand Oaks, CA: Sage.

Baym, N. K. (1997a). Identity, body, and community in on-line life [Review essay]. *Journal of Communication, 47*(4), 142–148.

Baym, N. K. (1997b). Interpreting soap operas and creating community: Inside an electronic fan culture. In S. Kiesler (Ed.), *Culture of the Internet* (pp. 103–120). Mahwah, NJ: Lawrence Erlbaum. (Original work published 1993)

Baym, N. K. (1998). The emergence of on-line community. In S. G. Jones (Ed.), *Cyber-Society 2.0: Revisiting computer-mediated communication and community* (pp. 35–68). Thousand Oaks, CA: Sage.

Baym, N. K. (1999). *Tune in, log on: Soaps, fandom, and on-line community.* Thousand Oaks, CA: Sage.

Beaubien, M. P. (1996). Playing at community: Multi-user dungeons and social interaction in cyberspace. In L. Strate, R. Jacobson, & S. B. Gibson (Eds.), *Communication and cyberspace: Social interaction in an electronic environment* (pp. 179–188). Cresskill, NJ: Hampton Press.

Becker, H. S. (1973). *Outsiders: Studies in the sociology of deviance.* New York: Free Press. (Original work published 1963)

Bellovin, S. (1998). Network and Internet security. In D. E. Denning & P. J. Denning (Eds.), *Internet besieged: Countering cyberspace scofflaws* (pp. 117–136). New York: ACM Press; Reading, MA: Addison Wesley.

Beniger, J. R. (1986). *The control revolution: Technological and economic origins of the information society.* Cambridge, MA: Harvard University Press.

Beniger, J. R. (1996). Who shall control cyberspace? In L. Strate, R. Jacobson, & S. B. Gibson (Eds.), *Communication and cyberspace: Social interaction in an electronic environment* (pp. 49–58). Cresskill, NJ: Hampton Press.

Biocca, F. (1997, September). The cyborg's dilemma: Progressive embodiment in virtual environments. *Journal of Computer-Mediated Communication, 3*(2). Retrieved August 2, 1999, from http://jcmc.huji.ac.il/vol3/issue2/biocca2.html

Birdwhistell, R. L. (1960). Kinesics and communication. In E. Carpenter & M. McLuhan (Eds.), *Explorations in communication* (pp. 54–64). Boston: Beacon Press.

Birdwhistell, R. L. (1970). *Kinesics and context: Essays on body motion communication.* Philadelphia: University of Pennsylvania Press.

Bolter, J. D. (1984). *Turing's man: Western culture in the computer age.* Chapel Hill: University of North Carolina Press.

Bolter, J. D. (1991). *Writing space: The computer, hypertext, and the history of writing.* Hillsdale, NJ: Lawrence Erlbaum.

Bolter, J. D. (1996). Virtual reality and the redefinition of self. In L. Strate, R. Jacobson, & S. B. Gibson (Eds.), *Communication and cyberspace: Social interaction in an electronic environment* (pp. 105–119). Cresskill, NJ: Hampton Press.

Brand, R. L. (1990, June 8). *Coping with the threat of computer security incidents: A primer from prevention through recovery* [Bulletin]. Livermore, CA: Computer Incident Advisory Capability (CIAC), U.S. Department of Energy. Retrieved February 28, 1999, from ftp://ciac.llnl.gov/pub/ciac/ciacdocs/primer.txt

Branscomb, A. W. (1995). Rogue computer programs and computer rogues: Tailoring the punishment to fit the crime. In G. Johnson & H. Nissenbaum (Eds.), *Computers, ethics & social values* (pp. 89–115). Englewood Cliffs, NJ: Prentice Hall.

Branscomb, A. W. (1996). Cyberspaces: Familiar territory or lawless frontiers. *Journal of Computer-Mediated Communication, 2*(1). Retrieved February 8, 1999, from http://jcmc.huji.ac.il/vol2/issue1/intro.html

Broadhurst, J. (1997). Gender differences in online communication. In M. D. Ermann, M. B. Williams, & M. S. Shauf (Eds.), *Computers, ethics, and society* (2nd ed.) (pp. 152–157). New York: Oxford University Press.

Bromberg, H. (1996). Are MUDs communities? Identity, belonging and consciousness in virtual worlds. In R. Shields (Ed.), *Cultures of Internet: Virtual spaces, real histories, living bodies* (pp. 143–152). London: Sage.

Brown, J. (1998, September 15). A kinder, gentler Usenet. *Salon.* Retrieved February 10, 1999, from http://www.salon.com/21st/feature/1998/09/15feature.html

Brown, J. (1999a, January 19). There goes the neighborhood. Are companies like GeoCities truly "building communities"—or just plastering ads on incomplete, out-of-date Web pages? *Salon.* Retrieved April 16, 1999, from http://www.salon.com/21st/feature/1999/01/cov_19feature.html

Brown, J. (1999b, March 25). Bringing mailing lists to the masses. *Salon.* Retrieved May 8, 1999, from http://www.salon.com/21st/feature/1999/03/25feature.html

Bruckman, A. (Ed.). (1994, April). Approaches to managing deviant behavior in virtual communities [Abstract of panel discussion presented at CHI 94 conference, Boston, MA]. *CHI 94 Companion, Association for Computing Machinery,* 183–184. Retrieved August 30, 1999, from http://www.acm.org/pubs/articles/proceedings/chi/259963/p183-bruckman/p183-bruckman.pdf

Bruckman, A. (Ed.). (1999, January). *Managing deviant behavior in online communities* [Abstract and transcript of online symposium held in MediaMOO]. Retrieved September 12, 1999, from http://www.cc.gatech.edu/~asb/mediamoo/deviance-symposium-99.html

Bruckman, A., Danis, C., Lampe, C., Sternberg, J., & Waldron, C. (2006, April). Managing deviant behavior in online communities [Abstract of panel discussion presented at CHI 96 conference, Montreal, Canada]. *Proceedings of CHI 2006 (Conference on Human Factors in Computing Systems),* 21–24. Retrieved August 17, 2006, from http://doi.acm.org/10.1145/1125451.1125458

Bruckman, A., & Resnick, M. (1995). The MediaMOO Project: Constructionism and professional community. *Convergence, 1*(1), 94–109. Retrieved December 28, 1998, from http://www.cc.gatech.edu/~asb/papers/convergence.html

Brunker, M. (2000, January 21). Mitnick goes free, but must remain totally unplugged. *MSNBC.* Retrieved September 3, 2001, from http://www.msnbc.com/news/178825.asp

Bunn, A. (1999, March 3). Molotovs and mailing lists. *Salon.* Retrieved May 8, 1999, from http://www.salon.com/21st/feature/1999/03/03feature.html

Burrows, R. (1997). Virtual culture, urban social polarisation and social science fiction. In B. D. Loader (Ed.), *The governance of cyberspace: Politics, technology and global restructuring* (pp. 38–45). New York: Routledge.

Cailliau, R. (2000, August 26). Opinion: Interview. *New Scientist.* Retrieved September 18, 2000, from http://www.newscientist.com/opinion/opinion.jsp?id=ns225317

Cairncross, F. (1997). *The death of distance: How the communications revolution will change our lives.* Boston: Harvard Business School Press.

Carnevale, P. J., & Probst, T. M. (1997). Conflict on the Internet. In S. Kiesler (Ed.), *Culture of the Internet* (pp. 233–255). Mahwah, NJ: Lawrence Erlbaum.

Carpenter, E. (1960). The new languages. In E. Carpenter & M. McLuhan (Eds.), *Explorations in communication* (pp. 162–179). Boston: Beacon Press.

Carpenter, E., & Heyman, K. (1970). *They became what they beheld.* New York: Outerbridge & Dienstfrey.

Carpenter, E., & McLuhan, M. (1960a). Acoustic space. In E. Carpenter & M. McLuhan (Eds.), *Explorations in communication* (pp. 65–70). Boston: Beacon Press.

Carpenter, E., & McLuhan, M. (Eds.). (1960b). *Explorations in communication.* Boston: Beacon Press.

Cascio, J. (1999, April 7). The ecology of computer viruses: Who was vulnerable to Melissa? Only users and companies who'd standardized on a software "monoculture"—like Microsoft's. *Salon.* Retrieved May 8, 1999, from http://www.salon.com/tech/feature/1999/04/07/melissa

Cathcart, R., & Gumpert, G. (1986). Mediated interpersonal communication: Toward a new typology. In G. Gumpert & R. Cathcart (Eds.), *Inter/media: Interpersonal communication in a media world* (3rd ed.) (pp. 25–40). New York: Oxford University Press. (Original work published 1983)

Cavazos, E. A., & Morin, G. (1994). *Cyberspace and the law: Your rights and duties in the on-line world.* Cambridge, MA: M.I.T. Press.

Chen, L. L.-J., & Gaines, B. R. (1998). Modeling and supporting virtual cooperative interaction through the World Wide Web. In F. Sudweeks, M. L. McLaughlin, & S. Rafaeli (Eds.), *Network and netplay: Virtual groups on the Internet* (pp. 221–242). Cambridge, MA: M.I.T. Press.

Chenault, B. (1998, May). Developing personal and emotional relationships via computer-mediated communication. *Computer-Mediated Communication Magazine, 5*(5). Retrieved May 13, 1998, from http://www.december.com/cmc/mag/1998/may/chenault.html

Chesebro, J. W., & Bonsall, D. G. (1989). *Computer-mediated communication: Human relationships in a computerized world.* Tuscaloosa: University of Alabama Press.

Cheung, J. L.-M. (1995). An exploratory study of computer-mediated communication as a social system: Internet Relay Chat (Master's thesis, University of Waterloo, Ontario, Canada, 1995). *Masters Abstracts International, 34*(01), 99.

Cicognani, A. (2003). Architectural design for online environments. In B. Kolko (Ed.), *Virtual publics: Policy and community in an electronic age* (pp. 83–111). New York: Columbia University Press. Retrieved August 2, 1999, from http://www.arch.usyd.edu.au/~anna/papers/kolko.html

Cisler, S. (1995, January). Can we keep community networks running? *Computer-Mediated Communication Magazine, 2*(1). Retrieved May 19, 1998, from http://www.december.com/cmc/mag/1995/jan/cisler.html

Clark, L. S. (1998). Dating on the net: Teens and the rise of "pure" relationships. In S. G. Jones (Ed.), *CyberSociety 2.0: Revisiting computer-mediated communication and community* (pp. 159–183). Thousand Oaks, CA: Sage.

CNN. (1999, April 8). Accused "Melissa" creator appears in court. Retrieved April 9, 1999, from http://cnn.com/TECH/computing/9904/08/melissa.charges.03

CNN. (1999, April 27). Chernobyl virus wreaks havoc in parts of Asia. Retrieved May 7, 1999, from http://cnn.com/TECH/computing/9904/27/computers.asia.virus/index.html

CNN. (2000, January 21). Legendary computer hacker released from prison. Retrieved January 26, 2000, from http://cnn.com/2000/TECH/computing/01/21/mitnick.release.01/index.html

CNN. (2005, March 25). Yahoo asks for ruling on censorship abroad. Retrieved March 26, 2005, from http://www.cnn.com/2005/TECH/03/25/yahoo.nazi.reut/index.html

Collins, M. (1992, Fall). *Flaming: The relationship between social context cues and uninhibited verbal behavior in computer-mediated communication.* Retrieved January 24, 1999, from http://star.ucc.nau.edu/~mauri/papers/flames.html

Coltman, T., & Romm, C. T. (1997, February). Factors affecting the quality of organizational computer mediated communication: A social network perspective. *Proceedings of Creative Collaboration in Virtual Communities '97*, University of Sydney, Australia. Retrieved February 19, 1999, from http://www.arch.usyd.edu.au/kcdc/conferences/VC97/papers/coltman.html

Computer Emergency Response Team (CERT). (1996a). *Anonymous FTP [file transfer protocol] abuses* [Bulletin]. Pittsburgh: CERT Coordination Center, Carnegie Mellon University. Retrieved February 21, 1999, from http://www.cert.org/ftp/tech_tips/anonymous_ftp_abuses

Computer Emergency Response Team (CERT). (1996b). *Email bombing and spamming* [Bulletin]. Pittsburgh: CERT Coordination Center, Carnegie Mellon University. Retrieved February 21, 1999, from http://www.cert.org/ftp/tech_tips/email_bombing_spamming

Computer Emergency Response Team (CERT). (1996c). *Spoofed/forged email* [Bulletin]. Pittsburgh: CERT Coordination Center, Carnegie Mellon University. Retrieved February 21, 1999, from http://www.cert.org/ftp/tech_tips/email_spoofing

Computer Emergency Response Team (CERT). (1997, October 2). *Denial of service* [Bulletin]. Pittsburgh: CERT Coordination Center, Carnegie Mellon University. Retrieved February 21, 1999, from http://www.cert.org/ftp/tech_tips/denial_of_service

Computer Emergency Response Team (CERT). (1998, May 26). *IP denial-of-service attacks* [Advisory CA-97.28]. Pittsburgh: CERT Coordination Center, Carnegie Mellon University. Retrieved March 7, 1999, from ftp://ftp.cert.org/pub/cert_advisories/CA-97.28.Teardrop_Land

Computer Ethics Institute. (1997). The ten commandments of computer ethics. In M. D. Ermann, M. B. Williams, & M. S. Shauf (Eds.), *Computers, ethics, and society* (2nd ed.) (pp. 313–314). New York: Oxford University Press.

Computer Incident Advisory Capability (CIAC). (1996, November 20). *Internet hoaxes: PKZ300, Irina, Good Times, Deeyenda, Ghost* [Bulletin]. Livermore, CA: Computer Security Technology Center, U.S. Department of Energy. Retrieved March 5, 1999, from http://ciac.llnl.gov/ciac/bulletins/h-05.shtml

Computer Incident Advisory Capability (CIAC). (1999a, January 11). *Internet hoaxes* [Bulletin]. Livermore, CA: Computer Security Technology Center, U.S. Department of Energy. Retrieved February 21, 1999, from http://ciac.llnl.gov/ciac/CIACHoaxes.html

Computer Incident Advisory Capability (CIAC). (1999b, February 10). *Internet chain letters* [Bulletin]. Livermore, CA: Computer Security Technology Center, U.S. Department of Energy. Retrieved February 21, 1999, from http://ciac.llnl.gov/ciac/CIACChainLetters.html

Condon, S. L., & Cech, C. G. (1996). Functional comparison of face-to-face and computer-mediated decision making interactions. In S. C. Herring (Ed.), *Computer-mediated communication: Linguistic, social and cross-cultural perspectives* (pp. 65–80). Amsterdam: J. Benjamins.

Conforti, R. (2001). An interview study of the role of computer-mediated relationships in the experiences and self development of a small group of women users of computer-mediated communication (Doctoral dissertation, New York University, 2001). *Dissertation Abstracts International, 61*(10), 3813 (UMI No. AAT 9992344).

Curtis, P. (1992). *LambdaMOO takes a new direction* [Memorandum to community from founder]. Retrieved August 13, 1998, from http://vesta.physics.ucla.edu/~smolin/lambda/laws_and_history/newdirection

Curtis, P. (1997). Mudding: Social phenomena in text-based virtual realities. In S. Kiesler (Ed.), *Culture of the Internet* (pp. 121–142). Mahwah, NJ: Lawrence Erlbaum.

Cutler, R. H. (1996). Technologies, relations, and selves. In L. Strate, R. Jacobson, & S. B. Gibson (Eds.), *Communication and cyberspace: Social interaction in an electronic environment* (pp. 317–333). Cresskill, NJ: Hampton Press.

Danet, B. (1998). Text as mask: Gender, play, and performance on the Internet. In S. G. Jones (Ed.), *CyberSociety 2.0: Revisiting computer-mediated communication and community* (pp. 129–158). Thousand Oaks, CA: Sage.

Danet, B., Ruedenberg, L., & Rosenbaum-Tamari, Y. (1998). Hmmm . . . where's that smoke coming from? Writing, play and performance on Internet Relay Chat. In F. Sudweeks, M. L. McLaughlin, & S. Rafaeli (Eds.), *Network and netplay: Virtual groups on the Internet* (pp. 41–76). Cambridge, MA: M.I.T. Press.

Danielson, P. (1996). Pseudonyms, mailbots, and virtual letterheads: The evolution of computer-mediated ethics. In C. Ess (Ed.), *Philosophical perspectives on computer-mediated communication* (pp. 67–93). Albany: State University of New York Press.

Data Communications Task Force. (1995, February 2). *Authenticated NYU-NET access to the Internet* [Bulletin]. New York: Academic Computing Facility, New York University. Retrieved February 21, 1999, from http://www.nyu.edu/acf/nyunet/tech/policy/access.html

Dean, D., Felten, E. W., Wallach, D. S., & Balfanz, D. (1998). Java security: Web browsers and beyond. In D. E. Denning & P. J. Denning (Eds.), *Internet besieged: Countering cyberspace scofflaws* (pp. 241–269). New York: ACM Press; Reading, MA: Addison Wesley.

December, J. (1995, January). Transitions in studying computer-mediated communication. *Computer-Mediated Communication Magazine, 2*(1). Retrieved May 19, 1998, from http://www.december.com/cmc/mag/1995/jan/december.html

December, J. (1996). Units of analysis for Internet communication. *Journal of Communication, 46*(1), 14–38.

December, J. (1997a, January). Notes on defining of computer-mediated communication. *Computer-Mediated Communication Magazine, 4*(1). Retrieved April 22, 1998, from http://www.december.com/cmc/mag/1997/jan/december.html

December, J. (1997b, February). Communities exist in cyberspace. *Computer-Mediated Communication Magazine, 4*(2). Retrieved April 22, 1998, from http://www.december.com/cmc/mag/1997/feb/last.html

DelFavero, J. (1997). When bad things happen to good accounts. *Connect Magazine*, Fall 1997, p. 18. New York: Academic Computing Facility, New York University. Retrieved February 21, 1999, from http://www.nyu.edu/acf/pubs/connect/fall97/FromPostFall97.html

DelFavero, J. (1998a). Dealing with spammers. *Connect Magazine*, Spring 1998, p. 19. New York: Academic Computing Facility, New York University. Retrieved February 21, 1999, from http://www.nyu.edu/acf/pubs/connect/spring98/Q&APostmasterSp98.html

DelFavero, J. (1998b). "As the e-mail bounces": An episodic drama for NYU. *Connect Magazine*, Fall 1998, p. 25. New York: Academic Computing Facility, New York University. Retrieved February 21, 1999, from http://www.nyu.edu/acf/pubs/connect/fall98/PostmasterFall98.html

DelFavero, J., & Losco, T. (1998). E-mail hoaxes: What threats are real. *Connect Magazine*, Summer 1998, p. 10. New York: Academic Computing Facility, New York University. Retrieved February 21, 1999, from http://www.nyu.edu/acf/pubs/connect/summer98/HelpCenterHoaxesSum98.html

Denning, D. E. (1996). Concerning hackers who break into computer systems. In P. Ludlow (Ed.), *High noon on the electronic frontier: Conceptual issues in cyberspace* (pp. 137–163). Cambridge, MA: M.I.T. Press.

Denning, D. E. (1998). Cyberspace attacks and countermeasures. In D. E. Denning & P. J. Denning (Eds.), *Internet besieged: Countering cyberspace scofflaws* (pp. 29–55). New York: ACM Press; Reading, MA: Addison Wesley.

Denning, D. E. (1999). *Information warfare and security*. New York: ACM Press; Reading, MA: Addison-Wesley.

Denning, D. E. (2000a, Autumn). Cyberterrorism. *Global Dialogue*. Retrieved March 17, 2001, from http://www.cs.georgetown.edu/~denning/infosec/cyberterror-GD.doc

Denning, D. E. (2000b, Fall). Reflections on cyberweapons controls. *Computer Security Journal, XVI*(4). Retrieved March 17, 2001, from http://www.cs.georgetown.edu/~denning/infosec/cyberweapons-controls.doc

Denning, D. E. (2000c, October). Disarming the Black Hats? When does a security tool become a cyberweapon? *Information Security Magazine*. Retrieved March 17, 2001, from http://www.cs.georgetown.edu/~denning/infosec/disarming-blackhats.html

Denning, D. E., & Denning, P. J. (Eds.). (1998a). *Internet besieged: Countering cyberspace scofflaws*. New York: ACM Press; Reading, MA: Addison Wesley.

Denning, D. E., & Denning, P. J. (1998b). Introduction. In D. E. Denning & P. J. Denning (Eds.), *Internet besieged: Countering cyberspace scofflaws* (pp. 1–10). New York: ACM Press; Reading, MA: Addison Wesley.

Denning, D. E., & Drake, F. (1995). A dialog on hacking and security. In G. Johnson & H. Nissenbaum (Eds.), *Computers, ethics & social values* (pp. 120–125). Englewood Cliffs, NJ: Prentice Hall.

Denning, D. E., & Lin, H. S. (Eds.). (1994). *Rights and responsibilities of participants in networked communities*. Washington, DC: National Academy Press.

Denning, P. J. (1998a). Electronic commerce. In D. E. Denning & P. J. Denning (Eds.), *Internet besieged: Countering cyberspace scofflaws* (pp. 377–388). New York: ACM Press; Reading, MA: Addison Wesley.

Denning, P. J. (1998b). The Internet after thirty years. In D. E. Denning & P. J. Denning (Eds.), *Internet besieged: Countering cyberspace scofflaws* (pp. 15–27). New York: ACM Press; Reading, MA: Addison Wesley.

Denning, P. J. (1998c). Passwords. In D. E. Denning & P. J. Denning (Eds.), *Internet besieged: Countering cyberspace scofflaws* (pp. 159–166). New York: ACM Press; Reading, MA: Addison Wesley.

Dery, M. (1993). Flame wars. *The South Atlantic Quarterly, 92*(4), 559–568.

Dery, M. (1996). *Escape velocity: Cyberculture at the end of the century*. New York: Grove Press.

Deuel, N. (1996). Our passionate response to virtual reality. In S. C. Herring (Ed.), *Computer-mediated communication: Linguistic, social and cross-cultural perspectives* (pp. 129–146). Amsterdam: J. Benjamins.

Dibbell, J. (1993, December 21). A rape in cyberspace: How an evil clown, a Haitian trickster spirit, two wizards, and a cast of dozens turned a database into a society. *The Village Voice*, pp. 36–42. Retrieved August 13, 1999, from http://vesta.physics.ucla.edu/~smolin/lambda/laws_and_history/VillageVoice.txt

Dibbell, J. (1996). Taboo, consensus, and the challenge of democracy in an electronic forum. In R. Kling (Ed.), *Computerization and controversy: Value conflicts and social choices* (2nd ed.) (pp. 552–568). San Diego, CA: Academic Press.

Dibbell, J. (1998). *My tiny life: Crime and passion in a virtual world.* New York: Holt.

Doheny-Farina, S. (1996). *The wired neighborhood.* New Haven, CT: Yale University Press.

Donath, J. S. (1996). *Inhabiting the virtual city: The design of social environments for electronic communities* (Doctoral dissertation, Massachusetts Institute of Technology, 1996). Retrieved May 7, 1999, from http://judith.www.media.mit.edu/Thesis

Donath, J. S. (1999). Identity and deception in the virtual community. In M. A. Smith & P. Kollock (Eds.), *Communities in cyberspace* (pp. 29–59). New York: Routledge.

Doyle, P., & Hayes-Roth, B. (1998). Guided exploration of virtual worlds. In F. Sudweeks, M. L. McLaughlin, & S. Rafaeli (Eds.), *Network and netplay: Virtual groups on the Internet* (pp. 243–263). Cambridge, MA: M.I.T. Press.

Drucker, S. J., & Gumpert, G. (Eds.). (1997). *Voices in the street: Explorations in gender, media, and public space.* Cresskill, NJ: Hampton Press.

Dsilva, M. U., Maddox, R., & Collins, B. (1998). Criticism on the Internet: An analysis of participant reactions. *Communication Research Reports, 15*(2), 180–187.

Dutton, W. H. (1996). Network rules of order: Regulating speech in public electronic fora. *Media, Culture & Society, 18*(2), 269–290.

Dyson, E. (1997). *Release 2.0: A design for living in the digital age.* New York: Broadway Books.

Edgar, S. L. (1997). *Morality and machines: Perspectives on computer ethics.* Boston: Jones and Bartlett.

Ehmen, B. (1996). *T'ai chi chu (or the yin-yang symbol).* Retrieved November 6, 2000, from http://www2.cybernex.net/~jefkirsh/symbol.html

Eisenstein, E. L. (1983). *The printing revolution in early modern Europe.* Cambridge: Cambridge University Press.

Elias, P. (1999, May 6). The case of the unhappy hacker. *ZDNet.* Retrieved May 7, 1999, from http://www.zdnet.com/zdnn/stories/news/0,4586,2254225,00.html

Ellul, J. (1964). *The technological society* (J. Wilkinson, Trans.). New York: Vintage Books. (Original work published 1954)

Elmer-Dewitt, P. (1996). Censoring cyberspace. In P. Ludlow (Ed.), *High noon on the electronic frontier: Conceptual issues in cyberspace* (pp. 259–262). Cambridge, MA: M.I.T. Press.

Emmet, E. R. (1968). *Learning to philosophize.* Harmondsworth: Penguin.

Ermann, M. D., Williams, M. B., & Shauf, M. S. (Eds.). (1997). *Computers, ethics, and society* (2nd ed.). New York: Oxford University Press.

Evans, M. (1999, July 9). Ontario judge rules against junk e-mail: "Netiquette" decision could set legal precedent. *The Globe and Mail.* Retrieved July 22, 1999, from http://globetechnology.com/gam/News/19990709/RSPAM.html

Fanderclai, T. L. (1995, January). MUDs in education: New environments, new pedagogies. *Computer-Mediated Communication Magazine, 2*(1). Retrieved May 19, 1998, from http://www.december.com/cmc/mag/1995/jan/fanderclai.html

Fernback, J. (1997). The individual within the collective: Virtual ideology and the realization of collective principles. In S. G. Jones (Ed.), *Virtual culture: Identity and communication in cybersociety* (pp. 36–54). Thousand Oaks, CA: Sage.

Figallo, C. (1998). *Hosting Web communities: Building relationships, increasing customer loyalty, and maintaining a competitive edge.* New York: John Wiley.

Fleming, P. J. (1990). Software and sympathy: Therapeutic interaction with the computer. In G. Gumpert & S. L. Fish (Eds.), *Talking to strangers: Mediated therapeutic communication* (pp. 170–183). Norwood, NJ: Ablex.

Foo, C. Y. (2006). *A qualitative study of grief play management in MMORPGs.* Unpublished doctoral dissertation, Curtin University of Technology, Perth, Australia.

Foo, C. Y. (2008). *Grief play management: A qualitative study of grief play management in MMORPGs.* Saarbrücken, Germany: VDM Verlag.

Foster, D. (1997). Community and identity in the electronic village. In D. Porter (Ed.), *Internet culture* (pp. 23–37). New York: Routledge.

Frank, L. K. (1960). Tactile communication. In E. Carpenter & M. McLuhan (Eds.), *Explorations in communication* (pp. 4–11). Boston: Beacon Press.

Freedman, D. H., & Mann, C. C. (1997). *At large: The strange case of the world's biggest Internet invasion.* New York: Simon & Schuster.

Frommer, M. (1987). How well do inventors understand the cultural consequences of their inventions? A study of: Samuel Finley Breese Morse and the telegraph, Thomas Alva Edison and the phonograph, and Alexander Graham Bell and the telephone (Doctoral dissertation, New York University, 1987). *Dissertation Abstracts International, 48*(05), 2979 (UMI No. AAT 8712485).

Fusaro, R. (1998, December 23). AOL claims victory in three spam suits. *CNN.* Retrieved December 23, 1998, from http://cnn.com/TECH/computing/9812/23/aolspam.idg

Gackenbach, J., Guthrie, G., & Karpen, J. (1998). The coevolution of technology and consciousness. In J. Gackenbach (Ed.), *Psychology and the Internet: Intrapersonal, interpersonal, and transpersonal implications* (pp. 321–350). San Diego, CA: Academic Press.

Gardrat, A. (1998). Another look at European Internet law. *Media Law & Policy, 7*(1), 27–32.

Garton, L., & Wellman, B. (1995). Social impacts of electronic mail in organizations: A review of the research literature. In B. R. Burleson (Ed.), *Communication Yearbook, 18*, 434–453. Thousand Oaks, CA: Sage. Retrieved February 21, 1998, from http://www.chass.utoronto.ca/~wellman/links/email.pdf

Gencarelli, T. F. (2000). The intellectual roots of media ecology in the work and thought of Neil Postman. *The New Jersey Journal of Communication, 8*(1), 91–103.

Gergen, K. J. (1997). How computers affect interpersonal relationships. In M. D. Ermann, M. B. Williams, & M. S. Shauf (Eds.), *Computers, ethics, and society* (2nd ed.) (pp. 137–151). New York: Oxford University Press.

Gibson, S. B. (1996). Pedagogy and hypertext. In L. Strate, R. Jacobson, & S. B. Gibson (Eds.), *Communication and cyberspace: Social interaction in an electronic environment* (pp. 243–259). Cresskill, NJ: Hampton Press.

Giedion, S. (1960). Space conception in prehistoric art. In E. Carpenter & M. McLuhan (Eds.), *Explorations in communication* (pp. 71–89). Boston: Beacon Press.

Giese, M. (1996). From ARPAnet to the Internet: A cultural clash and its implications in framing the debate on the information superhighway. In L. Strate, R. Jacobson, & S. B. Gibson (Eds.), *Communication and cyberspace: Social interaction in an electronic environment* (pp. 123–141). Cresskill, NJ: Hampton Press.

Giese, M. (1998). Constructing a virtual geography: Narratives of space in a text-based environment. *Journal of Communication Inquiry, 22*(2), 152–176.

Godwin, M. (1996a). Sex and the single sysadmin: The risks of carrying graphic sexual materials. In P. Ludlow (Ed.), *High noon on the electronic frontier: Conceptual issues in cyberspace* (pp. 291–300). Cambridge, MA: M.I.T. Press.

Godwin, M. (1996b). Virtual community standards: BBS obscenity case raises new legal issues. In P. Ludlow (Ed.), *High noon on the electronic frontier: Conceptual issues in cyberspace* (pp. 269–273). Cambridge, MA: M.I.T. Press.

Godwin, M. (1998). *Cyber rights: Defending free speech in the digital age.* New York: Random House.

Goertzel, B. (1998). World wide brain: Self-organizing Internet intelligence as the actualization of the collective unconscious. In J. Gackenbach (Ed.), *Psychology and the Internet: Intrapersonal, interpersonal, and transpersonal implications* (pp. 293–319). San Diego, CA: Academic Press.

Goffman, E. (1959). *The presentation of self in everyday life.* New York: Anchor Books.

Goffman, E. (1963). *Behavior in public places: Notes on the social organization of gatherings.* New York: The Free Press.

Gotved, S. (2000, September). *Newsgroup interaction as urban life.* Paper presented at the conference of the Association of Internet Researchers, Lawrence, KS. Retrieved September 11, 2000, from http://www2.cddc.vt.edu/aoir/papers/gotved-paper.pdf

Gozzi, Jr., R. (1999). *The power of metaphor in the age of electronic media.* Cresskill, NJ: Hampton Press.

Gozzi, Jr., R. (2000). Jacques Ellul on technique, media, and the spirit. *The New Jersey Journal of Communication, 8*(1), 79–90.

Grabowsky, P. N., & Smith, R. G. (1998). *Crime in the digital age: Controlling telecommunications and cyberspace illegalities.* New Brunswick, NJ: Transaction.

Griffiths, M. (1998). Internet addiction: Does it really exist? In J. Gackenbach (Ed.), *Psychology and the Internet: Intrapersonal, interpersonal, and transpersonal implications* (pp. 61–75). San Diego, CA: Academic Press.

Grohol, J. M. (1998). Future clinical directions: Professional development, pathology, and psychotherapy on-line. In J. Gackenbach (Ed.), *Psychology and the Internet: Intrapersonal, interpersonal, and transpersonal implications* (pp. 111–140). San Diego, CA: Academic Press.

Gronbeck, B. R. (2000). Communication media, memory, and social-political change in Eric Havelock. *The New Jersey Journal of Communication, 8*(1), 34–45.

Grossman, W. M. (1997). *Net.wars.* New York: New York University Press.

Guernsey, L. (1999, June 10). Rogues' gallery: Sneaky software. *The New York Times.* Retrieved June 12, 1999, from http://www.nytimes.com/library/tech/99/06/circuits/articles/10svir.html

Guernsey, L. (2001, January 11). Taking the offensive against cell phones. *The New York Times.* Retrieved January 11, 2001, from http://www.nytimes.com/2001/01/11/technology/11JAMS.html

Guisnel, J. (1997). *Cyberwars: Espionage on the Internet* (G. Masai, Trans.). New York: Plenum. (Original work published 1997)

Gumpert, G. (1987). *Talking tombstones and other tales of the media age.* New York: Oxford University Press.

Gumpert, G. (1990). Remote sex in the information age. In G. Gumpert & S. L. Fish (Eds.), *Talking to strangers: Mediated therapeutic communication* (pp. 143–153). Norwood, NJ: Ablex.

Gumpert, G., & Cathcart, R. (Eds.). (1979). *Inter/media: Interpersonal communication in a media world.* New York: Oxford University Press.

Gumpert, G., & Cathcart, R. (Eds.). (1982). *Inter/media: Interpersonal communication in a media world* (2nd ed.). New York: Oxford University Press.

Gumpert, G., & Cathcart, R. (Eds.). (1986a). *Inter/media: Interpersonal communication in a media world* (3rd ed.). New York: Oxford University Press.

Gumpert, G., & Cathcart, R. (1986b). Introduction. In G. Gumpert & R. Cathcart (Eds.), *Inter/media: Interpersonal communication in a media world* (3rd ed.) (pp. 9–16). New York: Oxford University Press.

Gumpert, G., & Cathcart, R. (1986c). Media, intimacy, and interpersonal networks. In G. Gumpert & R. Cathcart (Eds.), *Inter/media: Interpersonal communication in a media world* (3rd ed.) (pp. 161–168). New York: Oxford University Press.

Gumpert, G., & Drucker, S. J. (1996). From locomotion to telecommunication, or paths of safety, streets of gore. In L. Strate, R. Jacobson, & S. B. Gibson (Eds.), *Communication and cyberspace: Social interaction in an electronic environment* (pp. 25–38). Cresskill, NJ: Hampton Press.

Gumpert, G., & Drucker, S. J. (1997). Voices in the street: Explorations in gender, media, and public space. In S. J. Drucker & G. Gumpert (Eds.), *Voices in the street: Explorations in gender, media, and public space* (pp. 1–13). Cresskill, NJ: Hampton Press.

Gumpert, G., & Fish, S. L. (1990a). Introduction. In G. Gumpert & S. L. Fish (Eds.), *Talking to strangers: Mediated therapeutic communication* (pp. 1–9). Norwood, NJ: Ablex.

Gumpert, G., & Fish, S. L. (Eds.). (1990b). *Talking to strangers: Mediated therapeutic communication.* Norwood, NJ: Ablex.

Gurak, L. J. (1996, February). Toward broadening our research agenda in cyberspace. *Computer-Mediated Communication Magazine, 3*(2). Retrieved July 18, 1999, from http://www.december.com/cmc/mag/1996/feb/gurak.html

Gurak, L. J. (1997, May). Utopian visions of cyberspace. *Computer-Mediated Communication Magazine, 4*(5). Retrieved April 22, 1998, from http://www.december.com/cmc/mag/1997/may/last.html

Hafner, K. (1998, December 10). Tracking the evolution of e-mail etiquette. *The New York Times.* Retrieved March 4, 1999, from http://www.nytimes.com/library/tech/98/12/circuits/articles/10mail.html

Hafner, K., & Markoff, M. (1991). *Cyberpunk: Outlaws and hackers on the computer frontier.* New York: Simon & Schuster.

Halbert, D. (1997). Discourses of danger and the computer hacker. *The Information Society, 13,* 361–374.

Hall, E. T. (1959). *The silent language.* New York: Anchor Books.

Hall, E. T. (1966). *The hidden dimension.* New York: Anchor Books.

Hambridge, S. (1995, October). *Network working group request for comments 1855: Netiquette guidelines.* Retrieved January 10, 1999, from http://www.faqs.org/rfcs/rfc1855.html

Hambridge, S., & Lunde, A. (1999, June). *Network working group request for comments 2635: Don't spew, a set of guidelines for mass unsolicited mailings and postings (spam).* Retrieved September 25, 2000, from http://www.faqs.org/rfcs/rfc2635.html

Harmon, A. (1998, October 31). "Hacktivists" of all persuasions take their struggle to the Web. *The New York Times.* Retrieved September 9, 1999, from http://www.nytimes.com/library/tech/98/10/biztech/articles/31hack.html

Hauben, M. (1995, May). Exploring New York City's online community: A snapshot of NYC.GENERAL. *Computer-Mediated Communication Magazine, 2*(5), 9. Retrieved April 22, 1998, from http://www.december.com/cmc/mag/1995/may/hauben.html

Hauben, M. (1997, February). The netizens and community networks. *Computer-Mediated Communication Magazine, 4*(2). Retrieved April 22, 1998, from http://www.december.com/cmc/mag/1997/feb/hauben.html

Hauben, M., & Hauben, R. (1997). *Netizens: On the history and impact of Usenet and the Internet.* Los Alamitos, CA: IEEE Computer Society Press.

Havelock, E. A. (1982). *The literate revolution in Greece and its cultural consequences.* Princeton, NJ: Princeton University Press.

Haynes, C., & Holmevik, J. R. (Eds.). (1998). *High wired : On the design, use, and theory of educational MOOs.* Ann Arbor: University of Michigan Press.

Haythornthwaite, C., Wellman, B., & Garton, L. (1998). Work and community via computer-mediated communication In J. Gackenbach (Ed.), *Psychology and the Internet: Intrapersonal, interpersonal, and transpersonal implications* (pp. 199–226). San Diego, CA: Academic Press.

Healy, D. (1997). Cyberspace and place: The Internet as middle landscape on the electronic frontier. In D. Porter (Ed.), *Internet culture* (pp. 55–68). New York: Routledge.

Heberlein, L. T., & Bishop, M. (1998). Attack class: Address spoofing. In D. E. Denning & P. J. Denning (Eds.), *Internet besieged: Countering cyberspace scofflaws* (pp. 147–157). New York: ACM Press; Reading, MA: Addison Wesley.

Heim, M. (1993). *The metaphysics of virtual reality.* New York: Oxford University Press.

Heim, M. (1995, January). The nerd in the noosphere. *Computer-Mediated Communication Magazine, 2*(1), 3. Retrieved April 21, 1998, from http://sunsite.unc.edu/cmc/mag/1995/jan/heim.html

Herring, S. C. (1996a). Introduction. In S. C. Herring (Ed.), *Computer-mediated communication: Linguistic, social and cross-cultural perspectives* (pp. 1–10). Amsterdam: J. Benjamins.

Herring, S. C. (1996b). Posting in a different voice: Gender and ethics in computer-mediated communication. In C. Ess (Ed.), *Philosophical perspectives on computer-mediated communication* (pp. 115–145). Albany: State University of New York Press.

Herz, J. C. (1995). *Surfing on the Internet: A nethead's adventures on-line.* Boston: Little, Brown.

Hester, E. N. (1999, September 7). Flying in the age of air rage. *Salon.* Retrieved March 29, 2001, from http://www.salon.com/travel/diary/hest/1999/09/07/rage

Hiltz, S. R., & Turoff, M. (1993). *The network nation: Human communication via computer* (Rev. ed.). Cambridge, MA: M.I.T. Press. (Original work published 1978)

Holland, N. N. (1996, January). *The internet regression.* Retrieved January 21, 1999, from http://www.rider.edu/users/suler/psycyber/holland.html

Holmes, D. (1997a). Introduction: Virtual politics: Identity and community in cyberspace. In D. Holmes (Ed.), *Virtual politics: Identity and community in cyberspace* (pp. 1–25). Thousand Oaks, CA: Sage.

Holmes, D. (1997b). Virtual identity: Communities of broadcast, communities of interactivity. In D. Holmes (Ed.), *Virtual politics: Identity and community in cyberspace* (pp. 26–45). Thousand Oaks, CA: Sage.

Horn, S. (1998). *Cyberville: Clicks, culture, and the creation of an online town.* New York: Warner Books.

Horton, M. (1994, October 27). *Rules for posting to Usenet.* Retrieved March 5, 1999, from http://www.nonprofit.net/hoax/Rules.txt

Howard, J. D. (1997). *An analysis of security incidents on the Internet 1989–1995* (Doctoral dissertation, Carnegie Mellon University). Retrieved February 21, 1999, from http://www.cert.org/research/JHThesis

Hunkele, M., & Cornwell, K. (1997). The cyberspace curtain: Hidden gender issues. In S. J. Drucker & G. Gumpert (Eds.), *Voices in the street: Explorations in gender, media, and public space* (pp. 281–293). Cresskill, NJ: Hampton Press.

Hymes, C. (n.d.). *Don't spread that hoax!* Retrieved March 5, 1999, from http://www. nonprofit.net/hoax

Igbaria, M., Shayo, C., & Olfman, . (1998). Virtual societies: Their prospects and dilemmas. In J. Gackenbach (Ed.), *Psychology and the Internet: Intrapersonal, interpersonal, and transpersonal implications* (pp. 227–252). San Diego, CA: Academic Press.

Innis, H. A. (1951). *The bias of communication.* Toronto: University of Toronto Press.

Ito, M. (1997). Virtually embodied: The reality of fantasy in a multi-user dungeon. In D. Porter (Ed.), *Internet culture* (pp. 87–109). New York: Routledge.

Jacobson, R. (1996). "Are they building an off-ramp in my neighborhood?" and other questions concerning public interest in and access to the information superhighway. In L. Strate, R. Jacobson, & S. B. Gibson (Eds.), *Communication and cyberspace: Social interaction in an electronic environment* (pp. 143–153). Cresskill, NJ: Hampton Press.

Jacoby, N. (1999, November 29). Etiquette crisis at work: Employees say they've had enough of incivility, bad manners. *CNN.* Retrieved January 3, 2000, from http:// cnnfn.com/1999/11/29/life/q_manners

Johnson, D. R. (1996). Due process and cyberjurisdiction. *Journal of Computer-Mediated Communication, 2*(1). Retrieved February 8, 1999, from http://jcmc.huji.ac.il/vol2/ issue1/due.html

Johnson, D. R., & Post, D. G. (1996a, September). *And how shall the Net be governed? A meditation on the relative virtues of decentralized, emergent law.* Paper presented at the Conference on Coordination and Administration of the Internet, Harvard University, Cambridge, MA. Retrieved November 30, 2000, from http://www.cli.org/ emdraft.html

Johnson, D. R., & Post, D. G. (1996b). Laws and borders: The rise of law in cyberspace. 48 *Stanford Law Review,* 1367. Retrieved November 29, 2000, from http://www.cli. org/X0025_LBFIN.html

Johnson, D. R., & Post, D. G. (1997). The new "civic virtue" of the Internet. *First Monday 3*(1). Retrieved March 17, 2001, from http://www.firstmonday.dk/issues/issue3_ 1/johnson

Johnson, J. (1994). *Giga bites: The hacker cookbook: Underground delicacies for the quick-crunch, virtual reality, Zen-soaked, blaster nineties.* Berkeley, CA: Ten Speed Press.

Johnson, S. (1997). *Interface culture: How new technology transforms the way we create and communicate.* San Francisco, CA: HarperEdge.

Joinson, A. (1998). Causes and implications of disinhibited behavior on the Internet. In J. Gackenbach (Ed.), *Psychology and the Internet: Intrapersonal, interpersonal, and transpersonal implications* (pp. 43–60). San Diego, CA: Academic Press.

Jones, L. (1995, April 25). *Good Times virus hoax FAQ* [Frequently Asked Questions]. Retrieved March 5, 1999, from http://www.hr.doe.gov/goodtime.html

Jones, Q. (1997). Virtual-communities, virtual settlements & cyber-archaeology: A theoretical outline. *Journal of Computer-Mediated Communication, 3*(3). Retrieved February 8, 1999, from http://jcmc.huji.ac.il/vol3/issue3/jones.html

Jones, S. G. (1995). Understanding community in the information age. In S. G. Jones (Ed.), *CyberSociety: Computer-mediated communication and community* (pp. 10–35). Thousand Oaks, CA: Sage.

Jones, S. G. (1996, February). The last link: I'm online, you're online. *Computer-Mediated Communication Magazine, 3*(2). Retrieved May 13, 1998, from http://www.december.com/cmc/mag/1996/feb/last.html

Jones, S. G. (1998a). Information, Internet and community: Notes toward an understanding of community in the information age. In S. G. Jones (Ed.), *CyberSociety 2.0: Revisiting computer-mediated communication and community* (pp. 1–34). Thousand Oaks, CA: Sage.

Jones, S. G. (1998b). Introduction. In S. G. Jones (Ed.), *CyberSociety 2.0: Revisiting computer-mediated communication and community* (pp. xi–xvii). Thousand Oaks, CA: Sage.

Kaplan, C. S. (1999, July 16). An argument for "netiquette" holds up in court. *The New York Times.* Retrieved July 24, 1999, from http://www.nytimes.com/library/tech/99/07/cyber/cyberlaw/16law.html

Kaplan, C. S. (1999, August 20). Report questions government efforts against computer crime. *The New York Times.* Retrieved August 20, 1999, from http://www.nytimes.com/library/tech/99/08/cyber/cyberlaw/20law.html

Kaplan, C. S. (2000, August 11). French Nazi memorabilia case presents jurisdiction dilemma. *The New York Times.* Retrieved September 20, 2000, from http://www.nytimes.com/library/tech/00/08/cyber/cyberlaw/11law.html

Katsh, E. (1996, May). *The Online Ombuds Office: Adapting dispute resolution to cyberspace.* Paper presented at the National Center for Automated Information Research (NCAIR) Dispute Resolution Conference, Washington, DC. Retrieved August 1, 1999, from http://www.law.vill.edu/ncair/disres/katsh.htm

Kelly, K. (1997, November). Manners matter. *Wired News.* Retrieved January 24, 1999, from http://www.wired.com/wired/archive/5.11/manners_pr.html

Kiesler, S., Siegel, J., & McGuire, T. W. (1991). Social psychological aspects of computer-mediated communication. In C. Dunlop & R. Kling (Eds.), *Computerization and controversy: Value conflicts and social choices* (pp. 330–349). San Diego, CA: Academic Press. (Original work published 1984)

Kim, A. J. (1998, May). Killers have more fun. *Wired News.* Retrieved January 24, 1999, from http://www.wired.com/wired/archive/6.05/ultima_pr.html

Kim, A. J. (2000). *Community-building on the Web: Secret strategies for successful online communities.* Berkeley, CA: Peachpit Press.

King, S. A. (1995). *Effects of mood states on social judgments in cyberspace: Self focused sad people as the source of flame wars.* Retrieved January 21, 1999, from http://www.grohol.com/storm1.htm

King, S. A., & Moreggi, D. (1998). Internet therapy and self-help groups—the pros and cons. In J. Gackenbach (Ed.), *Psychology and the Internet: Intrapersonal, interpersonal, and transpersonal implications* (pp. 77–109). San Diego, CA: Academic Press.

Kirsh, E. M., Phillips, D. W., & McIntyre, D. E. (1996). Recommendations for the evolution of cyberlaw. *Journal of Computer-Mediated Communication, 2*(2). Retrieved February 8, 1999, from http://jcmc.huji.ac.il/vol2/issue2/kirsh.html

Kleinman, N. (1996). Don't fence me in: Copyright, property, and technology. In L. Strate, R. Jacobson, & S. B. Gibson (Eds.), *Communication and cyberspace: Social interaction in an electronic environment* (pp. 59–82). Cresskill, NJ: Hampton Press.

Kling, R. (1996a). Beyond outlaws, hackers, and pirates: Ethical issues in the work of information and computer science professionals. In R. Kling (Ed.), *Computerization and controversy: Value conflicts and social choices* (2nd ed.) (pp. 848–869). San Diego, CA: Academic Press.

Kling, R. (1996b). Social relationships in electronic forums: Hangouts, salons, workplaces, and communities. In R. Kling (Ed.), *Computerization and controversy: Value conflicts and social choices* (2nd ed.) (pp. 426–454). San Diego, CA: Academic Press.

Kobelius, J. (1999, March 15). Opinion: Antispam efforts smack of McCarthyism. *CNN*. Retrieved March 16, 1999, from http://cnn.com/TECH/computing/9903/15/antispam.idg

Kolko, B., & Reid, E. (1998). Dissolution and fragmentation: Problems in on-line communities. In S. G. Jones (Ed.), *CyberSociety 2.0: Revisiting computer-mediated communication and community* (pp. 212–229). Thousand Oaks, CA: Sage.

Kollock, P., & Smith, M. A. (1996). Managing the virtual commons: Cooperation and conflict in computer communities. In S. C. Herring (Ed.), *Computer-mediated communication: Linguistic, social and cross-cultural perspectives* (pp. 109–128). Amsterdam: J. Benjamins.

Kollock, P., & Smith, M. A. (1999). Introduction: Communities in cyberspace. In M. A. Smith & P. Kollock (Eds.), *Communities in cyberspace* (pp. 3–25). New York: Routledge.

Korenman, J., & Wyatt, N. (1996). Group dynamics in an e-mail forum. In S. C. Herring (Ed.), *Computer-mediated communication: Linguistic, social and cross-cultural perspectives* (pp. 225–242). Amsterdam: J. Benjamins.

Kramarae, C. (1998). Feminist fictions of future technology. In S. G. Jones (Ed.), *CyberSociety 2.0: Revisiting computer-mediated communication and community* (pp. 100–128). Thousand Oaks, CA: Sage.

Kraut, R., Steinfield, C., Chan, A., Butler, B., & Hoag, A. (1998). Coordination and virtualization: The role of electronic networks and personal relationships. *Journal of Computer-Mediated Communication, 3*(4). Retrieved February 8, 1999, from http://jcmc.huji.ac.il/vol3/issue4/kraut.html

Kupst, S., Mehravari, N., Olson, M., & Rush, S. (1997, February). Designing virtual co-location and collaborative environments via today's desktop videoconferencing technology. *Proceedings of Creative Collaboration in Virtual Communities '97*, University of Sydney, Australia. Retrieved February 19, 1999, from http://www.arch.usyd.edu.au/kcdc/conferences/VC97/papers/kupst.html

Lajoie, M. (1996). Psychoanalysis and cyberspace. In R. Shields (Ed.), *Cultures of Internet: Virtual spaces, real histories, living bodies* (pp. 153–169). London: Sage.

Langer, S. K. (1979). *Philosophy in a new key: A study in the symbolism of reason, rite, and art* (3rd ed.). Cambridge, MA: Harvard University Press. (Original work published 1942)

Lazar, J. (1999). *Online communities*. Retrieved July 30, 1999, from http://www.ifsm.umbc.edu/communities

Lazar, J. & Preece, J. (1998). Classification schema for online communities. *Proceedings of the 1998 Association for Information Systems Americas Conference*, 84–86. Retrieved July 30, 1999, from http://www.isworld.org/ais.ac.98/proceedings/track02/lazar.pdf

Lee, J. Y. (1996). Charting the codes of cyberspace: A rhetoric of electronic mail. In L. Strate, R. Jacobson, & S. B. Gibson (Eds.), *Communication and cyberspace: Social interaction in an electronic environment* (pp. 275–296). Cresskill, NJ: Hampton Press.

Leonard, A. (1997a, September 4). Spam bombers. *Salon*. Retrieved May 8, 1999, from http://www.salon.com/sept97/21st/spam970904.html

Leonard, A. (1997b, December 11). Pornutopia lost. *Salon.* Retrieved May 8, 1999, from http://www.salon.com/21st/feature/1997/12/cov_01feature.html

Leonard, A. (1998, October 30). The war for your e-mail box. *Salon.* Retrieved May 8, 1999, from http://www.salon.com/21st/feature/1998/10/cov_30feature.html

Leonard, A. (1999a, January 14). Prank takes down anti-impeachment site. *Salon.* Retrieved May 11, 1999, from http://www.salon.com/21st/log/1999/01/11log.html

Leonard, A. (1999b, April 21). Polynesian techno-porn. *Salon.* Retrieved May 8, 1999, from http://www.salon.com/tech/log/1999/04/21/polynesia_porn

Lessard, B., & Baldwin S. (2000). *Netslaves: True tales of working the Web.* New York: McGraw-Hill.

Levinson, P. (1997). *The soft edge: A natural history and future of the information revolution.* New York: Routledge.

Levinson, P. (1999). *Digital McLuhan: A guide to the information millennium.* New York: Routledge.

Levinson, P. (2000). McLuhan and media ecology. *Proceedings of the Media Ecology Association, 1,* 17–22. Retrieved January 8, 2012, from http://www.media-ecology. org/publications/MEA_proceedings/v1/McLuhan_and_media_ecology.html

Levinson, P. (2003). *Realspace: The fate of physical presence in the digital age, on and off planet .* New York: Routledge.

Levinson, P. (2004). *Cellphone: The story of the world's most mobile medium and how it has transformed everything!* New York: Palgrave Macmillan.

Levinson, P. (2009). *New new media.* Boston: Allyn & Bacon.

Levy, S. (1984). *Hackers: Heroes of the computer revolution.* New York: Doubleday.

Lipton, M. (1996). Forgetting the body: Cybersex and identity. In L. Strate, R. Jacobson, & S. B. Gibson (Eds.), *Communication and cyberspace: Social interaction in an electronic environment* (pp. 335–349). Cresskill, NJ: Hampton Press.

Littman, J. (1996). *The fugitive game: Online with Kevin Mitnick.* Boston: Little, Brown.

Littman, J. (1997). *The watchman: The twisted life and crimes of serial hacker Kevin Poulsen.* Boston: Little, Brown.

Lockard, J. (1997). Progressive politics, electronic individualism and the myth of virtual community. In D. Porter (Ed.), *Internet culture* (pp. 219–231). New York: Routledge.

Lofland, L. H. (1973). *A world of strangers: Order and action in urban public space.* New York: Basic Books.

Lofland, L. H. (1998). *The public realm: Exploring the city's quintessential social territory.* Hawthorne, NY: A. de Gruyter.

Ludlow, P. (Ed.). (1996). *High noon on the electronic frontier: Conceptual issues in cyberspace.* Cambridge, MA: M.I.T. Press.

Lum, C. M. K. (1996). *In search of a voice: Karaoke and the construction of identity in Chinese America.* Mahwah, NJ: Lawrence Erlbaum.

Lum, C. M. K. (2000a). Introduction: The intellectual roots of media ecology. *The New Jersey Journal of Communication, 8*(1), 1–7.

Lum, C. M. K. (Ed.). (2000b). The intellectual roots of media ecology [Special issue]. *The New Jersey Journal of Communication, 8*(1).

Lum, C. M. K. (2006a). Notes toward an intellectual history of media ecology. In C. M. K. Lum (Ed.), *Perspectives on culture, technology and communication: The media ecology tradition* (pp. 1–60). Cresskill, NJ: Hampton Press.

Lum, C. M. K. (Ed.). (2006b). *Perspectives on culture, technology and communication: The media ecology tradition.* Cresskill, NJ: Hampton Press.

Luther, S. F. (1997). "Can we talk"—Women's voices on shortwave radio worldwide. In S. J. Drucker & G. Gumpert (Eds.), *Voices in the street: Explorations in gender, media, and public space* (pp. 271–280). Cresskill, NJ: Hampton Press.

Mabry, E. A. (1998). Frames and flames: The structure of argumentative messages on the net. In F. Sudweeks, M. L. McLaughlin, & S. Rafaeli (Eds.), *Network and netplay: Virtual groups on the Internet* (pp. 13–26). Cambridge, MA: M.I.T. Press.

Machado, J. (1996). Netiquette 101. In M. Stefik (Ed.), *Internet dreams: Archetypes, myths, and metaphors* (pp. 135–141). Cambridge, MA: M.I.T. Press.

MacKinnon, R. C. (1995). Searching for the Leviathan in Usenet. In S. G. Jones (Ed.), *CyberSociety: Computer-mediated communication and community* (pp. 112–137). Thousand Oaks, CA: Sage.

MacKinnon, R. C. (1997). Punishing the persona: Correctional strategies for the virtual offender. In S. G. Jones (Ed.), *Virtual culture: Identity and communication in cyber-society* (pp. 206–235). Thousand Oaks, CA: Sage.

MacKinnon, R. C. (1998). The social construction of rape in virtual reality. In F. Sudweeks, M. L. McLaughlin, & S. Rafaeli (Eds.), *Network and netplay: Virtual groups on the Internet* (pp. 147–172). Cambridge, MA: M.I.T. Press.

Maltz, T. (1996). Customary law & power in Internet communities. *Journal of Computer-Mediated Communication, 2*(1). Retrieved February 8, 1999, from http://jcmc.huji. ac.il/vol2/issue1/custom.html

Marriott, M. (1999, June 10). Virus fighters on 24-hour, global guard. *The New York Times.* Retrieved June 12, 1999, from http://www.nytimes.com/library/tech/99/06/circuits/articles/10viru.html

Marvin, L.-E. (1995). Spoof, spam, lurk and lag: The aesthetics of text-based virtual realities. *Journal of Computer-Mediated Communication, 1*(2). Retrieved February 8, 1999, from http://jcmc.huji.ac.il/vol1/issue2/marvin.html

Mashima, R., & Hirose, K. (1996). From "Dial-a-Porn" to "Cyberporn": Approaches to and limitations of regulation in the United States and Japan. *Journal of Computer-Mediated Communication, 2*(2). Retrieved February 8, 1999, from http://jcmc.huji. ac.il/vol2/issue2/mashima.html

Maushart, S. (2010). *The winter of our disconnect: How three totally wired teenagers (and a mother who slept with her iPhone) pulled the plug on their technology and lived to tell the tale.* New York: Tarcher/Penguin.

McGrath, M. (1997). *Hard, soft & wet: The digital generation comes of age.* London: HarperCollins.

McIntosh, C. (1999, April 5). Protect yourself from the next Melissa. *CNN.* Retrieved April 5, 1999, from http://cnn.com/TECH/computing/9904/05/protect.idg

McKay, N. (1998, September 22). The golden age of hacktivism. *Wired News.* Retrieved September 9, 1999, from http://www.wired.com/news/news/politics/story/15129.html

McLaughlin, M. L., Osborne, K. K., & Smith, C. B. (1995). Standards of conduct on Usenet. In S. G. Jones (Ed.), *CyberSociety: Computer-mediated communication and community* (pp. 90–111). Thousand Oaks, CA: Sage.

McLuhan, M. (1964). *Understanding media: The extensions of man* (2nd ed.). New York: Mentor.

McNamara, P. (1999, April 6). Stopping the next Melissa. *CNN.* Retrieved April 8, 1999, from http://cnn.com/TECH/computing/9904/06/melissa.ent.idg

Mead, G. H. (1934). *Mind, self, and society: From the standpoint of a social behaviorist* (C. W. Morris, Ed.). Chicago: University of Chicago Press.

Meinel, C. P. (1998). *The happy hacker* (2nd ed.). Show Low, AZ: American Eagle.

Merkle, R. (1998). *The ultimate Internet terrorist: How hackers, geeks, and phreaks can ruin your trip on the information superhighway—and what you can do to protect yourself.* Boulder, CO: Paladin Press.

Meyrowitz, J. (1979). No sense of place: A theory on the impact of electronic media on social structure and behavior (Doctoral dissertation, New York University, 1979). *Dissertation Abstracts International, 40*(03), 1137 (UMI No. AAT 7918858).

Meyrowitz, J. (1985). *No sense of place: The impact of electronic media on social behavior.* New York: Oxford University Press.

Meyrowitz, J. (1986). Television and interpersonal behavior: Codes of perception and response. In G. Gumpert & R. Cathcart (Eds.), *Inter/media: Interpersonal communication in a media world* (3rd ed.) (pp. 253–272). New York: Oxford University Press. (Original work published 1979)

Meyrowitz, J. (2001). Morphing McLuhan: Medium theory for a new millennium. *Proceedings of the Media Ecology Association, 2*, 8–22. Retrieved January 8, 2012, from http://www.media-ecology.org/publications/MEA_proceedings/v2/Meyrowitz 02.pdf

Milgram, S. (1974). *Obedience to authority: An experimental view.* New York: Harper & Row.

Millard, W. B. (1997). I flamed Freud: A case study in teletextual incendiarism. In D. Porter (Ed.), *Internet culture* (pp. 145–159). New York: Routledge.

Miller, H. (1995). *The presentation of self in electronic life: Goffman on the Internet.* Retrieved January 21, 1999, from http://www.ntu.ac.uk/soc/psych/miller/goffman. htm

Miller, S. E. (1996). *Civilizing cyberspace: Policy, power, and the information superhighway.* Reading, MA: Addison-Wesley.

Mineo, B. (1998). Computer conferencing and online education: Uncovering the assumptions (Doctoral dissertation, New York University, 1998). *Dissertation Abstracts International, 59*(05), 1537 (UMI No. AAT 9832756).

Mitchell, W. J. (1995). *City of bits: Space, place and the infobahn.* Cambridge, MA: M.I.T. Press.

Mitra, A. (1997a). Diasporic Web sites: Ingroup and outgroup discourse. *Critical Studies in Mass Communications, 14*(2), 158–181.

Mitra, A. (1997b). Virtual commonality: Looking for India on the Internet. In S. G. Jones (Ed.), *Virtual culture: Identity and communication in cybersociety* (pp. 55–79). Thousand Oaks, CA: Sage.

Mnookin, J. L. (1996). Virtual(ly) law: The emergence of law in LambdaMOO. *Journal of Computer-Mediated Communication, 2*(1). Retrieved February 8, 1999, from http://jcmc.huji.ac.il/vol2/issue1/lambda.html

Moore, D. W. (1995). *The emperor's virtual clothes: The naked truth about Internet culture.* Chapel Hill, NC: Algonquin Books.

Morahan-Martin, J. (1998). Males, females, and the Internet. In J. Gackenbach (Ed.), *Psychology and the Internet: Intrapersonal, interpersonal, and transpersonal implications* (pp. 169–197). San Diego, CA: Academic Press.

Moran, T. P. (2010). *Introduction to the history of communication: Evolutions and revolutions.* New York: Peter Lang.

Morris, M., & Ogan, C. (1996). The Internet as mass medium. *Journal of Communication, 46*(1), 39–50.

MSNBC. (1999, April 30). CIH virus set to strike again. Retrieved May 1, 1999, from http://www.msnbc.com/news/264022.asp

Mumford, L. (1934). *Technics and civilization.* New York: Harcourt Brace Jovanovich.

Mynatt, E. D., Adler, A., Ito, M., & O'Day, V. L. (1997). Design for network communities. *Proceedings of SIGCHI, CHI 97.* Retrieved July 30, 1999, from http://www. acm.org/sigchi/chi97/proceedings/paper/edm.htm

The New York Times. (1999, April 7). Virus defendant to plead not guilty. Retrieved April 8, 1999, from http://www.nytimes.com/library/tech/99/04/biztech/articles/07 viru.html

The New York Times. (1999, April 9). Lawyer likens Melissa virus to graffiti. Retrieved April 9, 1999, from http://www.nytimes.com/library/tech/99/04/biztech/articles/ 009melissa.html

Nguyen, D. T. & Alexander, J. (1996). The coming of cyberspacetime and the end of the polity. In R. Shields (Ed.), *Cultures of Internet: Virtual spaces, real histories, living bodies* (pp. 99–124). London: Sage.

Nissen, B. (2000, November 15). Overworked, overwrought: "Desk rage" at work. *CNN.* Retrieved June 4, 2001, from http://www.cnn.com/2000/CAREER/trends/11/15/rage

Noonan, R. J. (1998). The psychology of sex: A mirror from the Internet. In J. Gackenbach (Ed.), *Psychology and the Internet: Intrapersonal, interpersonal, and transpersonal implications* (pp. 143–168). San Diego, CA: Academic Press.

Noone, R. M. (1986). The new reformation and the electronic media (Doctoral dissertation, New York University, 1986). *Dissertation Abstracts International, 47*(08), 2979 (UMI No. AAT 8625644).

Nystrom, C. L. (1973). *Toward a science of media ecology: The formulation of integrated conceptual paradigms for the study of human communication systems.* Unpublished doctoral dissertation, New York University.

Nystrom, C. L. (1978). Waiting: The semantics of transitional space. *Etc.: A Review of General Semantics, 35,* 245–253.

Nystrom, C. L. (1979). *Media ecology: Inquiries into the structure of communication environments.* Unpublished manuscript, New York University.

Nystrom, C. L. (1989). The crisis of narrative. *Translation Review, 29,* 2–4.

Nystrom, C. L. (2000). Symbol, thought, and reality: The contributions of Benjamin Lee Whorf and Susanne K. Langer to media ecology. *The New Jersey Journal of Communication, 8*(1), 8–34.

Office of Crimes Against Children. (n.d.). *A parent's guide to Internet safety* [Bulletin]. Washington, DC: Federal Bureau of Investigation. Retrieved March 19, 2001, from the Word Wide Web: http://www.fbi.gov/publications/pguide/pguidee.htm

Ohlson, K., & Harrison, A. (1999, March 30). "Melissa" mutates, becomes resistant to patch. *CNN.* Retrieved March 30, 1999, from http://cnn.com/TECH/computing/ 9903/30/melissamutate.idg

Oikarinen, J., & Reed, D. (1993, May). *Network working group request for comments 1459* [Memorandum defining protocol for Internet Relay Chat]. Retrieved November 26, 2000, from http://www.faqs.org/rfcs/rfc1459.html

Oldenburg, R. (1997). *The great good place: Cafés, coffee shops, community centers, beauty parlors, general stores, bars, hangouts, and how they get you through the day.* New York: Marlowe. (Original work published 1989)

Ong, W. J. (1982). *Orality and literacy: The technologizing of the word.* New York: Methuen.

Ostwald, M. J. (1997). Virtual urban futures. In D. Holmes (Ed.), *Virtual politics: Identity and community in cyberspace* (pp. 125–144). Thousand Oaks, CA: Sage.

Papert, S. A. (1980). *Mindstorms: Children, computers, and powerful ideas.* New York: Basic Books.

Paquin, B. (1998, October 26). E-guerrillas in the mist. *The Ottawa Citizen.* Retrieved September 9, 1999, from http://www.ottawacitizen.com/hightech/981026/1964496. htm

Parker, D. B. (1998). *Fighting computer crime: A new framework for protecting information.* New York: John Wiley.

Parks, M. R., & Floyd, K. (1996). Making friends in cyberspace. *Journal of Communication, 46*(1), 80–97.

Patkin, T. T. (1996). Constructing the virtual organization: Using a multimedia simulation for communication education. In L. Strate, R. Jacobson, & S. B. Gibson (Eds.), *Communication and cyberspace: Social interaction in an electronic environment* (pp. 167–177). Cresskill, NJ: Hampton Press.

Perkinson, H. J. (1991). *Getting better: Television and moral progress.* New Brunswick, NJ: Transaction.

Perkinson, H. J. (1996). *No safety in numbers: How the computer quantified everything and made people risk-aversive.* Cresskill, NJ: Hampton Press.

Perritt, Jr., H. H. (1996, May). *Electronic dispute resolution.* Paper presented at the National Center for Automated Information Research (NCAIR) Dispute Resolution Conference, Washington, DC. Retrieved August 1, 1999, from http://www.law.vill. edu/ncair/disres/PERRITT.HTM

Perrolle, J. A. (1991). Conversations and trust in computer interfaces. In C. Dunlop & R. Kling (Eds.), *Computerization and controversy: Value conflicts and social choices* (pp. 350–363). San Diego, CA: Academic Press.

Perry, G. M., Miller, P. A., Polak, V., & Edwards, M. L. (1998). Personal jurisdiction in cyberspace: Where can you be sued, and whose laws apply? *Media Law & Policy, 7*(1), 1–13.

Pfuhl, E. H., & Henry, S. (1993). *The deviance process* (3rd ed.). New York: A. de Gruyter.

Phillips, D. J. (1996). Defending the boundaries: Identifying and countering threats in a Usenet newsgroup. *The Information Society, 12,* 39–62.

Platt, C. (1997). *Anarchy online: Net sex net crime.* New York: HarperPrism.

Poster, M. (1997). Cyberdemocracy: The Internet and the public sphere. In D. Holmes (Ed.), *Virtual politics: Identity and community in cyberspace* (pp. 212–228). Thousand Oaks, CA: Sage.

Poster, M. (1998). Virtual ethnicity: Tribal identity in an age of global communications. In S. G. Jones (Ed.), *CyberSociety 2.0: Revisiting computer-mediated communication and community* (pp. 184–211). Thousand Oaks, CA: Sage.

Postman, N. (1976). *Crazy talk, stupid talk: How we defeat ourselves by the way we talk—and what to do about it.* New York: Delta.

Postman, N. (1979). *Teaching as a conserving activity.* New York: Dell.

Postman, N. (1982). *The disappearance of childhood.* New York: Delacorte.

Postman, N. (1985). *Amusing ourselves to death: Public discourse in the age of show business.* New York: Penguin.

Postman, N. (1988). *Conscientious objections: Stirring up trouble about language, technology, and education.* New York: Alfred A. Knopf.

Postman, N. (1992). *Technopoly: The surrender of culture to technology.* New York: Alfred A. Knopf.

Postman, N. (1996a). *The end of education: Redefining the value of school.* New York: Alfred A. Knopf.

Postman, N. (1996b). Epilogue: Cyberspace, shmyberspace. In L. Strate, R. Jacobson, & S. B. Gibson (Eds.), *Communication and cyberspace: Social interaction in an electronic environment* (pp. 379–382). Cresskill, NJ: Hampton Press.

Postman, N., & Weingartner, C. (1969). *Teaching as a subversive activity*. New York: Dell.

Postman, N., & Weingartner, C. (1971). *The soft revolution: A student handbook for turning schools around*. New York: Dell.

Poulsen, K. (1999, August 9). It's over—Mitnick finally sentenced. *ZDNet*. Retrieved September 8, 1999, from http://www.zdnet.com/zdnn/stories/news/0,4586,2311616, 00.html?chkpt=hpqs014

Poulsen, K. (2000, January 20). Hacker Mitnick released from prison. *ZDNet*. Retrieved September 3, 2001, from http://www.zdnet.com/zdnn/stories/news/0,4586,2425165, 00.html

Preece, J., & Ghozati, K. (1998). In search of empathy online: A review of 100 online communities. *Proceedings of the 1998 Association for Information Systems Americas Conference*, 92–94. Retrieved July 30, 1999, from http://www.isworld.org/ais. ac.98/proceedings/track02/preece.pdf

Preston, J. M. (1998). From mediated environments to the development of consciousness. In J. Gackenbach (Ed.), *Psychology and the Internet: Intrapersonal, interpersonal, and transpersonal implications* (pp. 255–291). San Diego, CA: Academic Press.

Puterman, S. (1995, July). *Extended essay* [IRC nicknames]. Retrieved January 24, 1999, from http://www.rucus.ru.ac.za/~simone/xessay.html

Quarles, P. O. (1986). Videotex and conceptions of knowledge: An historically-based model for identifying epistemological consequences of videotex (Doctoral dissertation, New York University, 1986). *Dissertation Abstracts International, 47*(12), 4127 (UMI No. AAT 8706331).

Rakow, L. (1997). The telephone and women's place. In S. J. Drucker & G. Gumpert (Eds.), *Voices in the street: Explorations in gender, media, and public space* (pp. 237–253). Cresskill, NJ: Hampton Press.

Randall, N. (1997). *The soul of the Internet: Net gods, netizens and the wiring of the world*. London: International Thomson Computer Press.

Raymond, E. S. (Ed.). (1991). *The new hacker's dictionary*. Cambridge, MA: M.I.T. Press.

Rayome, J. (1998, June). *IRC on your dime? What you really need to know about Internet Relay Chat (CIAC-2318)* [Bulletin]. Livermore, CA: Computer Incident Advisory Capability (CIAC), U.S. Department of Energy. Retrieved February 28, 1999, from http://ciac.llnl.gov/ciac/documents/CIAC-2318_IRC_On_Your_Dime.pdf

Reid, E. (1991). *Electropolis: Communications and community on Internet Relay Chat*. Honors thesis, Department of History, University of Melbourne, Australia. Retrieved August 7, 1997, from http://www.ee.mu.oz.au/papers/emr/work.html

Reid, E. (1995). Virtual worlds: Culture and imagination. In S. G. Jones (Ed.), *Cyber-Society: Computer-mediated communication and community* (pp. 164–183). Thousand Oaks, CA: Sage.

Reid, E. (1996a). Communication and community on Internet Relay Chat: Constructing communities. In P. Ludlow (Ed.), *High noon on the electronic frontier: Conceptual issues in cyberspace* (pp. 397–411). Cambridge, MA: M.I.T. Press.

Reid, E. (1996b). Informed consent in the study of on-line communities: A reflection on the effects of computer-mediated social research. *The Information Society, 12*, 169–174.

Reid, E. (1998). The self and the Internet: Variations on the illusion of one self. In J. Gackenbach (Ed.), *Psychology and the Internet: Intrapersonal, interpersonal, and transpersonal implications* (pp. 29–42). San Diego, CA: Academic Press.

Reid, E. (1999). Hierarchy and power: Social control in cyberspace. In M. A. Smith & P. Kollock (Eds.), *Communities in cyberspace* (pp. 107–133). New York: Routledge.

Reuters. (1999, March 31). Melissa tracked to user name "Sky Roket." *CNN*. Retrieved April 1, 1999, from http://cnn.com/TECH/computing/9903/31/computers.virus.reut

Reuters. (1999, April 30). Taiwan virus suspect free on lack of victims. *CNN*. Retrieved May 7, 1999, from http://cnn.com/TECH/computing/9904/30/virus.computer.reut/index.html

Reuters. (2000, June 16). Yahoo! rejects French court ban on Nazi sites. *The ISOC Forum, 6*(7) (July) [Monthly publication of the Internet Society. distributed electronically by membership@isoc.org].

Rheingold, H. (1993). *The virtual community: Homesteading on the electronic frontier.* New York: HarperPerennial.

Riley, P., Keough, C. M., Christiansen, T., Meilich, O., & Pierson, J. (1998). Community or colony: The case of online newspapers and the Web. *Journal of Computer-Mediated Communication, 4*(1). Retrieved February 8, 1999, from http://jcmc.huji.ac.il/vol4/issue1/keough.html

Rinaldi, A. H. (1994). *The net user guidelines and netiquette.* Retrieved January 24, 1999, from ftp://ftp.lib.berkeley.edu/pub/net.training/FAU/netiquette.txt

Rintel, E. S. (1995). *Nothing worth saying?: Communicatory freedom on Internet Relay Chat.* Retrieved November 14, 2000, from http://www.uq.edu.au/~ensrinte/work/irc/academic/rintel-es-nothing-worth-saying-1995.html

Rintel, E. S., & Pittam, J. (1997a, May). *Communicative and non-communicative silence on Internet Relay Chat: Management and function.* Paper presented at the annual convention of the International Communication Association, Montreal, Canada. Retrieved November 14, 2000, from http://www.uq.edu.au/~ensrinte/work/papers/silence-on-irc/rintel-es-silence-on-irc-1997.html

Rintel, E. S., & Pittam, J. (1997b). Strangers in a strange land: Interaction management on Internet Relay Chat. *Human Communication Research, 23*(4), 507–534.

Rodberg, S. (1999a, April 14). Balancing the dangers and the discoveries as students go online. *The New York Times.* Retrieved April 15, 1999, from http://www.nytimes.com/library/tech/99/04/circuits/articles/15tool.html

Rodberg, S. (1999b, April 15). Wiring the schools for e-mail and more. *The New York Times.* Retrieved April 15, 1999, from http://www.nytimes.com/library/tech/99/04/circuits/articles/15scho.html

Rodino, M. (1997). Breaking out of binaries: Reconceptualizing gender and its relationship to language in computer-mediated communication. *Journal of Computer-Mediated Communication, 3*(3). Retrieved February 8, 1999, from http://jcmc.huji.ac.il/vol3/issue3/rodino.html

Rose, H. (1996, December 13). *Internet Relay Chat FAQ* [Frequently Asked Questions]. Retrieved September 8, 1997, from http://www.irchelp.org/irchelp/altircfaq.html

Rose, L. (1995). *Netlaw: Your rights in the online world.* Berkeley, CA: Osborne McGraw-Hill.

Rosenberg, M. S. (1992). *Virtual reality: Reflections of life, dreams, and technology, an ethnography of a computer society.* Retrieved August 11, 1999, from ftp://sunsite.unc.edu/pub/academic/communications/papers/muds/muds/Ethnography-of-a-Computer-Society

Rosenberg, R. S. (1997). *The social impact of computers* (2nd ed.). San Diego, CA: Academic Press.

Roszak, T. (1986). *The cult of information: The folklore of computers and the true art of thinking.* New York: Pantheon Books.

Rushkoff, D. (1994). *Cyberia: Life in the trenches of hyperspace.* New York: HarperCollins.

Rushkoff, D. (2010). *Program or be programmed: Ten commandments for a digital age.* New York: OR Books.

Rutter, J., & Smith, G. (1999a). Ritual aspects of CMC sociability. In K. Buckner (Ed.), *Esprit i3 workshop on ethnographic studies in real and virtual environments: Inhabited information spaces and connected communities* (pp. 113–122). Edinburgh, Scotland: Queen Margaret College. Retrieved November 23, 2000, from http://les1.man.ac.uk/cric/Jason_Rutter/papers/Ritual.pdf

Rutter, J., & Smith, G. (1999b). *Presenting the off-line self in an everyday, online environment.* Retrieved November 23, 2000, from http://les1.man.ac.uk/cric/Jason_Rutter/papers/Self.pdf

Samarajiva, R., & Shields, P. (1997). Telecommunication networks as social space: Implications for research and policy and an exemplar. *Media, Culture & Society, 19*(4), 535–555.

Saulny, S. (2001, January 30). Umbrellas in their midst, New Yorkers ponder "rain rage." *New York Today.* Retrieved January 30, 2001, from http://www.nytoday.com/scripts/editorial.dll?&eeid=3917694&eetype=article&render=y

Savicki, V., Lingenfelter, D., & Kelley, M. (1996). Gender language style in group composition in Internet discussion groups. *Journal of Computer-Mediated Communication, 2*(3). Retrieved February 8, 1999, from http://jcmc.huji.ac.il/vol2/issue3/savicki.html

Schafer, R. M. (1986). The electric revolution. In G. Gumpert & R. Cathcart (Eds.), *Inter/media: Interpersonal communication in a media world* (3rd ed.) (pp. 368–380). New York: Oxford University Press. (Original work published 1977)

Scheinfeld, R. C., & Bagley, P. H. (1996, November 27). Long-arm jurisdiction: "Cybersquatting." *The New York Law Journal.* Retrieved May 1, 1999, from http://www.ljx.com/internet/1127squat.html

Scheinfeld, R. C., & Bagley, P. H. (1997, November 26). Emerging Internet trademark issues. *The New York Law Journal.* Retrieved May 1, 1999, from http://www.bakerbotts.com/practice/iptech/library/articles/emerging.html

Schnurr, L. E. (2000). Media and telecommunications regulation and the Internet: Regulate or strangulate? *Media Law & Policy, 8*(2), 11–27.

Schroeder, R. (1996). *Possible worlds: The social dynamic of virtual reality technology.* Boulder, CO: Westview Press.

Schroeder, R. (1997). Virtual worlds and the social realities of cyberspace. In B. D. Loader (Ed.), *The governance of cyberspace: Politics, technology and global restructuring* (pp. 97–107). New York: Routledge.

Schuchardt, R. M. (2000, June). *Understanding road rage.* Paper presented at the annual convention of the Media Ecology Association, Fordham University, New York, NY.

Schultz, Jr., E. E., Brown, D. S., & Longstaff, T. A. (1990, July 23). *Responding to computer security incidents: Guidelines for incident handling* [Bulletin]. Livermore, CA: Computer Incident Advisory Capability (CIAC), U.S. Department of Energy. Retrieved February 28, 1999, from ftp://ciac.llnl.gov/pub/ciac/ciacdocs/ihg.txt

Schwartz, T. (1973). *The responsive chord.* Garden City, NY: Anchor Books.

Scoblionkov, D. (1999, February 19). When candidates spam. *Salon.* Retrieved May 8, 1999, from http://www.salon.com/21st/feature/1999/02/19feature.html

Seabrook, J. (1997). *Deeper: My two-year odyssey in cyberspace.* New York: Simon & Schuster.

Selwyn, N. (2008). A safe haven for misbehaving? An investigation of online misbehavior among university students. *Social Science Computer Review, 26*(4), 446–465. Retrieved April 25, 2011, from http://ssc.sagepub.com/content/26/4/446

Sempsey, J. (1995, March). *The psycho-social aspects of multi-user dimensions in cyberspace: A review of the literature.* Retrieved January 24, 1999, from http://www.netaxs.com/~jamesiii/mud.htm

Shade, L. R. (1996). Is there free speech on the Net? Censorship in the global information structure. In R. Shields (Ed.), *Cultures of Internet: Virtual spaces, real histories, living bodies* (pp. 11–32). London: Sage.

Shade, L. R. (1997, February). Balancing the global through the local [Review of the book *The wired neighborhood*]. *Computer-Mediated Communication Magazine, 4*(2). Retrieved April 22, 1998, from http://www.december.com/cmc/mag/1997/feb/shade.html

Shallit, J. (1996). Public networks and censorship. In P. Ludlow (Ed.), *High noon on the electronic frontier: Conceptual issues in cyberspace* (pp. 275–289). Cambridge, MA: M.I.T. Press.

Shapiro, A. L. (1999, June 21). The net that binds: Using cyberspace to create real communities. *The Nation.* Retrieved June 26, 1999, from http://www.thenation.com/issue/990621/0621shapiro.shtml

Shaw, D. F. (1997). Gay men and computer communication: A discourse of sex and identity in cyberspace. In S. G. Jones (Ed.), *Virtual culture: Identity and communication in cybersociety* (pp. 133–145). Thousand Oaks, CA: Sage.

Shea, V. (1994). *Netiquette.* San Francisco, CA: Albion Books. Retrieved March 26, 2001, from http://www.albion.com/netiquette/book

Shimomura, T., & Markoff, J. (1996). *Takedown: The pursuit and capture of Kevin Mitnick, America's most wanted computer outlaw—by the man who did it.* New York: Hyperion.

Simmel, G. (1949). The sociology of sociability. *American Journal of Sociology, 55,* 254–261.

Simmel, G. (1950). The stranger. In K. H. Wolff (Ed.), *The sociology of Georg Simmel* (pp. 402–408). New York: Free Press.

Slatalla, M., & Quittner, J. (1995). *Masters of deception: The gang that ruled cyberspace.* New York: HarperCollins.

Slouka, M. (1995). *War of the worlds: Cyberspace and the high-tech assault on reality.* New York: Basic Books.

Smith, A. D. (1999). Problems of conflict management in virtual communities. In M. A. Smith & P. Kollock (Eds.), *Communities in cyberspace* (pp. 134–163). New York: Routledge.

Smith, C. B., McLaughlin, M. L., & Osborne, K. K. (1998). From terminal ineptitude to virtual sociopathy: How conduct is regulated on Usenet. In F. Sudweeks, M. L. McLaughlin, & S. Rafaeli (Eds.), *Network and netplay: Virtual groups on the Internet* (pp. 95–112). Cambridge, MA: M.I.T. Press.

Smith, M. A. (1992). *Voices from the WELL: The logic of the virtual commons.* Retrieved February 10, 1999, from http://netscan.sscnet.ucla.edu/csoc/papers/voices

Spafford, E. H. (1995). Are computer hacker break-ins ethical? In G. Johnson & H. Nissenbaum (Eds.), *Computers, ethics & social values* (pp. 125–135). Englewood Cliffs, NJ: Prentice Hall.

Spafford, E. H. (1998). Computer viruses. In D. E. Denning & P. J. Denning (Eds.), *Internet besieged: Countering cyberspace scofflaws* (pp. 73–95). New York: ACM Press; Reading, MA: Addison Wesley. (Original work published 1994)

Sprenger, P., Helft, D., & Yamada, M. (2000, May 29). French border patrol. *The Standard*. Retrieved October 1, 2000, from http://www.thestandard.com/article/display/0,1151,15387,00.html

Spring, T. (1999, March 31). The ten commandments of e-mail. *CNN*. Retrieved March 31, 1999, from http://cnn.com/TECH/computing/9903/31/commandments.idg

Sproull, L., & Faraj, S. (1997). Atheism, sex, and databases: The net as a social technology. In S. Kiesler (Ed.), *Culture of the Internet* (pp. 35–51). Mahwah, NJ: Lawrence Erlbaum. (Original work published 1995)

Sproull, L., & Kiesler, S. (1991). *Connections: New ways of working in the networked organization*. Cambridge, MA: M.I.T. Press.

Stamper, C. (1999, January 5). Prodigy prevails in libel suit. *Wired News*. Retrieved April 15, 1999, from http://www.wired.com/news/news/politics/story/17148.html

Stefik, M. (Ed.). (1996). *Internet dreams: Archetypes, myths, and metaphors*. Cambridge, MA: M.I.T. Press.

Sterling, B. (1992). *The hacker crackdown: Law and disorder on the electronic frontier*. New York: Bantam Books.

Sterling, B. (1998). Speech to the High Technology Crime Investigation Association [Lake Tahoe, November 1994]. In D. E. Denning & P. J. Denning (Eds.), *Internet besieged: Countering cyberspace scofflaws* (pp. 481–492). New York: ACM Press; Reading, MA: Addison Wesley.

Sternberg, J. (1998, March). *It's all in the timing: Synchronous versus asynchronous computer-mediated communication*. Paper presented at the annual convention of the New York State Communication Association, Montclair, NJ. Retrieved March 5, 2001, from http://homepages.nyu.edu/~js15/p-time.htm

Sternberg, J. (2000a, November). *Cyber places and their discontents: Dealing with misbehavior in online environments*. Paper presented at the annual convention of the National Communication Association, Seattle, WA.

Sternberg, J. (2000b, Fall). Minutes of the general business meeting of the Media Ecology Association. *In Medias Res, 2*(1), 14–17.

Sternberg, J. (2001). Misbehavior in cyber places: The regulation of online conduct in virtual communities on the Internet (Doctoral dissertation, New York University, 2001). *Dissertation Abstracts International, 62*(07), 2277 (UMI No. AAT 3022160).

Sternberg, J. (2002). The yin and yang of media ecology. *Proceedings of the Media Ecology Association, 3*. Retrieved January 8, 2012, from http://www.media-ecology.org/publications/MEA_proceedings/v3/Sternberg03.pdf

Sternberg, J. (2003). Cell phone as probe. *Explorations in Media Ecology, 2*(1), 15–17.

Sternberg, J. (2005). Legal dilemmas in transnational cyberspace. In A. Braga (Ed.), *CMC, identidades e género: Teoria e método* (pp. 213–233). Covilhã, Portugal: Universidade da Beira Interior. Retrieved October 15, 2006, from http://www.labcom.ubi.pt/livroslabcom/pdfs/braga_adriana_cmc.pdf

Sternberg, J. (2009). Misbehavior in mediated places: Using Goffman's analysis of situational proprieties to understand communication environments, *ETC: A Review of General Semantics, 66*(4), 433–442.

Stivale, C. J. (1997). Spam: Heteroglossia and harassment in cyberspace. In D. Porter (Ed.), *Internet culture* (pp. 133–144). New York: Routledge. (Original work published 1996)

Stoll, C. (1989). *The cuckoo's egg: Tracking a spy through the maze of computer espionage.* New York: Doubleday.

Stoll, C. (1991). Stalking the wily hacker. In C. Dunlop & R. Kling (Eds.), *Computerization and controversy: Value conflicts and social choices* (pp. 533–553). San Diego, CA: Academic Press. (Original work published 1988)

Stone, A. R. (1991). Will the real body please stand up? Boundary stories about virtual cultures. In M. Benedikt (Ed.), *Cyberspace: First steps* (pp. 81–118). Cambridge, MA: M.I.T. Press.

Strate, L. (1986). Media and the sense of smell. In G. Gumpert & R. Cathcart (Eds.), *Inter/media: Interpersonal communication in a media world* (3rd ed.) (pp. 428–438). New York: Oxford University Press. (Original work published 1982)

Strate, L. (1991). Heroes and humans: An examination of the relationship between media environments and conceptions of the hero (celebrity) (Doctoral dissertation, New York University, 1991). *Dissertation Abstracts International, 52*(12), 4134 (UMI No. AAT 9213200).

Strate, L. (1996a). Containers, computers and the media ecology of the city. *Media Ecology: A Journal of Intersections.* Retrieved December 6, 1999, from http://raven. ubalt.edu/features/media_ecology/articles/96/strate1/strate_1.html

Strate, L. (1996b). Cybertime. In L. Strate, R. Jacobson, & S. B. Gibson (Eds.), *Communication and cyberspace: Social interaction in an electronic environment* (pp. 351–377). Cresskill, NJ: Hampton Press.

Strate, L. (1999). The varieties of cyberspace: Problems in definition and delimitation. *Western Journal of Communication, 63*(3), 382–412.

Strate, L. (2006). *Echoes and reflections: On media ecology as a field of study.* Cresskill, NJ: Hampton Press.

Strate, L. (2011). *On the binding biases of time and other essays on general semantics and media ecology.* Fort Worth, TX: Institute of General Semantics.

Strate, L., Jacobson, R., & Gibson, S. B. (Eds.). (1996a). *Communication and cyberspace: Social interaction in an electronic environment.* Cresskill, NJ: Hampton Press.

Strate, L., Jacobson, R., & Gibson, S. B. (1996b). Surveying the electronic landscape: An introduction to communication and cyberspace. In L. Strate, R. Jacobson, & S. B. Gibson (Eds.), *Communication and cyberspace: Social interaction in an electronic environment* (pp. 1–22). Cresskill, NJ: Hampton Press.

Strate, L., & Lum, C. M. K. (2000). Lewis Mumford and the ecology of technics. *The New Jersey Journal of Communication, 8*(1), 56–78.

Suler, J. (1996–1999). *The psychology of cyberspace.* Retrieved June 13, 1999, from http://www.rider.edu/users/suler/psycyber/psycyber.html

Suler, J. (1997a, April). Knowledge, power, wisdom . . . and your very own asterisk: Wizards at the "Palace." In J. Suler, *The psychology of cyberspace.* Retrieved January 21, 1999, from http://www.rider.edu/users/suler/psycyber/wizards.html

Suler, J. (1997b, September). The bad boys of cyberspace: Deviant behavior in online multimedia communities and strategies for managing it. In J. Suler, *The psychology of cyberspace.* Retrieved January 21, 1999, from http://www.rider.edu/users/suler/psycyber/badboys.html

Sullivan, B. (1999, May 25). CIH virus set to strike again. *MSNBC.* Retrieved June 3, 1999, from http://www.msnbc.com/news/273347.asp

Surratt, C. G. (1996). The sociology of everyday life in computer-mediated communities (Doctoral dissertation, Arizona State University, 1996). *Dissertation Abstracts International, 57*(03-A), 1346.

Tang, P. (1997). Multimedia information products and services: A need for "cybercops"? In B. D. Loader (Ed.), *The governance of cyberspace: Politics, technology and global restructuring* (pp. 190–208). New York: Routledge.

Tankel, J. D., & Banks, J. (1997). Lifetime television and women: Narrowcasting as electronic space. In S. J. Drucker & G. Gumpert (Eds.), *Voices in the street: Explorations in gender, media, and public space* (pp. 255–270). Cresskill, NJ: Hampton Press.

Tapscott, D. (1998). *Growing up digital: The rise of the net generation.* New York: McGraw-Hill.

Templeton, B. (1994, November 2). *"Dear Emily Postnews" (Emily Postnews answers your questions on netiquette).* Retrieved March 5, 1999, from http://www.nonprofit.net/hoax/Emily.txt

Terkel, S. (1974). *Working: People talk about what they do all day and how they feel about what they do.* New York: Pantheon Books.

Thieme, R. (1997, February). Notes from the underground: An interview with Se7en. *Computer-Mediated Communication Magazine, 4*(2). Retrieved April 22, 1998, from http://www.december.com/cmc/mag/1997/feb/thieme.html

Thompsen, P. A. (1996). What's fueling the flames in cyberspace? A social influence model. In L. Strate, R. Jacobson, & S. B. Gibson (Eds.), *Communication and cyberspace: Social interaction in an electronic environment* (pp. 297–315). Cresskill, NJ: Hampton Press.

Tihor, S. (1998). Recent electronic attacks at NYU. *Connect Magazine,* Fall 1998, p. 21. New York: Academic Computing Facility, New York University. Retrieved February 21, 1999, from http://www.nyu.edu/acf/pubs/connect/fall98/TechAttacksFall98.html

Tillett, L. S. (1999, March 23). DOJ, IT industry team to fight cybercrime. *CNN.* Retrieved March 24, 1999, from http://cnn.com/TECH/computing/9903/23/crime fighters.idg

Turkle, S. (1984). *The second self: Computers and the human spirit.* New York: Simon & Schuster.

Turkle, S. (1995). *Life on the screen: Identity in the age of the Internet.* New York: Simon & Schuster.

Uncapher, W. (1999). New communities/new communication: Big Sky Telegraph and its community. In M. A. Smith & P. Kollock (Eds.), *Communities in cyberspace* (pp. 264–289). New York: Routledge.

United States Department of Justice. (2002, May 1). *Creator of Melissa computer virus sentenced to 20 months in federal prison* [Press release]. Retrieved January 15, 2011, from http://www.justice.gov/criminal/cybercrime/melissaSent.htm

United States Postal Inspection Service. (n.d.). *Chain letters* [Bulletin]. Retrieved March 5, 1999, from http://www.usps.gov/websites/depart/inspect/chainlet.htm

van Bakel, R. (1996, July). To surf and protect. *Wired News.* Retrieved January 24, 1999, from http://www.wired.com/wired/archive/4.07/es.cyberangels_pr.html

Vincent, C. (1992, November). *Collegiality in cyberspace: Case studies in computer mediated communication* [Electronic version]. Master's thesis, University of Tasmania, Australia. Retrieved September 8, 1997, from ftp://sunsite.unc.edu/pub/academic/communications/papers/irc/Collegiality-in-Cyberspace.txt

Von Rospach, C. (1999, January 28). *A primer on how to work with the Usenet community*. Retrieved February 10, 1999, from ftp://rtfm.mit.edu/pub/usenet-by-group/news.answers/usenet/primer/part1

Wachtel, E. (in press). *From cave walls to computer screens: The interplay of art, technology, and perception*. Cresskill, NJ: Hampton Press.

Wallace, J. D., & Mangan, M. (1997). *Sex, laws, and cyberspace: Freedom and regulation on the frontiers of the online revolution*. New York: John Wiley.

Waskul, D., & Douglass, M. (1997). Cyberself: The emergence of self in on-line chat. *The Information Society, 13*, 375–397.

Watson, N. (1997). Why we argue about virtual community: A case study of the Phish.Net fan community. In S. G. Jones (Ed.), *Virtual culture: Identity and communication in cybersociety* (pp. 102–132). Thousand Oaks, CA: Sage.

Weaver, A. E. (1996). A guide to safe sysop-ing: The church of Scientology, sysops & on-line service providers. *Journal of Computer-Mediated Communication, 2*(2). Retrieved July 19, 1999, from http://jcmc.huji.ac.il/vol2/issue2/weaver.html

Weinreich, F. (1997, February). Establishing a point of view toward virtual communities. *Computer-Mediated Communication Magazine, 4*(2). Retrieved April 22, 1998, from http://www.december.com/cmc/mag/1997/feb/wein.html

Weinstein, H. (2006, January 13). Yahoo's Nazi suit tossed. *Los Angeles Times*. Retrieved January 12, 2012, from http://articles.latimes.com/print/2006/jan/13/business/fi-yahoo13

Weizenbaum, J. (1976). *Computer power and human reason: From judgment to calculation*. New York: W. H. Freeman.

Wellman, B. (1997). An electronic group is virtually a social network. In S. Kiesler (Ed.), *Culture of the Internet* (pp. 179–205). Mahwah, NJ: Lawrence Erlbaum.

Wellman, B. (1999). The network community: An introduction. In B. Wellman (Ed.), *Networks in the global village: Life in contemporary communities* (pp. 1–47). Boulder, CO: Westview Press.

Wellman, B., & Gulia, M. (1999). Virtual communities as communities: Net surfers don't ride alone. In M. A. Smith & P. Kollock (Eds.), *Communities in cyberspace* (pp. 167–194). New York: Routledge.

Werry, C. C. (1996). Linguistic and interactional features of Internet Relay Chat. In S. C. Herring (Ed.), *Computer-mediated communication: Linguistic, social and cross-cultural perspectives* (pp. 47–63). Amsterdam: J. Benjamins.

West, R. & Turner, L. (2000). *Introducing communication theory: Analysis and application*. Mountainview, CA: Mayfield Publishing Company.

Whine, M. (1997). The far right on the Internet. In B. D. Loader (Ed.), *The governance of cyberspace: Politics, technology and global restructuring* (pp. 209–227). New York: Routledge.

Wiener, N. (1954). *The human use of human beings: Cybernetics and society*. New York: Da Capo Press. (Original work published 1950)

Wilbur, S. P. (1997). An archaeology of cyberspaces: Virtuality, community, identity. In D. Porter (Ed.), *Internet culture* (pp. 5–22). New York: Routledge.

Williams, M. (2000). Virtually criminal: Discourse, deviance, and anxiety within virtual communities. *International Review of Law, Computers & Technology, 14*(1), 95–104.

Williams, M. (2001). The language of cybercrime. In D. S. Wall (Ed.), *Crime and the Internet* (pp. 152–166). London: Routledge.

Williams, M. (2006). *Virtually criminal: Crime, deviance, and regulation online*. London: Routledge.

Willson, M. (1997). Community in the abstract: A political and ethical dilemma? In D. Holmes (Ed.), *Virtual politics: Identity and community in cyberspace* (pp. 145–162). Thousand Oaks, CA: Sage.

Wisebrod, D. (1995). Controlling the uncontrollable: Regulating the Internet. 4 *Media & Communications Law Review* 331. Retrieved July 24, 1999, from http://www. catalaw.com/dov/docs/dw-inet.htm

Wong, E. (2001, May 6). New rules for soccer parents: 1) No yelling. 2) No hitting ref. *The New York Times*. Retrieved June 4, 2001, from http://www.nytimes.com/2001/ 05/06/sports/06SPORTS.html

Wray, S. (1998, November). *Electronic civil disobedience and the World Wide Web of hacktivism: A mapping of extraparliamentarian direct action net politics*. Paper presented at the World Wide Web and Contemporary Cultural Theory Conference, Drake University, Des Moines, IA. Retrieved January 5, 1999, from http://www. nyu.edu/projects/wray/wwwhack.html

Yates, S. J. (1996). Oral and written linguistic aspects of computer conferencing: A corpus based study. In S. C. Herring (Ed.), *Computer-mediated communication: Linguistic, social and cross-cultural perspectives* (pp. 29–46). Amsterdam: J. Benjamins.

Zerubavel, E. (1981). *Hidden rhythms: Schedules and calendars in social life*. Berkeley, CA: University of California Press.

Zettl, H. (1996). Back to Plato's cave: Virtual reality. In L. Strate, R. Jacobson, & S. B. Gibson (Eds.), *Communication and cyberspace: Social interaction in an electronic environment* (pp. 83–94). Cresskill, NJ: Hampton Press.

Zgodzinski, D. (1999, May 5). The April Fools' stock hoax and the FBI. All these pranksters wanted to do was raise an alarm about Net investing. So why are they being investigated and sued? *Salon*. Retrieved May 5, 1999, from http://www.salon.com/ tech/feature/1999/05/05/stock_hoax

About the Author

A native New Yorker who grew up in Rio de Janeiro, Brazil, Janet Sternberg earned her Ph.D. in Media Ecology with Neil Postman at New York University. A former Fulbright scholar who holds a Bachelor of Arts in French and Spanish from Kirkland College and a Master of Arts in linguistics from Cornell University, Sternberg currently works in New York at Fordham University as Assistant Professor of Communication and Media Studies and member of Fordham's Latin American and Latino Studies faculty. She has also served as President of the Media Ecology Association. Sternberg has been online since acquiring her first computer, modem, and email account in 1984.